Management Systems and Organizational Performance

Management Systems and Organizational Performance

The Search for Excellence Beyond ISO9000

MARTIN F. STANKARD

QUORUM BOOKS
Westport, Connecticut • London

Library of Congress Cataloging-in-Publication Data

Stankard, Martin F.
    Management systems and organizational performance : the quest for
excellence beyond ISO9000 / Martin F. Stankard.
        p. cm.
    Includes bibliographical references and index.
    ISBN 1-56720-478-3 (alk. paper)
    1. Organizational effectiveness.   2. System analysis.   3. Organizational
learning.   4. ISO9000 Series Standards.   I. Title.
    HD58.9.S7385   2002
    658.4'013—dc21   2001057867

British Library Cataloguing in Publication Data is available.

Library of Congress Catalog Card Number: 2001057867
ISBN: 1-56720-478-3

First published in 2002

Quorum Books, 88 Post Road West, Westport, CT 06881
An imprint of Greenwood Publishing Group, Inc.
www.quorumbooks.com

Printed in the United States of America

The paper used in this book complies with the
Permanent Paper Standard issued by the National
Information Standards Organization (Z39.48-1984).

10 9 8 7 6 5 4 3 2 1

To Debbie

In the long run men hit only what they aim at. Therefore, though they should fail immediately, they had better aim at something high.

—Henry David Thoreau

Contents

Contents

Illustrations

Preface

A portfolio of a select group of publicly traded firms has consistently outperformed the Standard & Poor's 500 stock index by over 300 percent. Why do some organizations grow, both in size and in excellence and turn in stellar performances, while others that look similar do poorly; what makes the difference? What does it take to grow a business and to manage that growth with quality? Many years of research and consulting has shown that the answer lies in applying lessons learned from the study of systems to the management of organizations.

Don Evans, CEO of Baldrige award-winner Operations Management International (OMI), observed that CEOs should adopt the Baldrige high performance business model for two reasons. The first is that *this model clearly shows how to grow the business*. It links a focus on customers and market opportunities, empowerment of the workforce and excellent processes to rapidly improving business results. Don Evan's second reason for adopting the Baldrige business model is that at some point, *even the most capable CEO must build a management system to sustain growth and development of the business as it prospers and faces ever larger challenges.*

People hear or use the word "system," but fail to see how the concept of a system applies to their work in their organization. Consequently, they fail to use powerful but simple insights that come from understanding their business as a system. By viewing how the parts of their business work together as a whole, for example, by drawing them on a flow chart, they immediately see working relationships, bottlenecks and gain other insights into improvement. The appendix presents a simple analogy for explaining the high performance business system model to others. It also briefly summarizes many implications of viewing a business as a system.

Managers and consultants around the world now recognize the ISO9000 standard as the minimum requirement for maintaining customer satisfaction. The leaders among them accept the Baldrige criteria for performance excellence as the best validated model for organizational excellence, self-evaluation, and improvement. Whereas a technical committee of the International Organization for Standardization maintains the ISO standard, a government and industry partnership that includes representation from many of the most competitive organizations in the world, updates the Baldrige criteria annually. One standard, ISO9000, sets a baseline, the Baldrige outlines the full requirements for high performance management systems.

Several research studies show that as a group, organizations that satisfy the requirements of the Baldrige criteria excel in the marketplace as well as financially. While variation exists from firm to firm within the group, their overall performance as a group is outstanding. This book shares with readers the excitement of combining Deming's teachings about systems and continuous improvement with a performance excellence model. What results is a more compact, more business-oriented and more dynamic explanation of high performance than the Baldrige model and scoring system currently provides. It is also a model that takes advantage of the continual improvement requirements of the worldwide ISO9000 standard. Organizations that plan to meet this standard have a unique opportunity to excel beyond mere compliance to ISO9000. This book is written for such organizations.

The relatively static Baldrige model has six categories of management methods and their interactions that lead to a seventh category of outstanding results. Mechanisms of learning, innovation and improvement, which are central issues in truly understanding and creating organizational excellence, are treated indirectly through requirements for learning and sharing and the scoring concept of "increasing system maturity." Baldrige is properly nonprescriptive about what mechanism increases maturity within a real organization but does mention cycles of learning and improvement in passing.

Deming and others, in contrast, base organizational and individual learning on the use of cycles of continuous improvement (Plan, Do, Check, Act cycles) that lead to high performance. Lately this message of continual improvement has been taken up in the widely used ISO9000 quality management system standard. Adoption of these cycles update management methods and represent a start on embodying scientific methods within the management system. Those interested in gaining a competitive advantage from efforts to use the ISO9000 standard should find what they are looking for in the discussion of the golden and the capability-development cycles.

Part I of the book defines terms and introduces the concept of looking at your business as a social system. It presents a brief overview of the Baldrige model for performance excellence that gives you an intuitive grasp of your organization as a system. You can then use your new understanding of the system (Baldrige model) to see ways to re-engineer your own organization for high performance. The massive expansion of performance achieved through an integrated management system works on many levels.

Part I also raises the critical importance of individual values and high performance organizational values, as they influence behavior and provide the culture in which a high performance management system arises. After all, in a mechanical system, parts perform functions; in an organization, individuals, units and whole organizations make up a social system, all pursuing their own purposes.

Part II of the book introduces cycles of learning and improvement, the moving parts of a social system; high performance business organizations learn through these cycles to improve and innovate continuously. This part of the book also introduces the golden cycle—a companywide cycle of learning, innovation and improvement. The golden cycle links many elements from the Baldrige model into an organizationwide cycle for improved market and financial performance. The golden cycle provides the organizing mechanism by which a management system achieves eventual high performance (perhaps short of excellence).

For readers interested in international management system standards, the current revision of the ISO9000 standard provides a stimulus for building a golden cycle within an organization. For readers willing to go beyond mere compliance to the international standard, this book shows how you can turn the ISO9000 standard into a major opportunity for building the core of a high performance business. You must, however, understand enough of this book to aim for more than simple compliance to the standard. You will need to build a golden cycle of wealth-creating innovation within your firm.

Part III expands the discussion of cycles, adding three cycles that support and enable the golden cycle. Each of these supporting cycles takes a slice through relevant Baldrige categories and organizes learning and improvement relevant to those aspects of the business. The book shows how a high performance organization relies on learning through the action of these four dynamic cycles. The major integrating concept of this book is their relationship:

Sustained High Performance	=	Golden Opportunities to Create Wealth	+	Strategy and Motivation	+	World Class Capability	+	Risk/ Return Balance

The golden cycle identifies and aligns the business around wealth creation opportunities. The second cycle develops a common motivating purpose in the organization and deploys a strategy to capture opportunities. The third cycle improves capabilities—workforce, processes, suppliers and the management system—as necessary to execute the strategy and create wealth. At the highest levels of excellence, capabilities become world class in the sense that they permit the firm to compete successfully in the most demanding markets against the toughest competitors in the world. And last, the fourth cycle considers how information and analysis allow an organization to balance risk and return, because high returns must entail high risk, unless the organizational system offsets risk through improved forecasts and better decision making.

Working backward from these four cycles provides an idealized model of high performance to see what must be done today in your own organization. Chapter 9 also describes the highly interactive way in which an organization coordinates the separate cycles into a system.

Part IV provides a guide to action for pragmatic management readers. Chapter 10 tells the story of the actual experience of assessing a management system. It then concludes with a chapter on assembling and coaching teams to make changes in response to assessment findings and improve business performance. Teams chartered to follow up on improvement initiatives and action plans, solve two of the most pressing problems in a growing business. The first is how to make and manage the changes needed to keep growing, and the second is how to develop and season the management and leadership talent necessary to manage the growth. Teams of employees working together under a shared charter with coaching and appropriate training are the most intensive and effective hot house for growing and developing new leaders within an organization. The descriptions in chapters 10 and 11 are drawn from actual field experiences; there is no fiction in the writing.

Organizations are filled with leaders, but anyone who has laughed at a Dilbert cartoon realizes that not all managers are leaders. This book is written for managers that lead—not because they have important job titles, but because they are role models and coaches helping people they work with to do better and to become better, not only as individuals, but also as business frontrunners and as part of a larger society. This book aims to give you the explanations and "war stories" that you can use to help your organization change, grow and excel.

Acknowledgments

Since 1988, firms that have won the Baldrige Award for Performance Excellence have become the most trustworthy gurus of management performance in the United States. I am grateful to presenters at the annual Quest for Excellence Conference for sharing methods and insights that contribute immeasurably to the growth and competitiveness of U.S. enterprises. Many presenters from 3M Dental Products; AT&T Universal Card Services; Corning, Inc.; Federal Express; Globe Metallurgical; Los Alamos National Bank; Marlowe Industries; Merrill Lynch Credit Corp.; Operations Management International, Inc. (OMI); The Ritz-Carlton Hotel Co.; Solectron Corporation; Texas Name Plate, Inc. and Zytec Corp. have shown us the way to the management systems of the future. Insights shared by Dr. Ko Nishimura, CEO of Solectron (although I have never met him personally), have had the most influence on this book.

I would like to thank participants in American Society for Quality's "Baldrige Assessment" courses over the last nine years who have challenged me to study deeply the sources of high performance. I also am grateful to the several dozen firms and agencies that have invited me to assess their management systems and help coach their efforts to achieve higher performance.

Thanks are due to Jerry Christen, Kenneth F. Edwards, Brian and Tyler Fairbank, the late Robert K. Mueller, Robert Stankard and Richard Wells for reading and commenting on early versions of this manuscript. I especially thank Mark Alpert, who generously reviewed the final version of this book with me and made many helpful comments. My editor, Eric Valentine, also read and suggested many improvements in the book. My old friend Marjorie Jensen generously spent many weeks editing a draft of this book and her husband, Joel, suggested that I add the last chapter. Marj's hard work has added enormously to the book's organizational and editorial clarity.

Although many years have passed, it would be an injustice to omit a thank you to my teachers of long ago: Russell Ackoff, Richard Clelland, Morris Hamburg and the late Roger Sisson. I now see that these fine teachers at the University of Pennsylvania's Wharton School in the 1960s provided me with a whole system of learning and knowledge. Since the mid-1970s, the teacher from whom I have learned the most is the late W. Edwards Deming—through his writings and through subsequent discussions of his philosophy on the Internet. I am grateful to these teachers and to all the others who taught me.

Last, and most of all, I would like to thank my wife Debbie Tarsitano-Stankard, to whom I dedicate this book. She has taught me more than I can ever say about the human side of life and work. Since human feelings drive business progress, her contribution has been the greatest of all. Debbie has truly been my "inner help" with her insightful questions and suggestions. I also want to thank my son David Stankard, who first suggested the bicycle analogy for explaining the system that appears in the Appendix.

I cannot do justice to all those who have taught me the lessons on which this book is based; I apologize if I have inadvertently overlooked someone deserving of acknowledgment.

PART I

Management Systems

CHAPTER 1

See Your Business as a System

A system is a whole that cannot be divided into independent parts. . . . The performance of a system is not the sum of the performance of its parts taken separately, but the product of their interactions.

—Russell L. Ackoff, *The Democratic Corporation*

The outstanding profitability performance of a growing number of firms is not accidental—these firms profit because they have built world-class management systems. This does not mean that there is anything mechanical or bureaucratic in the way they operate. Quite the opposite; these firms shape their processes and methods so that they work together for high performance. These firms perform well because they are designed to grow in profit, size and management capability. Their managers focus on the behaviors, strategies, processes and measures that must work together as a system to find and satisfy customers, as the following true story shows.

A few years ago, a manager from of one of the world's largest investment-banking houses came to a course on measuring management systems against a business model known as the Baldrige Criteria. When asked what brought him to the class he said that his firm had been making hundreds of millions of dollars investing in Swedish firms. He explained that the Swedish government regularly surveys its citizens on their satisfaction with goods and services in their economy. His firm used the government data to search for companies that systematically were raising customer satisfaction faster than their competitors. Once identified, the investment firm sent analysts to interview management and determine if the firm had systematic methods to raise customer satisfaction. The investment bankers then bought stock in the firms with the best system for pleasing customers. They had found that increasing customer satisfaction was a reliable leading indicator of profit growth.

The banker went on to say that when the Baldrige award was introduced in the late 1980s, his firm brought its stock-picking strategy into the U.S. stock market by investing in Baldrige award winners. It had done extremely well buying stock in firms that had just won Baldrige Awards. (As reported at the Baldrige Award Conference in 2001, this group of firms as a whole has historically outperformed the Standard & Poor's 500 by over 400 percent.) The banker concluded by saying that he was attending the Baldrige course to find out how to identify firms that were building Baldrige award-winning management systems—before they won awards. His firm wanted to invest in such promising companies before the broader market recognized that these firms were preparing for high long-term profit performances.

There has been much progress in management over the last forty years: the rise of marketing as a profession; the introduction of computer and telecommunications technology to process data and speed information flow; the development of strategic planning and strategy; the expansion of industrial research; the introduction of powerful project management tools; the development of quality as a competitive weapon and the widening use of process management to deliver market-breaking quality and service at low cost. Whatever your position in the organization you may have helped lead efforts to adopt some or all of these progressive methods. Yet, a single integrating concept encompasses all these important developments and trends, and one hardly sees a coherent essay or article on this concept in business and management journals. This single concept, which becomes ever more important as businesses and the world grow more complex, is the concept of a system—a collection of parts that work together as a whole in order to carry out a defining purpose. This book's main purpose is to help you look at your own business as a system and to introduce that view to others in your company. Then, when you grasp the system view, you can begin working toward a better system. This work consists of comparing your organization to a high performance model and then making organizational improvements in an annual cycle of assessment and follow-up.

This book also explains how to use a widely accepted standard or model to help your organization progress toward truly high performance. Assessment reveals your organization's relative strengths and opportunities for improvement as a basis for planning changes in your management methods. Then follow-up organizes teams of employees to act on the most significant opportunities for improvement. Such regular, systematic assessments are crucial to sustained high performance in the current competitive climate. So this book seeks to give you a point of view, an understanding of systems and a process of improvement that helps you evolve your management system to higher and higher levels of performance. Those higher levels of performance and the demands made by your management system may lead you to focus on detailed management specialties. However, the driving purpose is to have a system of management that is equal to the task of generating excellent organizational performance for all stakeholders.

The greatest single step that you in organizational leadership can take toward building a growing, high performance business is to see organizational performance as the result of a system, not the result of isolated methods and decisions. The next important step is to use the *Baldrige Criteria for Performance Excellence* as a template to study your management system and improve it. This book shares lessons that managers of Baldrige winners have learned as they took these steps to build world-class management systems. It targets organizational leaders who think about the needs of their organization as a whole—and who want examples, true stories and insights they can use to stimulate that type of thinking in others.

You can use this book to develop new awareness of a business or organization as a system, so that systems assessment approaches can be used to (re)design your organization's management system for better performance.

Many books talk about what is new; this book mainly organizes proven ideas and methods into a more powerful management system. It helps you understand *why* a management system works well, providing a foundation for genuine innovation and invention. This book gives you the insights you need to take your organization—as it is now—and mobilize its transformation into a system that benefits all concerned. The book synthesizes several threads of contemporary management thinking and practice (e.g., quality management, customer focus, system assessment, organizational learning, knowledge management and innovation). All are valuable, useful and insufficient by themselves. They must be fit into a larger understanding of organizational performance. To see the whole management system, this book first gives you an intuitive, everyday understanding of systems so you understand why they work. Then it guides you through examples of high performance systems elements to see how to improve your own organization, using cycles of learning, improvement and innovation.

WHAT IS A SYSTEM VIEW?

When you think about your business as a system you can gain a better understanding of the "whys" of the business world than you can from analogies that model organizations as machines, living beings or even armies. A system view enables you to innovate beyond any existing model into ever higher performance systems. Thinking of a business as a system turns managers and leaders into designers of better, more robust, more profitable businesses and ways to manage them. In addition, system concepts allow people in a firm to recognize, diagnose and discuss more precisely what changes will improve results.

Mintzberg and Van der Heyden (1999) present an easy way to conceptualize a system view of your business by drawing a flow chart of its elements. All systems are made of parts, so the business flow chart will depict how two or more elements work together as a whole. The elements of your management system (such as market surveys, leaders, management behavior, strategic planning, workforce, processes, information flows, analyses, and so on) each show up as a box or other symbol on the flow chart. Arrows between pairs of symbols show how each pair of elements works together within your business. In his book, *The Democratic Corporation*, Ackoff (1994) defines five conditions that must be satisfied for this whole to be a system.

1. *The whole must serve a mission or purpose.* The mission of a business might be to find and satisfy customers at a profit. (A nonprofit or a government organization might omit the profit elements from its defining purpose.) In pursuing its mission, a system may perform functions within larger systems—industries, professions, society or the economy. For example, an organization plays a role within the economy by sharing wealth it creates with those who provide resources to it. It may play a role in society when it provides work opportunities and training that help people develop personally and professionally into better employees and individual members of society. It may play a role within a profession or industry by setting ethical and professional standards and sharing knowledge. However, functions such as sharing wealth, developing human resources, or leading an industry or profession, define the organization's roles within larger economic, social or industry systems. Such functional roles supplement but do not replace the mission of the organization, which defines its purpose as a system.

2. *Every element (symbol on the flow chart) can impact how well the whole performs its mission.* For example, a bank has many parts that affect its performance: lending, credit, information systems, retail operations and the like. If, hypothetically, a bank also employed an economist but left him or her out of all business processes, then firing the economist would not affect performance under most conditions; the economist is therefore not part of the system. The economist in such a case is an accessory to the system.

To apply this test to your business you would ask of each element on your flow chart, how deleting that element would affect the ability of the whole to carry out its mission. If your answer for any element is that it has no effect, you can erase it from the diagram of the system. So, for example, you might ask does market research help the business carry out its mission (to find and satisfy customers)?

After tracing through your hypothetical flow chart you would answer "yes." Market research seeks to understand your customers and those you want as customers. Arrows on your diagram would show that market research information enhances marketing, advertising and new product development. Enhancing these improves your business's ability to find and satisfy customers, which is part of its mission. If you were to cut market research out of your business (delete it from the flow chart) your business's ability to carry out its mission would suffer. So market research is part of the system. (Can you imagine what the flow chart must look like if market research is not part of the system, but is an accessory?) Every element shown on the business flow chart would have to pass this type of test. Any that fail the test are left off the business diagram, as they are not part of the system.

3. *Many elements must work together to carry out the mission of the whole no matter what environment it operates in; each element is essential for success, but no element can carry out the mission alone.* For example, a profitable business must be assembled from a set of units. Even a bare bones business must generate demand, produce goods and services to satisfy it and keep revenues and costs in balance. If you take any of those essential parts out of the business, the whole business cannot serve its mission, which is to earn a profit by satisfying customers. However, none of those essential parts, marketing, production, selling or finance alone can replace the whole business.

For any given business scenario, you can trace through the imaginary business flow chart deciding which elements must work together to carry out the mission of the whole. Each of the elements you identify is essential to the mission. If a single one of these elements, for example the sales department, could accomplish the whole mission by itself, you do not have a system. However, if you do have a system, omitting any element, such as the sales department, impedes the whole from accomplishing its mission. The sales department is an essential part of the whole, but cannot replace it.

To see how this works, take the situation in which a competitor begins winning away your best customers. Referring to your hypothetical flow chart, you trace out how your business will pursue its mission (finding and satisfying customers at a profit) in what is now a competitive environment. As you trace links through the business flow chart they gradually connect all elements that must work together to let your business succeed in its mission even though the environment has changed. For example, you might trace out how market research, finance, engineering, production, marketing and distribution can work together to come up with better products and marketing strategies to restore competitive success. Although each element (market research, finance, etc.) is essential to the success of the whole, no one of them alone can carry out the whole mission. Moreover, some functions, such as the legal department or the company economist, are not essential in at least some environments.

When elements on the business flow chart interact with elements outside your business you have to include environmental factors in looking at your business as a system. For example, your business may rely on suppliers or the Internet to help achieve its mission. Elements surrounding your business over which you have no control, such as the competitor in the example above, make up its environment. When success in achieving your business's mission depends on environmental elements such as suppliers or the Internet, the business is referred to as an *open system*. Other factors in the environment, such as competitors that influence your business performance, but which you do not interact with, define the *context* of the system. In business, it often is helpful to think of the system as consisting of several businesses: your suppliers, your business and your customers form THE system. When thought of this way, your business can be seen to operate as an open system within a larger supply chain.

4. *No element of the system has an independent effect on how well the whole carries out its mission.* The effect of any system element on the whole depends on how it works with at least one other element of the system. On the business flow chart, arrows show how inputs (links) from other parts of the system influence an element's role in pursuing the mission. For example, inputs from marketing and accounting to engineers designing your new product influence product performance and customer value. Marketing supplies engineering with such data as customer requirements, preferences, estimated volumes, competitive features and pricing. Accounting

inputs would include cost, investment and profit margin data. No matter how ingenious the engineers, their impact on the overall business mission depends on the quality of input received from accounting and marketing. In turn, the input from accounting and marketing depend on how these elements of the system perform (which depends on still another level of inputs, and so on.) These dependencies among elements of a system cause bottlenecks and create leverage points in businesses that motivate a system view of the business.

The statement—parts of a business that work in isolation are not part of a system—parallels the idea that no element of a system works alone. For example, a sales organization employs fifty salespersons working in their respective territories. If the salespeople do not interact directly or indirectly, they are not a system. They are a group of salespeople, and the overall result is just the sum of the individual efforts. However, once high- and low-volume sales producers form into teams to share knowledge, test new sales approaches and support each other's selling efforts, they perform as a system with the mission of expanding the sales of the whole sales force. The act of working together makes them part of a system to pursue a mission—more sales.

5. *The effect of each subset of business elements on the whole mission depends on the behavior of at least one other subset.* For example, the effect of the information system in the business flow chart depends on how effectively the training system prepared people to analyze data to make sound decisions. The effectiveness of the training system in turn depends on whether the personnel selection system chose employees capable of learning quickly. The effectiveness of the personnel selection system depends on how effectively the planning system anticipated future skill needs. The planning system's effectiveness depends on how effectively the leadership system defined future directions and opportunities, and so on. The effectiveness of parts of a system depends on how they work with other parts of the same system.

Much of the gain in performance you can obtain from viewing your own business as a system will come from understanding and exploiting these interdependencies. For example, opportunities interact with a firm's capabilities. The firm's success, given opportunities within its capability, depends on whether it can come up with a successful strategy and execute it. Chapter 5 will identify critical sets of dependencies in the form of system cycles that produce learning, innovation and improvement that fit together into a high performance management system.

Unlike other system models (e.g., computers, machines or even living organisms), a business is a *social* system. In the 1960s, Russell L. Ackoff, then of Penn's Wharton School, was one of the first to talk about understanding businesses as social systems. (Jay Forrester also spoke of and analyzed organizations as systems during the 1960s. However, Forrester approached business from the point of view of mathematical control theory, rather than Ackoff's treatment of them as social systems founded on purpose, communication, cooperation, learning and conflict.)

Ackoff articulated the vision of purposeful individuals whose behavior in organizations depends on communication, choice, learning and conflict/cooperation. A social system is made up of individuals and departments that have purposes, not just functions. As such, parts of the system can learn, develop and improve upon how they perform their business functions while constantly pursuing whole-system purposes (missions). In Ackoff's view, it is this learning, development, improvement and cooperation in pursuit of an ideal or ideals that help a so-so business turn itself into a social system capable of producing excellent performance from the interplay of ordinary elements.

The extraordinary, sustained high performance of the Baldrige award winners as a group has resoundingly proven Ackoff's social system view to be sound. These forty plus firms have shown how using a system view of their organizations to guide improvement leads to stronger management systems, capable of generating and managing growth. Organizations recognized for building high performance management systems by winning the Baldrige award have shown that they achieve organizational excellence without sacrificing the development of the capabilities and talents of all members of their workforce. They achieve outstanding profits yet they still contribute to the development and enhancement of their surrounding communities and the environment. They approximate the ideal of a social system in Ackoff's sense.

The system view is not an academic abstraction; it is a practical tool to be used in guiding improvement and managing performance. Viewing your business as a system gives you a practical way to ask the right questions—ones that reveal where change efforts yield maximum payoff with minimum resources. This view helps identify where parts are disconnected (or not aligned for the best performance) from your whole organization. The right questions also address what types of people and behavior are needed for high performance. The view of the whole—the system view—links several dimensions, from high-level strategy to work processes, from leadership behavior to daily production and office work. The simplest way to see how these pieces fit into a system is to develop a flow chart of your business that shows both the flow of work and the feedback of lessons learned to improve that flow. (To see one of the earliest examples of such a flow chart, the interested reader can refer to the diagram on p. 4 of Deming's book, *Out of the Crisis*, which reproduces the flow chart he drew for members of the Japanese Keidanren in 1950 [Deming 1989].)

In their Quest for Excellence presentation, Baldrige award winner OMI (2001) implemented the system view of its business by preparing a network flow model of 150 processes that make up its business. This Linkage of Processes (LOP) model shows how work flows from suppliers through three "mainstay" processes to reach the firm's eventual customers. Feedback about customer experience with the resulting services returns back to senior executives who work as a team to plan improvement initiatives for the mainstay processes. The senior executives of the firm use this flow chart to plan for the business. This simple LOP model, as OMI refers to it, provides a clear example of what this book refers to as a "golden cycle." OMI chose to define its golden cycle around its core of "mainstay processes." The following example tells of an executive who built a similar cycle around an emphasis on planning.

A management consultant with a background in banking took an executive position to help turn around the performance of a bank. He created an annual planning cycle and then hired consultants to help with the issues that arose during planning. This banker, however, used the consultants as teachers. He built the lessons learned from consultants into repetitive process improvement cycles driven by his firm's annual planning. By creating a companywide cycle he dramatically boosted company performance. Over several years, he built his organization (which had delivered satisfactory performance for decades) into a system for achieving high business performance.

This executive hit many rough spots in building his company's management system. He had to win allies. He listened to the opposition and resolved legitimate problems. He developed project management and change management skills in those who worked on improvement teams. The biggest surprise, however, was that he kept revolutionary change moving forward through gradual, evolutionary steps that formed an annual cycle of improvement. He started with a small pilot project to improve an important process. After a success with that pilot, he expanded on that first success. By learning from each success and expanding involvement to include more and more people, he expanded the cycle over several years into an enterprisewide management system.

The transformation of this executive's firm took several years (and is detailed in chapter 5 as the Yankee Bank case). He was committed to achieving high performance in the long term in order to stimulate the growth of his bank. It was this commitment to help his organization learn whatever it needed, from whomever could teach it, year after year for more than five years that made this individual and his organization's performance outstanding. Of course the ability to keep the business running smoothly as he built on opportunities and upgraded management and processes helped make his a success story. He combined the skills of both a committed leader and a very good manager. His two sets of skills—the ability to link planning, improvement and listening to customers *and* generating better and better results—enabled his organization to excel, even though he could not possibly have taken personal charge of every detail. Thus his leadership achieved results in five years that many decades of previous management did not.

The systems view is long term, not a quick fix. The gradual approach, using every lesson learned to improve the system of management and make the next cycle easier and more effective, works better than any other large organizational change model. A cyclic approach gives your people time to learn and to build on what they learn. It gives you and other leaders time enough to see what improvements you need to make in your management system. Furthermore, a simple improvement cycle almost guarantees that every repetition produces progress. It takes dedication to create these cycles and build a management system, but they are worth the effort because shareholders, employees, customers, suppliers and managers all benefit—especially the employees. Finally, although the task of management can easily outgrow even the ablest manager, that same manager can build a system that no reasonable rate of growth can outrun because the learning and improvement cycles keep the system even with expanding needs of a growing business.

This book refers to a management system based on company-wide cycles of profit improvement and wealth creation, with a focus on innovating for customers, as the golden cycle. Each cycle leaves customers, employees, other stakeholders and the whole business better off than when it began. The lesson from the banker's experience above shows the power of managers as builders of management systems; it also offers convincing evidence of the durability of management systems as executives who participated in building the original system went off to head other firms and took their insights with them. What's more, the man who built the initial management system went on to adapt the same system very successfully to an organization ten times the size of that bank.

You do not need managerial supermen to build a high performance management system; the system performs because its design enables ordinary people to deliver extraordinary results consistently. High performance *does*, however, require managers who understand, use and improve the system. Most organizations already have the building blocks in the form of management approaches and capabilities; they just stop short of linking what they have into a continuous cycle, which can amplify the performance of the whole. It is this "connecting the dots" and getting all parts working together that permanently boosts management effectiveness and business performance.

The beauty of basing business improvement on cycles of learning, improvement and innovation in a management system is that it ties separate elements into the whole. No element needs to be radically new or innovative, yet by behaving as a system, the whole produces radically new and innovative results. But how can you measure your management system's ability to produce such results?

Before moving on to the subject of high performance, a few definitions might help clarify the important concepts. This book distinguishes between *businesses, organizations* and *social systems,* although the terms may seem synonymous. A *business* is what the shareholders own. So a business is property and often represents someone's investment in hopes of earning a return. Please think of the system view you were invited to imagine earlier in this chapter. Within this system view, the sequence of assets, work and management processes and business relationships that generate revenue, cost and operational results such as return on investment (ROI), define the business.

Referring also to your hypothetical system's view, the term *organization* refers to the network of people, teams and units that work in, supply or partner with each other within the business. Although organization members may own the business, the business is the reason the organization exists. A key difference between an organization and a social system lies in the type of power within the network of relationships. Organizations usually allocate authority and responsibility, which define each element's "power over" neighboring elements. For example, the relationships among the officers and personnel of a military unit form an organization with well-defined ranks and degrees of "power over" known as command and control.

Within a *social system,* the coin of the realm is "power to" or capability; each element of the social system enhances every other element's "power to" accomplish its own purpose while enhancing the pursuit of the purpose of the whole system. So, for example, scientists in a field like chemistry each share their knowledge and scientific discoveries with colleagues through publications, conferences and the Internet. Sharing in this way expands other scientists' power to make further discoveries and contribute knowledge. No scientist has power over other scientists, but as a whole scientists fit together into a social system in which any scientist's power to discover enhances and expands the power of discovery for all other members of the social system of science. This collective sharing of knowledge expands the capability of the whole of science to explain real phenomena and enhances society through the use of that knowledge. Yet this progress arises from individual efforts of people to learn, share and be recognized for what they do.

In the same way, discovery and sharing of knowledge within an organization can enable high performance within that organization. The accumulation and use of knowledge within the organization, however, does not inevitably lead to improved organizational life and output. It takes a systematic effort to translate useful knowledge into new products, processes and business results. This fact defines management's role as builders of the management system that simultaneously limits and promotes business progress. The capacity of a management system to acquire and use new knowledge to create customer value and competitive advantage drives future business success; knowledge and practice are hard to copy and so, are hard to compete against.

The networks of management elements that do the planning, deciding, directing, coordinating, communicating, allocating and analyzing, make up its *management system*. The purpose of a management system is to link all parts of the business and organization in ways that encourage individuals to excel, as they work together to help the business excel and contribute to excellence in the surrounding environment. Understanding cause and effect within the business and its processes forms the foundation on which the business creates wealth. An effective management system creates and shares that wealth. If the organization's purpose does not include profit, as in education or healthcare, the management system maximizes other relevant performance objectives derived from the organization's mission.

When business, organization, and management system work together for the betterment of all in the organization they become a *social system*. When members of an organization work together to build up a business, assemble a system to manage it, develop their own individual capabilities, and contribute to the higher development of their environment, they are building a social system focused on that business. By enabling a business to create wealth, its management system strengthens the rationale for the organization and can allocate resources to allow the organization to evolve into a social system; one of the purposes of the social system is finding ever more valuable and uplifting missions for the business to pursue. All of these: business, organization, management and social systems, coexist at the same time and place within a high performance organization. They are simply different slices of reality through a complex high performance system.

One stepping stone on the path to organizational excellence is achievement of a new level of understanding—something that W. Edwards Deming called by the unfortunate name of "profound knowledge" (Deming 1993). The shift to high performance can be slow because of bottlenecks in the training and education of people who must work in organizations and within management systems designed on principles that impede the emergence of high performance. However, the lessons of the firms that have made the transition to high performance are not earth-shattering. In many cases the lessons learned from seeing business as a system are embarrassingly obvious. One of these lessons is that great people working in a lousy system produce mediocre to poor results, but average people working purposefully within an excellent system produce outstanding results. Another such lesson can be posed as the question: Why should customers be loyal to a business that its employees do not trust or think worthy of loyalty?

High Performance: Doing More with Less

A high performance business is a business that accomplishes with a 100-employee organization what another business needs 150 or 200 people to accomplish. Here is a simple example of high performance to stimulate your thinking. Just contrast a 100-person organization that attracts and pleases customers with superior customer value, productivity and quality against a 200-person organization in the same industry that has 40 percent customer dissatisfaction, constant employee and customer turnover, frantic and fearful management and business results to match—and you will understand what high performance is about. What factors let 100 people in one organization outdo twice as many working in a different, but similar looking organization? It is the way the parts work together as a whole so that the system achieves its mission or purpose more effectively that leads to high performance.

Now you have an introduction to the idea of a business as a social system, how a purpose defines the system's boundaries and how its overall performance comes from how its parts work with each other to pursue that purpose. The next step is to relate this understanding to your business and what you must do to improve its performance. Chapter 2 relates system thinking to two management system models: ISO9000 and the Baldrige framework. Since the purpose of this book is to show you how competitive leadership depends on improving your management system, most of the discussion in the following chapter is on the Baldrige model and the outstanding results achieved by businesses that have pursued it.

CHAPTER 2

Business Excellence and Its Payoff

> It would be better for everybody to work together as a system, with the aim for everybody to win.
>
> —W. Edwards Deming, *The New Economics*

Excellent business performance accumulates from sustained, long-term improvements. The kind of continual improvement capability needed to start toward high performance is actually a requirement of the current revision of the ISO9000 quality system standard. By embodying systematic and ongoing improvement in a worldwide management standard, the International Organization for Standardization (known by the abbreviation, ISO) has opened the door for firms all over the world to begin their journeys to excellent performance. While the ISO9000 standard makes a start, it alone is insufficient to achieve durable competitive advantage and high performance; its scope is too narrow.

Business excellence requires two things. The first is a company-wide capability to plan and deploy improvements focused on achieving strategic objectives. The current ISO standard does require firms to build a continuous improvement capability, however its improvement focus is narrowed to customer satisfaction and process performance without regard to overall competitive strategy and the need for profitability. This narrow scope of the ISO standard leads to the second requirement for excellence which is to balance improvements across four main areas: (1) economic opportunity and wealth creation (profitability), (2) strategies and motivation to realize the opportunities, (3) capabilities to execute the strategies and, (4) use of information and analysis to balance risk of loss with financial return.

In contrast to ISO9000 (which is a sound standard for its narrower purpose) the Baldrige business excellence framework considers all requirements shown to be necessary and sufficient for high performance. The Baldrige framework catalogs the elements in a full management system capable of competing against the toughest competitors in any market in the world. An organization that measures up to this standard is world-class; it goes beyond just those elements needed for registration to the ISO standard. This marks the first time in American business management that any well-regarded authority has attempted to catalog the "genome" of a highly competitive business. When you compare your firm's management system to the Baldrige model, you hold it up to a comprehensive and holistic standard to reveal its strengths and shortcomings. All strengths in your system enhance its effectiveness, just as every gap and shortcoming limits its competitiveness and presents an opportunity for improvement.

For example, the Baldrige framework asks you to "describe how your organization provides effective performance management systems for measuring, analyzing, aligning, and improving performance at all levels and in all parts of your organization." The ISO9000 standard also requires a factual approach to making process, product quality and customer satisfaction decisions. ISO goes on to require that records be maintained as proof to auditors that management did what they said they planned to do. However, measurements and recordkeeping that will satisfy an ISO9000 audit team often stops short of meeting the full-range performance needs of your business. Establishing what data, analyses and information your business needs to excel goes beyond the limits of ISO9000 to look at the whole business as a system (not just its product-, process-, and customer satisfaction-related elements). If you want to gain significant competitive advantage you must improve beyond minimum ISO9000 requirements in the directions suggested by a more complete model. The validated management methods and insights from excellent firms that have won Baldrige awards show how others have achieved excellence by building management systems beyond ISO9000. For this reason, this book adopts the Baldrige model as the basis for high performance.

Excellence requires managers to become leaders, change makers, and coaches in order to build a management system that will gain genuine competitive advantage. Where do these leaders draw their guidance? For lack of anything better, the answer is the experiences of firms that have won the Baldrige award. Knowing a little about the Baldrige performance excellence framework will help managers in developing a more powerful and durable management system.

OVERVIEW OF PERFORMANCE EXCELLENCE

Beginning in the late 1980s, a new method arrived to gauge and improve management systems and business performance. The Malcolm Baldrige National Quality Award, formed under joint industry and government sponsorship, offers three benefits. It prescribes a consensus set of requirements that a high performance management system must meet and a framework for gauging a given management system against; it provides a common language and a testing ground to showcase firms with truly great management systems and results; and it elevates whole companies (or at least their management systems) to the status of teachers.

Over forty Baldrige award-winning organizations have shared their methods and described their management systems publicly as role models for others to learn from. Firms that have built world-class management systems such as the Ritz-Carlton Hotel Co., OMI, Inc., Solectron Corp., Corning, Inc., and many more share what they know and show the way. Over the last thirteen years, twenty or more nations around the world have adopted versions of the Baldrige model for their own national competitiveness improvement efforts, confirming its usefulness across different cultures and economic situations.

A system view of your business will help you clarify how the major parts of your business, such as leadership, strategy, workforce and processes work together to achieve high performance (or do not). This chapter provides only a brief, high-level introduction to the *Baldrige Criteria for Performance Excellence* as a guide to its contents. To boost your confidence in the award-winning companies used as examples throughout the book, this chapter also summarizes research on the outstanding market and financial performance of firms striving to develop excellent management systems.

Reproduced from the 2001 *Baldrige Criteria for Performance Excellence* (NIST 1991–2001), Figure 2.1 fits the seven category-level components of the Baldrige framework together into a cohesive system referred to as the Baldrige management system model. The

Figure 2.1
Baldrige System Relationships

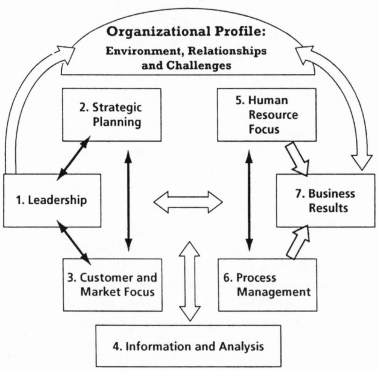

six categories labeled leadership, strategic planning and the like (categories 1 through 6) list requirements known as *approach and deployment* items. Approach and deployment items ask how your firm's methods and processes and their linkages meet stated requirements for high performance. For example, one item that deals with work systems asks that you: *"Describe how your organization's work and jobs, compensation, career progression, and related workforce practices motivate and enable employees and the organization to achieve high performance."* The methods your business actually uses to address this requirement are called approaches. (Business magazine articles that focus on how a leading business works rather than on personalities usually describe management approaches.) The seventh category, business results, contains four *result* items that give your firm the opportunity to show results that prove your approaches yield success in the areas of customer satisfaction, product and service performance, financial and market results, human resource development and organizational productivity and effectiveness. Together the six approach and deployment and the single result categories outline the full requirements of a high performance management system. These requirements are a model or template against which you can compare your organization's management system and performance to spot its strengths and the areas for improvement.

If someone asks you—why bother with the Baldrige model—the short answer is that it makes sense and it works. Figure 2.1 shows a flow from leadership and strategic opportunity (at the left) to business results (on the right). To understand how the model works, it helps to think of the framework in Figure 2.1 as having three elements or subsystems. The first is the strategic triad on the left of the figure, which orients the organization to its future by providing direction and purpose. The second is the result triad on the right, which develops and operates capabilities in the workforce, processes and systems of the organization. The link between the two, an alignment subsystem, uses action plans coordinated with a scorecard of financial and nonfinancial data and information to align all parts of the management system properly so they work with, not against, each other. These two major triads and their alignment work as a system to generate results that go far beyond what any of the methods could produce in isolation.

In the following description of the performance excellence system and its elements, the *italicized quotations* below are directly from the *Baldrige Criteria*. (Readers interested in a much simplified explanation of the Baldrige framework are referred to the appendix.)

Strategic Management Triad

The strategic triad of the management system links the three categories on the left side of Figure 2.1: 1. leadership, 2. strategic planning and 3. customer and market focus into a steering mechanism for the whole organization. Quoting from the *Baldrige Criteria*:

> *1. The **Leadership** Category examines how your organization's senior leaders address values, directions, and performance expectations, as well as a focus on customers and other stakeholders, empowerment, innovation, and learning. Leadership also considers how your organization addresses its responsibilities to the public and supports its key communities.*

The leadership category is about interacting with and attracting people in your organization to change, to winning, and ultimately to excelling. Leaders at all levels of an organization orchestrate change by working with customers and employees and understanding and tapping their motivations. Leaders also own responsibility for planning; they set high standards, and shape strategies based on a reliable understanding of customer and market trends as well as organizational capabilities. As an organization shifts to high performance, its leaders must learn to coach rather than direct. Leading in a high performance organization is about listening to those doing the work, observing them, seeing the problems and opportunities for improvement and giving coaching and help that works. Leaders also set the standards of behavior, both for individuals and for high performance values—so people know what is expected of them. Leaders periodically check progress against plans and expectations by conducting reviews. In these reviews they recognize and praise those who have earned the status of role models for others to emulate. When people are well led, they feel that someone cares, and that they know what they are doing, why it is important, and where they can get help when they need it.

*2. The **Strategic Planning** Category examines how your organization develops strategic objectives and action plans, deploys them and measures their progress.*

Your business cannot serve all customers in all markets offering all service and product combinations, through all distribution channels and at all price points; strategic choices must be made. The leadership of your firm works backward from identified goals in order to decide on strategic choices. These choices consider two factors. The first is what product or service qualities your organization can deliver that will attract and hold customers. The second is how your business's capabilities measure up against other firms competing for those same customers and revenue. To ensure progress in the planned direction, the business develops a road map, its strategic plan. The strategic plan maps the route from where the business is today to the more desirable future. It connects the strategy with actions and decisions in each unit so that the whole organization works the strategy in a coordinated fashion.

*3. The **Customer and Market Focus** Category examines how your organization determines requirements, expectations and preferences of customers and markets. It also includes how you build relationships with customers and determine the factors driving customer acquisition, satisfaction and retention and business expansion.*

The concept of *customer value* provides a long-term foundation for revenue growth as an input to planning. (This book uses the term *customer value* when talking of benefits a customer gets from a product or service in order to distinguish it from the word *value* used to describe what an individual or organization considers important.) Customers choose products and services that maximize the benefits they experience. In concept, customer value equals the benefits that customers get from buying and using your product or service minus what they pay you. Customers choose your products and services when they get more positive customer value from you than elsewhere. (Please do not confuse the best customer value with lowest price; top customer value offers customers the greatest benefits they can experience for the going price.) In this sense a Ritz-Carlton hotel room at $300 per night is a tremendous customer value for luxury-oriented guests in many hospitality markets. At the opposite extreme of a commodity product, a load of gravel from Granite Rock Co., at the going market price is a tremendous customer value to road builders because the firm's "Granite Express" service saves nearly twenty minutes loading time on each trip. The service makes picking up truckloads of sand and gravel as easy as a visit to an ATM. So both a luxury producer for the carriage trade and a commodity supplier of sand and gravel excel by finding ways to offer customers greater customer value as part of a growth and profit strategy.

In short, the strategic triad involves leaders in learning about customers and markets and in shaping strategic plans to offer greater customer value and to expand revenue. The plans consider the needs and capabilities of all stakeholders in order to maximize accomplishment and profitability. Implementing the strategy involves leaders in setting expectations, reinforcing both individual and high performance values, and coaching progress toward the objective. This feeds into the working end of the system, the Result Triad.

The Result Triad

Producing and selling products and services supplies the cash flow and profits to fund plans and investments that push the business forward. Similarly, the result triad links the three Baldrige categories that drive your immediate business results: 5. human resource focus, 6. process management and 7. business results. These categories provide the motive power that propels your business toward its strategic objectives.

5. The **Human Resource Focus** Category *examines how your organization motivates and enables employees to develop and utilize their full potential in alignment with your organization's overall objectives and action plans. Also examined are your organization's efforts to build and maintain*

a work environment and an employee support climate conducive to perfor-mance excellence, and personal and organizational growth.

Your organization's workforce—its employees—operates or "works in" your business's processes. Methods for identifying the characteristics of your best performing employees and for select-ing new employees with similar characteristics, as well as job de-sign and work assignment are critical to producing good business results. Human resource practices must themselves align with strat-egy and with daily operating needs of the workforce. This includes assessing training needs, arranging for or delivering that training, measuring and understanding employee motivation and satisfac-tion and implementing programs to raise workforce morale and well-being. Increasingly, demands of high performance call for in-volvement of the workforce in innovation, assuming responsibility for customer satisfaction, and for making decisions that can affect costs and profits. When backed up by sound training and coach-ing, such workforce empowerment provides people with more sat-isfying jobs, gets better results, and cuts the cost of supervisory overhead. This powerful combination does much to boost overall performance. Of course, in the result triad, results also depend on the actual work itself—your processes.

6. *The **Process Management** Category examines the key aspects of your organization's process management, including customer-focused design, product- and service-delivery, key business and support processes. This category encompasses all key processes and all work units.*

As the workforce develops, the organization develops in paral-lel as it adopts ever improving processes. In simple terms, operat-ing processes are the work designs or recipes your business follows to turn what it buys into products and services that meet your cus-tomers' needs. If you follow a poor process you will achieve poor results. To generate better business results takes two kinds of changes in processes: remedies for faults so that more things go right and improvements and innovations that make a process even better. The kinds of specialization and job simplification that indus-trial engineering used as a basis for designing work processes has now become obsolete in many cases. End-to-end re-engineering of key processes raises customer value and cuts out waste and error, driving costs down.

Processes are a locus of organizational learning. The workforce learns to use processes through training and by accessing process documentation. The combination of workforce practice and process effectiveness drives business performance. Improvements in processes therefore must be reflected in changes in training, documentation, and workforce skills. New and better technology usually enters into the business through processes. When well-motivated and well-led employees work with capable and continuously improving processes, they generate ever better results.

*7. The **Business Results** Category examines your organization's performance and improvement in key business areas—customer satisfaction, product and service performance, financial and marketplace performance, human-resource results, and operational performance. Also examined are performance levels relative to those of competitors.*

As your organization shows improvements you can measure them in market share, customers satisfied, income, expense, quality, and productivity. A business improves as it operates, by learning and using what it learns to innovate and improve until it achieves levels that exceed the competition. As long as work on processes yields a flow of process changes that improve process performance, business results improve. As you and other managers and leaders alter your firm's directions and refine its processes, you vary the balance among its parts. The third part of the management system links the strategic triad together with the result triad to ensure that they work well with each other. The final elements that complete the whole system are alignment and integration of the parts into an effective whole.

Alignment and Integration

The third and last major component of a high performance management system aligns the future direction of the strategic triad with the operational and result-oriented result triad, to unify organizational efforts into an integrated system. Two companywide elements perform this alignment function within a business management system: (1) developing action plans to deploy strategies that meet the firm's challenges and (2) relying on information and analysis for plans, priorities and decisions. Between the left and right triads, the information and analysis category serves as a foundation for the management system that aligns all parts of the system with overall objectives and provides feedback and information for corrective action and control.

*4. The **Information and Analysis** Category examines your organization's information management and performance measurement systems and how your organization analyzes performance data and information.*

The first companywide element for aligning your management system consists of the goals, objectives and measurements of progress from the information and analysis category of the Baldrige framework. Shown at the bottom of Figure 2.1, information and analysis feeds facts on actual progress by all work units forward for review by your firm's leaders, tightening alignment of all the business units. As part of their participation in action planning, managers throughout the organization define measures to show how their units link with their strategic responsibilities. These measures include financial data, but usually balance accounting information with nonfinancial data on customers, process performance, suppliers, cycle times, as well as workforce skill and capability.

Measurable goals and targets for improvement defined during action planning guide the collection of data and information throughout the business. Regularly comparing actual results against plans produces another benefit—systematic learning. The learning improves everyone's understanding of what factors make a difference in results and what cause-and-effect relationships drive your business performance. In particular, the framework of strategic planning, deployment, aligning/measuring and correcting/learning form the principal cycle of high performance in the business. Creating this cycle within your business should be the objective of efforts to develop an ISO9000: 2000 compliant management system.

Involving all organizational units in deploying strategy is the second element that ties the strategic front end to the tactical back end of a business. Units take the strategy and come up with action plans and goals that transmit steering forces from your organization's strategy to action and changes throughout the organization. The arc at the top of Figure 2.1 represents a link between strategies and actions that addresses the firm's opportunities, challenges and relationships with customers and others, throughout all the firm's units. Each unit's participation in action planning to implement strategy helps to link its capabilities to, and align its change efforts with, your firm's strategic objectives. The process of connecting strategic planning with planned changes in the business (workforce, suppliers, products, processes, etc.) also involves process owners and unit managers in setting goals and expectations. This network of strategies, action plans and measurable goals aligns the firm's units and processes to overall direction and creates a framework for measuring progress.

You now have an overall insight into the high performance business model and the seven categories of requirements that define it. These categories are themselves broken down into more detailed requirements known as items. Items in turn are spelled out in several areas to address. In all, the 2002 criteria have seven categories containing eighteen items and twenty-nine areas to address. There are minor changes from year to year at the item and area levels, as the criteria are updated to reflect new discoveries. No management system meets all requirements of the performance excellence model, so the next section describes how Baldrige recognizes different system capabilities.

MANAGEMENT SYSTEM MATURITY

Some management systems produce better results than others. Some firms may be just starting to link improvement projects with planning. Other firms, with more mature management systems, have years of experience in coordinating innovation and improvement with strategic planning and measurement. A second aspect of the Baldrige framework, called scoring, systematizes these differing levels of maturity into a summary of the management system's relative competitiveness. Although in school a perfect test score is

100, an assessment of a perfectly competitive management system scores 1,000 points. Baldrige scores let you assess the relative competitiveness of your management approaches and results using a repeatable, objective, scoring system.

The criteria express requirements for two types of items: *approach-and-deployment* or *results*. Approach-and-deployment items describe the management methods your firm actually puts into use (or deploys) and how they work. So, for example, a firm may have sound approaches for maintaining customer relationships, but be in the early stages of deployment because they only use these approaches with large national accounts. Result items contain tables and graphs of the business results that your approaches produce and compare them to benchmarks or competitors where possible. Continuing the example, the company may be able to show good customer satisfaction and loyalty in national accounts, but has no results to show for other customers. Approach, deployment and results make up three dimensions of the scoring system that quantifies the maturity of your firm's management system elements. Figure 2.2 shows the three dimensions and their relationships: planned approaches must be deployed, creating an expectation of results; checking compares actual results with expected, leading finally to evaluation and refinement in preparation for another cycle. The terms approach, deployment and results, along with the relationships shown in Figure 2.2, provide a vocabulary for talking about what is going on inside the management system. They are defined as follows:

Approach—what method or process does your business use in relation to a particular requirement of the Baldrige criteria? For example, process management approaches explore how your firm manages its operations to turn out high quality consistently at ever lower cost. Process management also asks for such information as how your firm innovates to create customer value and improve performance.

Deployment—how does your business use a particular approach to address requirements of the criteria that are relevant and important to your business? Deployment considers where your company uses its approaches to meet both its own business

Figure 2.2
Relationships among Baldrige Scoring Dimensions

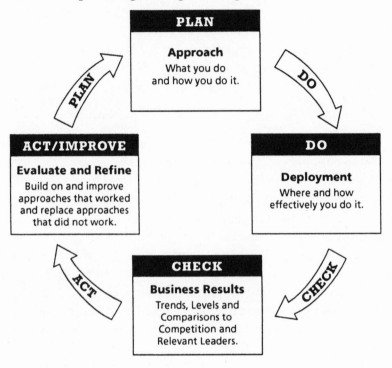

needs and the requirements of the criteria. Needs of the business, in turn, are defined by its environment, context, organizational relationships, strategic challenges and improvement system.

Results—what measurable improvements in performance trends and levels result from your firm's deploying its approaches? Usually firms new to performance improvement show outstanding improvement trends; year to year progress moves from poor levels of performance upward. As firms begin to excel, however, improvement trends level off, but at comparatively high levels. Result items seek benchmarks or comparisons with your competitors' results to establish how good your results are.

Recognizing Maturity of Approaches

The parts of a management system—for example, management methods, data used and actions taken—are not static. They evolve and improve their performance over time—or, as a Baldrige expert might pontificate, they "achieve higher levels of maturity." As better performing parts become more closely integrated into your business, maturity and performance of the whole management system rises. Some businesses get along with immature elements in their management systems or with actual gaps where no systematic approaches exist. Managers compensate for deficiencies and system gaps by doing the best they can when they need to, and hope that their best is good enough. When faced with gaps in a management system, performance boils down to individual (often heroic) effort to compensate for those gaps.

When you compare your management system against the high performance model, the news is seldom all good or all bad; all systems of management include both strengths and areas for improvement. The following scenario outlines the increasing maturity of a hypothetical customer service approach.

1. *No systematic approach*—"do the best you can." Even in the best firms, things go wrong, and customers complain. A firm just starting out may take customer complaints as they come: whoever receives each complaint does the best he or she can to make the customer happy or passes the complaint along to someone else. As the business grows, the function of servicing customers with complaints may be located in a specialized customer service unit (usually referred to euphemistically as the complaint department), which develops information systems and processes to resolve customers' complaints quickly and effectively. (This represents the state of the art in many businesses that occupy niches or compete against local or regional peers.)

2. *Beginning of a systematic approach*—resolves complaints systematically once they come in. Instead of asking everyone to do the best they can when customers complain, the firm sets standards for complaint resolution. It bases its standards on an

understanding of how customers want to be treated, what they care about, and what the firm must do to make them happy. The firm then trains its customer contact staff in methods of resolving complaints, and provides them with the supporting information and access to systems that let them restore customer good will (the state of the art in well-managed businesses currently at the top of regional markets.)

3. *A sound approach*—treats each complaint as an opportunity to make the customer happier and more loyal than if the upset never occurred. This approach goes beyond the specific customer complaint by seeking ways to prevent upsets that customers complain most about. The firm begins to organize its systems and processes to operate in "improvement mode," taking improvement steps and making changes that anticipate, avoid, and prevent complaints. For example, every month an improvement team counts up the complaints to find the number one cause of customer upsets—often referred to as "ouches." Once the team knows its top problem, it investigates the organization's processes or product designs to find its cause. By working with management to remove this "ouch" at its cause, it makes an improvement for future customers. Once it verifies that its action was effective, the team repeats the whole process on the next most damaging "ouch." Such a sound approach signifies that this firm is probably competing successfully in national or export markets and is in the early stages of generating superior customer satisfaction and loyalty results.

4. *A well-integrated and mature approach*—integrates complaint identification and prevention with planning and improvement priority setting throughout the organization. The organization goes beyond resolving complaints and recovering customer good will and loyalty. To boost performance still further, the firm's methods analyze complaint data against customer loyalty and retention to relate improvements to increased revenue and profitability. The strategic planning process uses these analyses as one of several inputs as it develops customer-focused plans. (This level of approach is the state of the art in

a world-class firm, one that competes successfully against the top competitors in any market in the world.)

When you compare your management methods against the performance excellence model, the results lead you directly to actions that you can take to improve your business. For example, suppose you compare your customer service approaches against the model and find that, while each unit has practices and procedures, you lack overall standards, common methods, training and data collection; in short, you lack a systematic approach to customer service. The service experience of customers doing business with you depends on which practices and procedures they encounter—some worse than others.

The implication of continuous improvement is that your business takes one step up on the maturity ladder from where it operates now. In the example that move would be from having no systematic approach to full deployment of a systematic and effective customer service approach. The model does not tell you how—it is nonprescriptive. Developing and deploying a systematic customer service approach across all points of customer contact will advance the maturity of your approach, deployment and results. The business justification for such an action is that you would expect a systematic and effective customer service approach to improve customer retention, leading to more revenue and higher future profits. Figure 2.2 shows how the approach, deployment, results and refinement fit together into a cycle of improvement.

At a higher level of competitiveness, if some units already have a systematic approach to customer service while others do not, the next step is to refine your existing best practice, deploy it to all units, measure the results and make it a part of your management system. As your management methods attain each step on the maturity scale, they give you a plateau from which to advance your management system to the next higher level of effectiveness and competitiveness.

Most firms quit progressing toward more effective management systems when they feel that their management methods are good enough to be competitive. For example, if your customers insist that your quality management system be compliant to ISO9000, most firms improve their relevant management approaches until they can get a registrar to issue a certificate of compliance. After registration they coast and maintain compliance with the standard. However, once all supplier management systems are similarly registered, none of the suppliers has a competitive advantage over its competitors. If your business operates in competitive markets that demand ever higher performance, your organization must evolve more mature management systems just to survive. In some highly competitive international markets only outstanding management systems survive at all.

The ability to recognize the relative maturities of your business system's approaches and of your whole system takes a broader concept of how to evaluate and improve your management system. Baldrige answers this need through a scoring system that can be used to diagnose your opportunities for improving management approaches with high precision. Chapters 10 and 11 will cover this topic in detail. Now that you have a sense of a system's maturity, the next section explains how the Baldrige scoring system lets you quantify maturity and competitiveness.

The Scoring System

To quantify levels of management system maturity, the Baldrige framework outlines expectations for "good, better and best" responses to each item requirement. (Each item has a point weight such as 45 points or 80 points; the sum of these item weights equals a total theoretical maximum of 1,000 points.) Scoring refers to the process of assigning percentage ranges (0 percent, 10 percent to 20 percent, etc.) to indicate relative maturity and effectiveness of an approach. The assignments of scores are guided by these good, better and best expectations. If the approach being scored has the "good" characteristics, but not the "better" or "best," it will earn a score of 20 percent, or 30 percent out of 100 percent. If the approach has most of the characteristics of the "best," then it will earn a score in the 80 percent to 90 percent area. The sum of all 18 individual item point weights times their percentage scores indicates the maturity of your firm's management system compared with the 1,000-point Baldrige model.

Table 2.1 shows how numeric scores signify different levels of approach maturity. Scores in increments of 10 percent range from a low of 0 percent, signifying no systematic approach to a requirement, to a maximum of 100 percent, signifying an appropriate, effective, systematic approach, deployed thoroughly, and well integrated into the management system.

As your business improves its use of information and analysis throughout your organization, it becomes possible to measure business results beyond financial results. Evaluation of these results provides an important confirmation of the effectiveness of the management system. Once again, the scoring system relies on a "good," "better" and "best" characterization of result trends, levels and comparisons to competitors as a guide to assignments of percentage scores. Table 2.2 shows the progression of maturity in results

Table 2.1
Various Levels of Approach Maturity

Approximate Scoring Range	Approach Description	Deployment Description
Little or no evidence of approach (score of 0% to 10%)	Reacts to complaints quickly and promptly	Examples here and there
Low (score of 20% to 30%)	Audits processes occasionally	Several customer groups, products, locations
Medium (score of 40% to 60%)	Audits processes regularly and follows up on findings	Most important service processes and some support processes covered with effective, prevention-based methods and controls.
High (score of 70%+)	Measures key customer and employee satisfaction drivers, re-engineers all processes accordingly, reviews and improves re-engineering approach regularly	All main product, service, and support processes covered with refined and innovative prevention-based methods and controls

Table 2.2
Various Levels of Result Maturity

Approximate Results Maturity	Result Description
Little or no evidence of favorable results (score of 0%)	No results or poor results
Low (score of 10% to 30%)	A few good results, but neither trends nor comparisons to competitors or benchmarks
Medium (score of 40% to 60%)	Good improvement trends in most indicators, better than some benchmarks
High (score of 70%+)	Excellent trends/levels in all indicators and better than relevant (tough) benchmarks

and how it correlates with percentage scores on corresponding items. The evaluation of results depends on factors such as: current performance levels compared with benchmarks and competitors; how broad, rapid, and important the measures are that show improvement; and whether your firm sustains its improvement and high performance over time.

Your management system's overall maturity and therefore competitiveness lies on a scale between 0 and 1,000 points. The higher its score, the more competitive your firm and the more rapidly it improves key indicators of market effectiveness and operational performance. For example, a management system that scored 50 percent on each of the 18 Baldrige items earns 500 points out of 1,000; a firm that scored 30 percent on each item would earn 300 in total. Other things being equal, a firm with a 500-point management system will significantly out-compete and out-perform a firm with a 300-point management system. The more mature 500-point management system links more highly developed approaches into a more effective system than its less mature 300-point competitor.

Because the upper end of the Baldrige scoring range (600 to 1,000 points) sets a world-class standard, Baldrige scores usually disappoint American managers encountering them for the first time. In U.S. schools, a passing grade is usually 70 percent. Initially, many managers expect that, if their firm is already doing pretty well, it should get a passing grade—which their experience suggests would be 70 percent; they hope to see Baldrige scores of about 700 out of 1,000 points. Unfortunately, many successful firms—even some that regard themselves as "world class"—learn from comparing their management system to the performance excellence standards that they score only 200 to 300 points out of the 1,000 possible. This score implies that these firms' management systems are beginning to meet requirements for high performance, but gaps in approaches or deployment prevent their methods from systematically working everywhere necessary. Even very successful firms often learn that their management systems fall short in several areas when compared to a world-class standard. The news that their business success depends more on competitive and external factors than on their management systems is often hard for managers to swallow. (Unfortunately, it is nevertheless true.)

High performance firms in the United States that have calibrated their management systems against the Baldrige criteria earn a score of about 500 to 600 points on a 1,000-point scale. Unfortunately, almost all U.S. firms—even those with management systems registered to earlier versions of ISO9000—score only about 200 to 300 on that 1,000-point scale. A management system certifiable to the current ISO9000 standard should be able to earn between 350 and 400 points on the 1,000-point Baldrige system maturity scale. However, the issue is not the number of points on a measurement scale.

The ultimate prize in business is market leadership and customer, employee and shareholder loyalty. A minimum Baldrige score to achieve durable competitive advantage against relatively strong competition lies in the region of a 350 to 450-point Baldrige score. It is a fact that most firms prosper with much *weaker* management systems. However, you should not mistake good luck for good management. Firms with 300-point management systems can prosper as long as they compete against other firms also running 300-point management systems. However, they run into trouble as soon as one of those competitors improves its management system up to 400 points and then to 500 points, thus changing the competitive situation.

Less mature management systems rely on reactive approaches much like the prizefighter holding his arms up, protecting his face and head from an opponent's jabs. Each time the opponent jabs, the boxer fends off the jab as best he can. The firm that reacts to jab after jab prospers as long as the competition does no better. But, as our consumer electronics and auto industries found when the Japanese entered their U.S. markets years ago, competing against firms like Toyota with world-class management systems is difficult even for firms as historically successful as GM, Ford and Chrysler. High performance firms leave the reactive mode of managing behind and adopt an improvement approach; they spend a greater proportion of their resources on improving and innovating than they spend reacting to "ouches" from omissions of the past. The current revision of ISO9000 now requires that firms institute ongoing improvement of the quality management system and product and service delivery processes. However, any firm able to meet this narrow requirement for improvement need not stop with processes, customer satisfaction and management responsibility. It can use the high performance business model to guide improvement in planning, technology, workforce development, supply chain and any other area of the management system that bottlenecks growth in revenue and profits.

In contrast with ISO9000, Baldrige does not require that management methods be formal or documented in great detail. Approaches used in small firms may be quite informal, while larger firms often rely on formal methods. Baldrige requires that your management methods be appropriate, effective, and well integrated and that they meet your firm's needs. For example, one small firm holds an annual management retreat to formulate its strategies into action plans, and all participants enter their plans and deadlines into day-planners. Checks with managers throughout the organization revealed that the whole organization used these day-planners to plan and track all plans and activities. This informal but effective approach deployed strategy and action plans in all parts of the firm. Such an informal approach effectively met the small firm's needs; however, a large firm would rely on a more formal approach to deploy its strategy and action plans. ISO9000's requirements for formal documentation and record keeping are designed to facilitate independent audits, which are not customary when building a high performance management system. So if you start out to build a high performance management system and you also want to earn registration to ISO standards, you may have to formalize certain aspects of your system and data to allow for the necessary audits. Next we will move on to the payoff from improving your management system's maturity.

EVIDENCE OF THE PAYOFF

In order to banish any doubts about the payoff from developing a *high performance management system,* this chapter presents the conclusions of three research studies on business performance of firms with award-winning management systems. Without a systematic basis for corporate performance, business results become a matter of luck. Author C. K. Prahalad cited a 1991 study by Electronic Data Systems (EDS) which found that only 40 percent of the 1970 Fortune-500 firms were still alive and well in 1991 (Hamel and Prahalad 1994). What happened to the 300 or so dropouts from the list of leading firms of the 1970s? Either their luck ran out or someone else tried harder, had better luck, and bought them out. Relying on good luck for long-run business success should make both managers and investors uncomfortable. Relying on good luck is not a long-term business strategy. These three studies will demonstrate that a well-designed system of management can produce sustained growth and good performance. The first of the three studies concerns the stock market performance of firms that have been awarded the Baldrige Award for Performance Excellence, which implies that their management systems scored roughly 600 to 700 points on the maturity scale.

NIST Studies of Financial Payoff

Each year for the last six years, the government agency NIST, which runs the Baldrige award, has reported on its "Baldrige Stock Index" (NIST 2000, 2001). The index is a fictitious mutual fund of publicly traded firms that have earned a Baldrige award. This index thus provides an estimate of the payoff from investing in organizations with high performance management systems. To assess the performance of award-winning firms, NIST invested a hypothetical $1,000 in the common stock of each 1988-1999, publicly traded Baldrige award recipient, in the year it applied for the award.

NIST found in its 1999 study that the group of whole-company winners—ADAC Laboratories (1996), Eastman Chemical Co. (1993), Federal Express Corp. (1990), Motorola, Inc. (1988) and Solectron Corp. (1991 and 1997)—outperformed the S&P 500 by 4.8 to 1, achieving a 1,101 percent return on investment compared to a 228 percent return for the S&P 500.

A comparable investment in a group made up of the six whole-company winners plus the parent companies of eighteen subsidiary winners outperformed the S&P 500 by about 3.8 to 1, achieving an 841 percent return on investment compared to a 222 percent return for the S&P 500.

Even seventy firms that have received site visits from a team of Baldrige examiners outperformed the S&P 500 by approximately 2 to 1, achieving a 351.52 percent return compared to a 174.68 percent return for the S&P 500. The group of fourteen whole-company site-visited applicants outperformed the S&P 500 by almost 2.2 to 1, achieving a 390.71 percent return compared to a 180.23 percent return for the S&P 500.

As this book goes to press, NIST has announced that the stock study updated to 2001 has shown that the "Baldrige Index" sustained its outperformance of the S&P 500 for the seventh year. The whole-company award winners maintained a 4.4 to 1 lead and the larger set of whole-company and subsidiary winners came in at 4.2 to 1.

Despite the NIST study's findings, managing a company, its quality, and productivity as a system may not guarantee success. For example, small firms may be subject to external shocks, and larger firms may face formidable competitors that also use world-class management systems. Either situation can upset performance, even though the company's system is excellent. However, the NIST study provides strong evidence that systematic quality management leads to outstanding returns in many business areas, including stock market performance.

There is one case where a Baldrige award winner went out of business. The famous Wallace Co. experience—in which a small-business Baldrige award winner later failed—shows that even a firm with an excellent management system faces hazards. In Wallace's case, its industry went into a slump, and failing competitors began dumping inventory at bargain prices. Wallace's loyal customers could not resist the temptation of buying product for less than half Wallace's cost and they left Wallace to take advantage of the fire sale prices. To make matters worse, as Wallace was coping with extreme price competition its bank withdrew its line of credit; management was unable to replace that credit line before time ran out and had to sell the firm. None of these contingencies had its cause in the management system. (However, the Wallace Company's management system could be faulted for not handling external or environmental risk adequately.)

The NIST stock study confirms the strategy of the Wall Street investment bankers who had been systematically investing in Baldrige winners (mentioned in chapter 1). However, skeptics may argue that the performance of Baldrige winners relative to the S&P 500, results from conditions in industries in which the winners operate. Perhaps the Baldrige award-winning firms were just lucky and happened to be in high growth or highly profitable industries. What is true? You can see from the next study, which accounts for industry and economic factors.

Hendricks and Singhal Study of Award-Winning Firms

A major scientific study by Hendricks and Singhal (1997) covered firms that have won any publicly recognized quality management award (not just Baldrige, but state, consulting firm and publicly recognized customer quality awards). This study is compelling, because it compares performance not against an arbitrary stock market index, but against carefully chosen control firms selected by industry and time period to be comparable to the award-winning study firms.

The research considered awards for Total Quality Management (TQM); defined as a customer-focused program of continuous improvement and organizational innovation (a definition less stringent than the criteria for a Baldrige-based management system). The study's intent was to replace published "studies" of TQM, generally based on surveying managers' perceptions of the benefits or demerits of TQM, with audited accounting data from published financial statements. They sought data on all quality award-winning firms between 1983 and 1993, assuming that winning a public quality award means that a firm had implemented "an effective Total Quality Management (TQM) System." Quality awards are based on independent assessments of management methods, rather than on financial results, so relying on a quality management award eliminates the possibility of favoritism toward firms that were already financial star performers.

Hendricks and Singhal compared award winners versus matched nonaward winners to eliminate the effects of industry and economic trends on performance. They studied a broad spectrum of U.S. business sectors, finding 335 firms in 180 SIC codes that met all their criteria. The 335 "study" firms (1) had won an award, (2) had available at least six years of published accounting and operating data, and (3) had at least one comparable firm to use as a control. The control firms were roughly the same asset size, had publicly available performance data for the same time, no public award for TQM, and operated in the same 2-digit SIC code. Since the study assumed that it takes five years for a firm to build an award-winning management system, the researchers studied a period from six years before study firms won their awards to three years after—a total of ten years. The study found five statistically significant results:

- Four measures—operating income, and the ratios of operating income to assets, operating income to sales, and operating income per employee—all improved significantly in the year just before winning the award. From the time of implementing TQM (one year before winning an award) to three years later, the study firms outperformed their controls on operating income by 35 percent. Over the whole study period (from six years before the award until three years after it), the TQM firms outperformed the control firms by 107 percent on operating income.

- Sales per employee between study and control firms hardly differed at all. However, once a firm wins a recognized quality award, its sales begin to outperform the matched control firms; over the long term, the TQM firms outperformed the controls on sales growth by an average of 64 percent. In contrast, TQM versus control comparisons on cost as a percentage of sales showed the TQM firms only outperformed the control firms by 1.27 percent, which was barely significant (a difference that small could happen just by luck in one out of ten comparisons).

- Study firms increased the ratio of capital investment to assets significantly more than did the control firms—up 9 percent. Apparently, firms that implement TQM make significantly higher investments than do their non-TQM peers in the same industry.

- Employment at the TQM firms rose a highly significant 17 percent more than that at the control firms, meaning that the TQM firms added employment.

- Total assets of TQM firms were up 45 percent more than the assets of the controls for the 10-year study period.

The researchers concluded that implementing a management system capable of earning a public quality management award "clearly improves the operating performance of firms relative to industry peers who do not upgrade management systems." The performance of firms after they win one of these awards is clearly better than the performance of comparable firms that win no awards.

Second Hendricks and Singhal Study of Award-Winning Firms

In a sequel to their earlier study, Hendricks and Singhal (2001) studied how stock market prices were impacted by deployment of a TQM system. Their method once again was to take a firm's receipt of a quality award as the signal that the firm had a high performance management system in place. Their research considered stock market valuations of a sample of nearly 600 award-winning firms, each matched with a control firm (by market capitalization and/or industry) that did not win an award. They considered what would happen if an investor bought and held a fixed amount of each firm's stock and obtained the following stock market results:

- Buying and holding stock in the award-winning firms over the four years prior to their award slightly outperformed buying and holding stock of the matched control firms for the same time period. A buy and hold investment in the award winners to-be was up 99.33 percent while the control firms rose by 92.58 percent over the four-year implementation period (during which each TQM firm was assumed to be investing in upgrading its management system). The negligible difference between study and control investments indicates that the cost of developing a sound management system neither helps nor harms a firm's stock valuation during the period before full deployment of the system.

- The award winners significantly outperformed the non–award-winning controls over a five-year period when their high performance management systems were in place. Stock prices of the award winners rose by 117.66 percent over the five-year period while the stock prices of the same-industry controls were up 79.82 percent. This difference in performance is statistically significant meaning that there is little possibility it is simply due to chance.

- The average difference in stock market performance between each award winner versus its control company (averaged across nearly 600 such pairs) was 37.84 percent. The odds that a difference of this size could occur by chance are about 40 to 1 against.

- Not all award winners did extremely well in comparison with their matched controls. Although the average performance difference just cited was nearly 38 percent in favor of the award winners, the median difference (across the nearly 600 pairs of firms) was only 17.27 percent in favor of the award winners. The big difference in average versus median share price gains implies that the best performing award winners outpaced their controls by a wide margin. (The average includes each data point with an equal weight; so a few really big gainers can pull the average up. The median, however, is only the middle observation out of a group of data points so it is insensitive to the best and worst performances.)

Although the researchers do not speculate, the fact that the best award winners far outperformed their peers is consistent with the hypothesis that some of the award winners clobbered their industry competitors. They might do this by offering better quality at lower cost. For example, using a hypothetical one to ten quality scale to rate goods and services, suppose most of the award winners attained quality levels of nine in industries where competitors without such systems already produced quality rated at eight. The competitive advantage (and presumably relative stock performance) of the award winners, being one notch above the competition, would be relatively small. However, if the award-winning firm turned out quality at a nine level in an industry where competitors (including the control firm) produced a five or six quality rating, customers would see the difference. In such a scenario, the control firms would lose market share to the award winners, causing their relative stock market performances to diverge.

- Some observers criticize a buy and hold investment criterion by pointing out that if an award winner had a good year early in the study period, compounding on the new higher share price could make the award winners look as though they were outperforming the controls, when the only source of different performance was compounding of the early good results. To adjust for this the researchers looked at month-to-month changes in performance. They found that the award winners outperformed their controls by an average of 0.5 percent per month over the entire history studied. This difference could only have occurred by chance in one instance out of 100, so the monthly average return is statistically better for the firms using a quality management system.

- The researchers also studied the relative outperformance in the early months of operation of the TQM system versus later results after winning awards. Although the award winners outperformed their controls during both periods, as time went on they widened the margin of outperformance versus the control companies. The authors conclude that the stock market systematically underestimates the worth of deploying a sound quality management system and catches on to the benefits only after they show up in results much later.

After seeing proof that an effective quality and performance management system can lead your firm to high performance, what do you need to know next? You need to know that even managers in firms that say they want to achieve high performance frequently fail. They fail in thousands of small ways for a few big reasons as the following incident shows.

A chief executive opened a meeting with his management team on the subject of Baldrige assessment and improvement; he gave a moving talk about his aspirations for their organization to achieve excellence. As the meeting went on, one of his managers told a story about how a clerk in the tax department used an obsolete typewriter to fill in paper forms that word processing could not handle. Her typewriter broke and she had been complaining about the need to repair it for over six months with no action. Everyone looked at the CEO expecting a reaction; he did not bat an eyelash on hearing of this clerk's plight and made no comment. That incident made an impression; what a message it sent, and what a wasted opportunity to stress what really matters! How can an organization excel as a whole while its upper managers do not recognize their professional and personal responsibility to help its members succeed as individuals in their jobs?

Those trying to transform businesses to achieve the kinds of results shown in the three studies above often fail because they do not understand what is really important. Despite more than ten years of struggling with ISO9000 and TQM, many organizations simply lack an understanding of people and why they resist change. Processes and people that have worked with them for years will push back against change. Overcoming this resistance takes less pushing and more learning at all levels, but especially learning the importance of eleven high performance values. (The ISO9000 standard refers to a subset of eight as its management principles.) These high performance values form a sound and permanent foundation for the management system. They guide you when there are no strict rules and they keep you focused on what is important for success. The next chapter reveals the importance of high performance organizational values—standards of behavior—in shaping the development of an organizational social system.

CHAPTER 3

High Performance Values

Try not to become a man of success but rather to become a man of value.

—Albert Einstein

Whatever affects one directly, affects all indirectly. I can never be what I ought to be until you are what you ought to be. This is the inter-related structure of reality.

—Martin Luther King, Jr.

The fact that your organization is a social system sets it apart from physical or biological systems. People working within a social system are purposeful; they have to know how to behave in myriad daily situations. The organizational or cultural forces that shape their purposes and behaviors are known as *organizational values*. Other values such as honesty, integrity, accountability, respecting others and the like are characteristics of individuals and will be referred to as *individual values*. People must generally be selected for their individual values; a thief hired by an organization that considers honesty important is unlikely to become a saint just by working there. However, once hired, members of an organization learn organizational values from the "four Ps"—praise, promotion, privilege and punishment. Whatever behavior earns praise, wins promotions or privileges becomes important. Whatever is punished becomes unimportant.

The simplest way to understand the role of organizational values in shaping an organization's performance is to look at a case where the organization is deficient in a key organizational value. The following example of a utility that was losing market share after deregulation shows how organizational values shape high performance behavior and conversely, a gap in organizational values can depress performance.

The utility company in question experienced disappointing revenue growth for several years after deregulation ended its monopoly in certain markets. Falling revenue forced three rounds of staff reductions in three years. In order to turn things around, senior managers decided to assess their management system against the Baldrige model. Among other requirements, an item in the customer and market focus category of the criteria asks how a firm systematically (1) measures customer satisfaction and (2) relates various levels of customer satisfaction to likely purchase, customer loyalty, and referral behavior. Most organizations fill up several pages describing how they measure customer satisfaction and use the data to plan market opportunities and better customer relationships. However, this firm only needed one line to state honestly: "We are too busy to measure customer satisfaction and use the information in planning improvements." Of course, the feedback report cited the lack of systematic attention to customer satisfaction as a gap and therefore an opportunity for improvement. Linking systematic measures of customer satisfaction to planning and improvement would help the firm reverse its market share loss and resume growth.

However, when you think about the utility's system deficiency more deeply, the real opportunity for improvement was to plug a gap in organizational values. Top management had a blind spot; their actions signaled to people that selling, cost cutting, and boosting financial results were urgent priorities, surveying how happy customers were became low priority by default. If management really considered customer satisfaction important, they would ask that it be measured and they would stress the need to improve satisfaction in order to build customer loyalty. The practical implication of this insight is that if top executives made customer satisfaction important in this firm (say by measuring it and linking performance bonuses to higher satisfaction), they probably would not be losing customers, and there would be less need for downsizing and cost cutting. But unfortunately, the message received was that if people spent time and money on customer satisfaction, but could not tell management what was happening with sales and costs on a weekly basis, they could lose their jobs. Customers responded to this indifference by switching to the competition in droves.

This organizational value gap—failing to make customer satisfaction important in everyone's work—blinded the organization's search for ways to strengthen customer relationships and halt declining market share. This gap loosened the firm's hold on future income in order to boost profits now. Such a gap is not likely to cause this business to fail quickly (in fact this firm was acquired by another company). However, closing the gap by adopting customer-driven behaviors would have gone a long way to halting customer attrition and sales decline, and put revenue and profit back on an uptrend.

An organization proves that it considers customer-driven excellence important when it sacrifices something to put that organizational value into action. As you look over your organization, ask yourself what you have really sacrificed for. Sometimes the sacrifice may be to listen to customers, especially unhappy ones (your own and your competitors'), when you would rather not. Horst Schulze, formerly COO of The Ritz-Carlton Hotel Co., tells the story of how his organization won numerous awards for being the best hotel chain, even though his customer comments ratings suggested that there were many areas for improvement. Because he considered customer satisfaction more important than the praise of hotel critics, Schulze coached his organization to continue driving for excellence in serving guests. Encouraging staff to find ways to anticipate customer wants and needs even after winning top industry awards led to many innovative methods that attract and provide guests with genuine care and comfort in a luxury environment. This puts the company still further ahead with its own guests.

Not surprisingly, behaviors—like focusing on customers—show up across high performance firms in all industries. Such behaviors, ingrained in your firm's culture, become your *high performance values*. High performance values are shared across the whole organization, so they are organizational, rather than individual. Most wall plaques in corporate lobbies state company values as integrity, accountability, respect for individuals, open communication, fairness and the like. These are individual values. Organizational values summarize lessons your organization has learned about what things are important (often learned the hard way rather than by studying the successes). The utility incident shows how an organizational values gap led honest, high integrity, hard working people to ignore or neglect things that were critical to the organization's survival. Organizational values gaps often arise from a single-minded reliance on performance appraisal through the four Ps— pay, promotion, privilege and punishment. In the long run, any business that does not consider customer satisfaction important will eventually fail in the marketplace. In the utility example, the organization's purpose had shrunk down to delivering short-term profits, ignoring that the profit came from unhappy customers who could choose other service providers.

Being customer focused is one of the primary survival organizational values of every successful business; after all, customers put money into the business. Sometimes, managers have to experience a blinding flash of the obvious before adopting organizational values that are essential for long-term survival, let alone high performance. Comparing your management system against the performance excellence model can provide such a blinding glimpse of the obvious. Assessment feedback often points out inconsistencies between what an organization says is important and what it actually rewards and does. Identifying and resolving contradictions between these values and the firm's actions strengthens your business's foundation for high performance.

Years of observing high performance organizations have revealed eleven high performance values that they share. The list of high performance organizational values has evolved as understanding of excellent business performance has grown, so the eleven are not carved in stone. As your organization faces tougher market, competitive, and technological demands, it will learn for itself why each high performance value is important in strengthening its management system. This learning and adoption of high performance values separates successful organizations from the failures in a given competitive environment. The following thumbnail sketch describes the evolution of the eleven high performance values and gives you a sense of the role each value plays in developing a high performance management system.

HIGH PERFORMANCE VALUES EVOLVE FROM MEETING CHALLENGES

Profit and cash flow help ensure business survival; so valuing business results responds to the basic need to survive. The importance of profit performance provides a starting point in the following story of how high performance organizational values arise in response to demands on an organization. Suppose that you organize a firm to carry out a good business idea, perhaps it is a new way to deliver childcare services, just for example. Your purpose may be to pursue this idea with a passion, because you really care about children—not just your own—but all children who need care while their parents work. Along with really caring for the welfare and development of the children you serve, your business needs to be profitable in order to remain in business. While your mission is to care for children, in organizational value terms your commitment must also focus on *business results*—measured by how much your revenue exceeds expense.

Making financial results your dominant commitment presents you with few options for improving business performance. To raise profits in this situation, you seek low wage employees, lower-cost facilities and suppliers, and charge prices as high as parents will pay. Although these behaviors raise your financial results, they also cause undesirable side effects, such as:

- Seeking cheaper facilities and suppliers turns suppliers into adversaries; they supply lower quality products and services. Less expensive facilities and locations may raise parental concerns about the safety of their children and the aesthetics of your service. This will not attract future business.

- Hiring lower-paid employees or cutting wages attracts less capable employees and demoralizes your workforce. Unhappy workers soon leave for better jobs, forcing you to hire and train replacements. Staff turnover not only upsets the children, and their parents, but also raises your employment and supervision costs. Again, this is not good for business in the long run.

Despite these side effects, focusing your attention on results still leaves you able to compete as long as your products and services are no worse than your competition.

The picture changes radically, however, when some competitor offers your customers a real choice. For example, a new firm hits on the idea of running a childcare center right on the site of an employer for whom most of your customers work. The employers prefer your competitor because on-site childcare helps them retain many of their best people who need convenient childcare to be able to work. The competitor also hires the best staff available because inferior childcare will displease parents. In one stroke your customer base of parents gets a high quality, subsidized childcare option available conveniently located right where they work at about the price they pay you. This competitor has used innovation and new insights into the economics of childcare to give customers more customer value, and to enlist employers as partners in reducing their employees' childcare worries. Many of your customers switch to this new competitor because it is convenient and they expect their children to benefit from higher quality staff and programs.

You must respond quickly or see your customer base and revenue shrink. But responding only from your commitment to boost business results will only worsen your competitive disadvantage and put you out of business sooner. For example, trying to cut costs and prices further to hold customers and remain profitable is likely to reduce quality and drive customers away even faster. So, competitive tactics based only on an analysis of business results hurts your ability to fight off the new, higher customer value competition. Such a crisis forces you to behave in new ways to survive. You must focus on (1) *results as well as on creating value* by paying attention to what customers get that benefits and interests them in order to counter competition and achieve good business results in the longer run.

Competition teaches you to be as committed to customers as you are to business results or you will go out of business. Soon you are investigating the full range of what the customers want, and how you can enlist cooperation from employers in your area to open on-site branches of your childcare center. You explore your own employer partnerships and find out what employers, parents, and children want and need. Your behavior shows that your firm is learning the high performance value of (2) *customer-driven excellence*. As you offer services based on what customers want you to excel at, you also must commit to (3) *organizational and personal learning*, which means learning to do new things in better ways. Adding two new commitments to your original high performance value, business results, leads you to innovations that delight current customers and successfully defend you from the competitive attack. Acting on these organizational values results in: a steady flow of improvements in service to customers; better work and service processes; employees who aspire to do a good job; and better skills and education that lets your workforce attain higher personal goals. You have also redefined local employers as your partners in offering good quality childcare as a benefit to their employees. Partnering with employers is important because your partners help you stay up with and pull ahead of the competition.

Because you now recognize the importance of learning, you realize that you must select creative people who want to learn, experiment, and innovate in how they care for children. You begin identifying top performing child care workers; you also find out what pay and working conditions you have to offer to attract the best to your organization. Once you attract the best childcare providers, you need to retain them. If they stay with you, they cannot work for competitors, and their creativity and innovation make them assets in your business. Consequently, you listen to your workforce as they listen to children and parents. Soon the workforce suggests ways to deliver more customer value to parents, employers and children for less cost. You also work with vendors of supplies, training materials, professional staff, your space, and others with whom your business partners. You measure and improve your customers' satisfaction; as satisfaction improves, so does customer loyalty, positive referral and your competitiveness. You gain advantage from (4) *valuing employees' and other partners' help*. This commitment to cooperating with your partners and employees becomes a high performance organizational value, which helps you come up with services and products that offer customers significantly more customer value.

As you run out of easy improvements, you find that staying ahead of competition forces you to search for ways to attract new customers, and for new ways to excel in quality and operational performance to keep them happy. To expand your employees' and suppliers' knowledge and improvement skill, you set up teams of employees and managers to study every area of the business that generates cost or provides customer value, and draw on the knowledge of those working closest to the opportunities. Your team members seek opportunities to generate more customer value or less cost, or both. Soon people become proficient in gathering and analyzing data in order to (5) *manage by facts*. Creative ideas and opinions are always welcome, however facts are needed on what makes a difference in costs and customer value in order to provide a steady flow of improvements. Your growing understanding of which factors in your service drive customer satisfaction accelerates improvements in business results. Process improvement becomes an organizationwide "must do," while gathering and analyzing facts produces new knowledge that drives creativity and innovation.

At this point, you also redesign the role of managers in your centers into coaches and teachers and away from boss or supervisor roles. As managers learn to manage by facts they can teach employees to control their own work. Giving employees measurements and tools that let them control their own work processes frees up managers' and supervisors' time for innovating products and services, and the processes that deliver them. Improvements no longer take hit-or-miss tinkering with your business. Instead, you see the business as a whole—as a system. You see how your firm and the people who work in it, rent to it, or supply it must learn and cooperate. You design the system so that all stakeholders share in the prosperity brought about by high quality childcare that excels for its customers. All of your organization (employees, suppliers, processes, etc.) seeks to cooperate on serving customers better and keeping them loyal. Cooperation might provide more flexible facilities arrangements, technological innovations that let parents view their children even from their desk at work, staff workshops to share lessons learned, and many other large and small win-win opportunities.

Seeing the whole organization as a system leads you to manage the parts in the best interest of the whole system. You now have developed a (6) *system perspective*, which seeks to align all units of the organization with the overall interest of the organization and all its participants. By this stage of development you would be managing your organization as a companywide system. It possesses all of the methods and organizational values to begin rapid improvement in business results; for the first time, your system focus lets you create a companywide improvement cycle. This golden improvement cycle consists of:

1. Planning strategic opportunities and improvements annually, based on what might attract and please customers and deliver better childcare;

2. Making the improvements in products, services and processes on a pilot basis to test them;

3. Checking the results of the pilot against your original projections and expectations; learning what worked from the results of the pilot test; and,

4. Scaling up what worked well, and seeking a better theory of what pleases customers to replace ideas that did not work out as expected.

Each repetition of this cycle leads the organization to a greater understanding of what pleases customers. Thus the system view produces an organizationwide cycle of learning and improvement known generally as a Plan, Do, Check, Act/Improve (PDCA/I) cycle. This golden cycle defines the main interactions of the management system as it pursues higher performance and better business results. The golden cycle, however, depends on customer-driven excellence, learning and managing by fact, key organizational values that you have already seen.

Your system view also leads you to define employers as partners, making them part of the whole system. Employers who hire parents; parents who want their children to have excellent care; and children who are the primary reason for your business all participate in the system, along with your staff, managers, supervisors and other stakeholders. The organizational values of your organization have expanded far beyond the original mission of providing childcare to make a profit, but you are now well on your way to doing just that with excellence.

As you improve, your competition improves also. You invent ways to outdo their best; your competitors—if they are to survive—also learn and improve. Each round of competition offers better market choices to customers. Gradually, both you and your competitors speed up the pace of innovation. New offerings and improvements in customer service levels take less and less time to market. To remain competitive, your firm becomes flexible, responsive, and fast—in sum, (7) *agility* has become important. Each competitive improvement invites your response. As staff innovate in one childcare center, lessons learned are shared with all other locations with minimum delay; the more agile your firm becomes, the sooner you can offset any competitor's advantage. In addition to making your organization more agile, this sharing of lessons learned demonstrates a commitment to organizational learning, driven by personal learning of your most innovative staff.

As your firm evolves toward a position of market leadership it becomes more proactive about creating new opportunities. Your firm's management stops simply reacting to fend off competition. To continue progressing, you (8) *innovate*, shifting from working on what already exists, to inventing a better future. Innovations may build on insights into what is stimulating, creative, and helpful to the development of children in your care. You might innovate in the area of what happens inside the childcare center—its curriculum, for example. Or you might run counter to low price competitors by innovating your hiring, training and development processes in ways that differentiate your childcare providers from low-wage baby sitters that less expensive competitors employ in their operations.

Shifting from market follower to market leader requires (9) *visionary leadership* to mobilize change by focusing on where your organization wants to go. Orienting your organization toward a vision ensures that you do not waste time and effort pursuing temptations for quick and easy profits that lead into blind alleys. The vision also provides a (10) *focus on the future*, which helps you make long-term commitments that position your firm for long-term success. Corporations seeking childcare services as a benefit for their employees want partners with a future, not fly-by-night operators with no plans beyond the next payroll. Employers must know where your organization is going before they will partner with you by setting aside or leasing space, or offering your service as part of their human resource package.

In many small but important ways your firm's success also depends on its reputation within the communities where you hire employees, find customers and suppliers, and develop professional contacts. Treating these communities as important, you identify ways to help them; you do good things and avoid doing anything harmful. You become more public-spirited and responsible, focusing on (11) *public responsibility and citizenship* in each of your organization's communities. Gradually, as customers and partners sing your company's praises, your reputation brings in new business by word of mouth. Having a reputation as a place where people enjoy their jobs and develop personally, also gives you an advantage over the competition in hiring top quality staff. Not only has your management system evolved to organizational excellence, but your reputation for excellence attracts excellent staff in a virtuous cycle. The secret of success is to aim high and rise to the challenges.

The above fable shows how an organization's set of core organizational values expands as its management system moves up the maturity scale to high performance. Each high performance value emerges as the organization learns how to respond to requirements imposed by competition, technology, stakeholders' concerns, or other challenges. As members of your organization act on what is important for the organization to achieve high performance, they show what organizational values they are committed to. An organizational value does not tell people how to act. But pervasive actions and behavior across an organization does tell you what that organization values. So organizational values and individual commitments drive behavior.

The decade-long scenario above portrays the evolution of a hypothetical firm's organizational values. Note that each added high performance value benefits the organization by ensuring its evolution in the direction of excellence under ever changing conditions. A high performance firm blends and stresses some high performance values more than others, as necessary to maintain ongoing improvement. The specific management system that evolves in your organization depends on which organizational values dominate your firm's culture and how the people of the organization act upon those organizational values. Each high performance value fits in and enhances the effectiveness of the other organizational values, expanding your firm's competitive capability.

The eleven high performance organizational values introduced by the childcare example above play a critical role in integrating management system elements into a system for performance excellence. Organizational and certain individual values also are a rallying point for key individuals in transforming a firm to high performance. As an organization learns what is important for success, it spots those employees whose individual values fit with what the organization needs; it also spots employees whose individual values conflict with what is becoming important. One duty of leaders throughout the organization is to weed out those with incompatible values before these people's individual values lead them to work around or sabotage vital changes.

Readers interested in fuller explanation of these high performance values are referred to the full definitions of the core values in the Baldrige criteria. Those readers interested in the ISO9000 management system standard will recognize that the eight principles underlying the system standard are virtually identical with their Baldrige counterparts. This means that most management methods motivated by Baldrige core values (the eleven high performance organizational values above) will be consistent with the requirements of the ISO standard. Now that you have seen how your organization's values guide development of your management system, the next section shows how high performance values support system cycles of learning and improvement that drive performance improvement.

CYCLES EMERGE FROM ORGANIZATIONAL VALUES

The United States built a marvelous nation out of a population of immigrants that valued economic opportunity for all, individual responsibility, and freedom of speech, religion and action. Our shared national values have shaped our society. In the same way, what your business considers important and commits its energy, enthusiasm and creativity to shapes its management system and culture. If you are committed to excelling for customers, then you will generate your business results through that customer commitment. If you are committed to learning, then you will improve processes and individual skills through that learning commitment. If you consider improvement important, you will measure improvement in key results and analyze data to understand what drives better results. If you think it is important to put these commitments together in an organizational system, you have discovered the key to high performance. So progress in management arises through your commitments to what is important to achieve high performance. Commitment to anything less produces less.

Just as your firm learns the importance of high performance values when confronted with ever more challenging business requirements, adoption of strong organizational values stimulates higher management system effectiveness. In a business, people who really hold high performance values—such as putting customers first, or taking organizational and personal learning seriously—will organize themselves, if they must, to put those values into action. Your people can learn to put organizational values to work more rapidly, however, once they adopt a systematic approach to learning such as the PDCA cycle of continuous improvement.

Organizational values, especially the eleven high performance values, are a generalized commitment rather than a specific design. They guide how parts of a business behave toward each other. A cycle that combines the important behaviors for high performance focuses the business on continuously expanding its wealth-creating potential by inventing newer and better ways of pleasing customers. Institution-alizing these high performance values allows a continuous cycle of wealth creation to arise when an organization begins managing all of its elements as a *system* focused on finding sources of *customer-driven excellence* while *learning* to improve processes by analyses of *data*. The importance of the four *italicized* high performance values above is that they are all necessary before you can build a durable management system for generating wealth. Omitting any one of the four central organizational values: system view, customer-driven excellence, organizational and personal learning, or management by fact, breaks the cycle of learning and innovation.

In Part I, you have seen how to look at your business as a system. You have also gained an overview of the Baldrige model, which provides a template for checking your management system. Finally, this chapter has emphasized the role that individual and especially organizational values play in the evolution of your management system. Now, what about these "cycles"?

The concept is simple: The interconnectedness of a system's parts means that causes and effects can form a ring or circle in which eventual effects return later to affect their own causes. If you ignore the existence of cycles within your business system, your "reasonable and rational business decisions" may lead not to improvement but to a mess. What is reasonable and rational in isolation often ignores your firm's interconnected feedback loops. Something happening in one part of your business can set off a chain of linked events that eventually returns to belt you in the back of the head. To see this clearly think of the last time you tried to make a large scale change that was reasonable and rational. Chances are that you had a number of surprises, few of them pleasant and all of them at least once or twice removed from what you intended to change.

The cure? Use cycles of learning and improvement to upgrade your organization's management methods and performance. Part II will explain in detail how these cycles of learning and improvement boost performance. The next few chapters on cycles present a new and more dynamic approach to organizing the elements of a management system for performance excellence than the seven-category Baldrige model presented earlier.

PART II

Cycles of High Performance

CHAPTER 4

Cycles of Learning, Innovation and Improvement

We know that all things work together for good to those that love God and who are called to his purpose.

—Saint Paul, *Romans 8:28*

An organization that cannot *learn and improve systematically* cannot benefit from seeing its business as a system. It cannot effectively put the eleven high performance values to use. It may use the Baldrige model as a template to find opportunities to improve, but will not turn those opportunities into business results. Its quality management system may be registered to ISO9000, but it will not progress beyond mere compliance to the standard and so will yield no competitive advantage. The missing element is the performance advancement process itself.

Systematic learning and improvement is not new; over eighty years ago Walter Shewhart, working at Bell Telephone Laboratories, laid the foundation for modern process improvement. But putting learning, innovation and improvement to systematic use on the scale of a whole business is very new. The idea is to make learning and improvement an ongoing and routine part of all aspects of daily life in your organization by building it into a repetitive cycle.

Ongoing activities such as annual planning, new product development, investment and personnel development all go on in cycles. Some cyclical patterns arise from your firm's daily work: sell one, make one, ship one, bill one, service one—and then do it over and over and over again, in a cycle that produces revenue. All of these repetitious cycles accomplish their purposes, but without necessarily improving how well they work. However, a learning and improvement cycle organizes a steady, focused accumulation of knowledge and effort across your enterprise to produce excellent results as years go by and as environmental and economic conditions change.

Within an organization, cycles of behavior that produce steady, purposeful learning and improvement also provide *durable* (not momentary) high performance in your organization. Organizations that have achieved and sustained high performance through good times and bad have instituted ongoing patterns of behavior that continuously improve their capability to produce good results. Cycles link static parts of your business into a dynamic whole that works as a system. Since learning takes time, the more your organization knows, the longer it will take competitors to catch up, so you achieve a lasting competitive advantage.

VIRTUOUS CYCLES

A "virtuous" cycle leaves your organization better off at its end than when the cycle started. For example, high performance service firms (such as Disney or The Ritz-Carlton Hotel Co.) often pay relatively low wages when compared with competitors yet they have spectacular service and high employee loyalty. They create a virtuous cycle based on providing a good place to work, which attracts the best employees. The high quality workforce is trained to render superior service to customers, which boosts customer loyalty and sales revenue. By eliminating causes of employee dissatisfaction, they cut employee turnover, which reduces hiring and training costs. Thus, a cycle revolving around satisfied employees in good jobs gives great service, lowers cost, widens the firm's performance advantage, and increases employee job security—a virtuous cycle in which employees, customers and business owners all win.

Some management standards for quality systems require that management operate a cycle of improvement. The auto industry standard for supplier firms (known as QS-9000) mandates that supplier firms adopt a virtuous cycle of continuous process improvement. The worldwide ISO9000 standard similarly mandates continual improvement in a network of processes to maintain customer satisfaction with product and service quality. These system standards often provide firms with their first encounter with ongoing cycles of learning and improvement—admittedly at the level of manufacturing and service processes, rather than in the management system itself.

The most durable and powerful virtuous cycle is known as the *Plan, Do, Check, Act cycle* of continuous improvement attributed to Shewhart. This Plan, Do, Check, Act cycle (often just called the PDCA cycle) is the prototype for most virtuous cycles in business. Historically, W. Edwards Deming popularized this cycle, first in Japan during the 1950s and then in the United States during the 1980s and 1990s (Deming 1989). In recent years some have renamed the "check" step of the cycle to stress the need for "study" in the sense of investigation and learning, while the term "improve" is often substituted for the final step, act. Both *Plan, Do, Study, Act* (PDSA) or *Plan, Do, Study, Improve* (PDSI) refer to the same PDCA cycle. This book uses the PDCA initials because managers all over the world recognize and understand that the initials "PDCA" describe continuous improvement. Here is how the PDCA cycle works.

CONTINUOUS-IMPROVEMENT CYCLE

Figure 4.1 shows the PDCA cycle, summarizing the scientific method for generating human knowledge into a few words and a simple diagram. Spears and Bowen reported finding the scientific method—Plan, Do, Check, Act—at the heart of the most competitive production system in the world (Spears and Bowen 1999). It shows up in how Toyota simplifies even the simplest tasks needed to build a reliable car at low cost. Short summaries of the four stages of the PDCA cycle follow.

The *Plan* stage of the continuous-improvement cycle uses inductive thinking. That is, it starts with observations of specific events

Figure 4.1
The Continuous Improvement Cycle

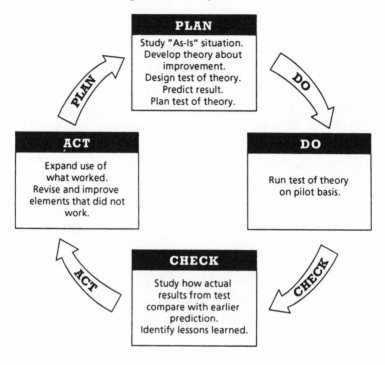

and arrives at a more general theory. For example, from observing how people use your product or service, you might develop a theory about how you can improve on your business as it is now (referred to as the as-is situation). The word theory refers to strongly held opinions about what might work better than the as-is. The specific area to be improved is unimportant; it might improve product, design, service, process, or method. The PDCA cycle works for all of these. To see how the cycle works, take the example of how Walt Disney is said to have invented the daily parade, which is such a popular attraction at Disney theme parks.

As the story goes, Walt Disney himself was hosting the opening of Disney World in Orlando, Florida. To celebrate the opening of the park, management decided to stage a parade with all of the park's cartoon characters, Mickey, Minnie, and so forth, marching with musical groups down Main Street. As host, Walt Disney was to ride in an open car waving to the crowd. When the parade marched down Main Street, there was quite a crowd, and Disney noticed smiles on the faces of all the onlooking guests lining the parade route. Without calling it a theory, Disney had the idea that all the people coming to Disney World would enjoy their stay more if they too could see a parade of Disney characters.

His theory was that there should be an opening day parade every day in the park to delight guests and make them want to return soon. (Such a proposed change from the way things are is often referred to as the "should-be" process.) Now planning a test of the theory is easy. All that the Disney Company had to do was to announce the daily parade, put it on, and see how many guests in the park showed up at parade time, lining Main Street to watch the characters march by. So, the prediction from the theory was that staging a daily parade would attract and entertain park guests. This would make them more likely to want to come back to Disney World. From this prediction, it is easy to set up measurements in result areas such as parade attendance, and surveys of guest intention to repeat visits. The theory also predicts that longer-term measures of customer loyalty and repeat visits would also improve.

To minimize disruption when any organization tests a should-be process, it is usual to plan a pilot test that provides a reality check on an improvement theory. In the Disney case, they probably considered the first few weeks of daily parades to be their pilot. If guests in the park ignored the parade, park managers would have to reject Walt Disney's theory and look for other attractions to keep guests delighted with their time at Disney World. A well-planned pilot test also lets organization members perfect their should-be process (putting on a parade every day may seem easy, but takes considerable coordination.) Finally the pilot lets everyone check both performer and customer reactions to the new parade process to learn how to improve the should-be process further. So, pilot testing daily parades gave the company the experience it needed to evaluate its longer-term business case and make needed improvements. Now with a plan for the pilot test of the should-be process, a prediction of results, and a plan for measuring the result the cycle moves on to its second stage—Do.

During the cycle's *Do* stage, you set up and run the pilot test of the should-be process, daily parades in this case, to give the new methods a fair chance to work. (This test is like an experiment that tests a hypothesis.) During the *Do* stage you would also measure the performance of the new business process on a sample of guests to see how well they liked it. The test must run long enough to see whether it increases or decreases guest repeat visits to the park. With the experience of running a pilot test of the should-be process, and with result measurements taken during the pilot, the cycle moves on to its third stage that *checks* the results of the test against the original plan and prediction. In the Disney case, the story does not go into how they checked whether the parades were a success, but anyone who has been to a Disney parade, knows that they were.

The *Check* stage of the cycle involves studying the measurements of results from the new process to learn whether the predicted improvements worked out. In this case, park managers would listen to what guests and parade participants liked and disliked about the parade and then go back to the drawing board. Comparing actual test results for attendance, satisfaction, and intention to return, against predictions made in the planning produces one of two outcomes:

- Ah-Ha: the should-be business process produces results as good as hoped for during planning; this confirms Walt Disney's thinking. Note that confirming Walt's original theory about improvement implies that expanding the parade idea to other Disney locations would be an improvement over the no-parade as-is situation.

- Oh-Oh: the actual results differ significantly from predicted; Walt Disney's theory about the should-be process was not confirmed. Based on their investigation of why the predicted results did not occur, park managers would come up with a better theory of what might please guests and a new should-be process based on what they learned from testing the last theory. When it happens, being proved wrong produces an uncomfortable feeling—which, more often than not, leads to the final stage of the cycle—Act.

Nothing ever works quite right the first time; the final, *Act* stage of the PDCA cycle depends on what lessons were learned during the check stage. If test results worked out as predicted, they boost confidence in expanding the use of the should-be process. In that case, Disney might standardize the new parade process and deploy it to other parks. If, however, the test shows that the new process falls short of predicted results, then park managers need to revise their thinking on what might delight guests. They would then repeat the PDCA cycle.

Repeating the PDCA continuous improvement cycle gradually accumulates practical knowledge about what works to please customers (or some other objective). Sharing each lesson learned throughout your firm, multiplies the return on your investment in the PDCA cycle that discovered each improvement. The new knowledge and skill gets more and better results with less effort. Unfortunately, implementing the cycle at the whole-business level means getting annual planning, market research, process owners, accountants and those working in the processes aligned with each other and focused on the common objective and carrying out their respective roles in the cycle.

One surprising fact about the PDCA continuous improvement cycle is that it is extremely hard to implement in a real organization. Leadership for change often conflicts with the management quest for stability and control that produces consistent results. Continuous improvement takes widespread cooperation and occasional persuasion, abetted by changing performance appraisal methods to reinforce cooperation. Although a cycle of continuous improvement represents change and is not easily implemented, the current ISO9000 standard requires firms to make a start on continual improvement. This is a first step in the right direction.

PDCA is an elementary form of the scientific method, which begins with a theory and a prediction—but, just as early scientists took hundreds of years to learn how to test theories against measurements, it often takes years for organizations to find the blend of leadership and management that lets them improve continuously. This balance between leadership and management partially explains why no other automobile firm has been able to duplicate

Toyota's production success. One method of stimulating cooperation to get a continuous improvement cycle rolling is to tie all senior management bonuses to measurable improvements they can
only make if they all cooperate. From experience of Baldrige award
winners, applying about 40 percent weight to organizationwide improvement measures such as customer retention, seems to be the
magic level for determining bonuses.

Although companywide continuous improvement sets up a cycle
of growth and wealth creation within your business, this chain reaction can have adverse side effects. One paradoxical side effect of
successful quality- and productivity-improvement is that when
managed improperly improvement can put out of work the very
people whose ideas and energy drive the success!

THE IMPROVEMENT PARADOX

Successful quality and performance improvement can actually turn
around later and hurt your company when you achieve success. John
Sterman of MIT's Sloan Business School described a paradox that
arises when quality and productivity improvements increase capacity
faster than the rate of sales growth and employee attrition (Stankard
1996a). Sterman's "Iron Law of Layoffs" says that as long as the following relationship is true, no layoffs occur in an enterprise:

Productivity Improvement Rate	$<$	Rate of Sales Growth	$+$	Employee Attrition Rate

Sterman's "Iron Law" says that sales growth must expand faster
than productivity increases or some employees will have too little
to do, unless they leave voluntarily by attrition. If productivity expands faster than new work comes in, employees with too little
work may lose their jobs. Here is an example.

Suppose a wildly successful improvement program cuts error
rates and boosts companywide productivity by 20 percent per year.
If sales grow 5 percent per year, some employees soon have too little
work. If attrition is low (e.g., 5 percent) because people are happy
and better jobs are scarce, productivity gains of 20 percent versus
sales growth and attrition of 10 percent (5 percent sales growth + 5

percent attrition) implies about 10 percent slack in the workforce. Once surplus employees exist on the payroll, short-term profit pressures lead to layoffs. Laying off 10 percent of the workforce damages employee morale, weakens employee trust and reduces participation, which undermines further improvement efforts.

The success strategy of seeking quick results actually plants seeds of future failure for an improvement program. In working with firms like Ford Motor Co., and National Semiconductor, Sterman finds that quality improvement tends to be sold on the basis of immediate successes in cutting defects and customer dissatisfaction. The quickest, easiest opportunities to show improvement usually appear in operating areas, because these people are in one place, and they are used to working together; they can pilot test improvements quickly and learn from each test.

When asked to recommend a way out of the improvement paradox, Sterman advised "improvement must be integrated with pricing, strategy, and HR policy." This kind of improvement takes "impressive management with a good sense for the big picture." Sterman's study of successful companies finds that they are either in rapidly growing markets (rapid growth sops up the extra capacity), or they control the sequence and pace of improvement programs to create new demand for the extra capacity that their improvement program generates. Sterman says that sustainable improvement programs also have de-emphasized short-term results.

The improvement story differs for overhead processes that develop new products or make your company easy to do business with (order processing, billing, customer servicing). These processes can be improved just like operating processes; however, changing new product development (or any other overhead process) raises organizational complications. More functions get involved—marketing, finance, sales, operations, customer service, suppliers, even customers. A process like new product development spans more layers of your organization and crosses more boundaries. Meetings are hard to schedule, people do not know one another or are not used to working together. Improvement cycles take longer, so learning is slower. Instead of pilot testing a new process for a week or a month, as you can in operations, pilot testing a new product development cycle can take a year or longer.

When you delay improvements in demand-creation processes, you just postpone sales growth. As a result, sales growth from new products and new market development turns out to be just the right place for you to begin an improvement cycle. In contrast, an improvement strategy that seeks quick increases in output leaves complex processes (like new product development or demand creation) for later, because they take too long to improve.

The more your improvement program increases output productivity, the sooner demand creation becomes your performance bottleneck. "In the short run, if a quality program is successful in doubling productivity, the firm has two basic choices: (1) Try to increase market share or (2) Try to create new products and services that will absorb the extra capacity," says Sterman. Attracting new market share is difficult unless your market is growing. "Competitors usually react quickly to counter price cuts or increased advertising, so management is forced to shift focus to developing new products that can increase sales." What's more, expanding the sales force when you do need more sales will not work either, because it adds cost as well as sales, and new sales people need time to become proficient.

Now that you understand the continuous improvement cycle, here are a few examples of cycles at work.

EXAMPLES OF CYCLES THAT CREATE WEALTH

Cycles are dynamic sequences of events within your business system that reconcile opposing forces. There are many examples of virtuous cycles currently in the workplace. These following vignettes describe cycles in retailing and in knowledge-based business sectors.

A Virtuous Service Quality Cycle

Top managers of a retail operation put out customer-comment cards near cashiers and said to customers, "You Tell Us—Rate Our Service." Originally, the cards were a goodwill gesture; eventually, the program's expense grew to many thousands of dollars annually and took up hundreds of hours of management time, as each card was read and discussed and its author asked what the store could do to make that customer happy. The program responded to hundreds of individual incidents per week (across several hundred outlets). Seeing that the program had become a time-waster, the CFO decided either to make it useful or end it.

The first step in making customer feedback more useful was to stop treating each card as an isolated incident and look for overall patterns instead (Stankard 1981). A staffer began tabulating the rate of cards returned per 1,000 sales transactions. In some stores, the rate was rather low; those stores had no process for keeping their "take one" cardholders stocked. Other stores had two or three times the average rate; clerks in these stores were told to hand cards to any customers who commented favorably on service in the store, so many more customers sent in comments—all favorable.

Within six months of standardizing in-store card locations and training stores not to bias results, patterns in the favorable/unfavorable ratio showed up for each store; some stores systematically made customers happier than others. Before the tracking program began, individual complaints about store employees were often put into personnel files, demoralizing employees severely, and the firm made little constructive use of favorable comments other than occasionally to post them on staff lounge bulletin boards. The firm decided to publish customer feedback tabulations monthly to all stores. Upper management tracked the results and began evaluating store managers' performance partly on their stores' customer satisfaction ratings.

Soon, store managers from stores getting low ratings began seeking help from managers in stores with higher ratings. Gradually, over time, a gradual upward trend developed in the rate of customer satisfaction throughout the chain; the rate of dissatisfied customer comments dropped steadily. Management also noticed that when a manager from a unit with good customer ratings took over a unit with poor ratings, customer satisfaction would gradually improve over six *months*. In contrast, when a manager from a poorly run unit transferred to a store with high customer satisfaction, ratings began slipping within six *weeks*. As this example shows, simple feedback can stimulate learning and improvement. Also, virtuous and adverse cycles work on their own timetables; deterioration was fast acting while improvement accumulates more slowly in the same system.

The Industrial Engineering Learning Curve

Another example of a virtuous cycle became the basis for many companies' strategies during the 1960s and 1970s, when mass markets for commodity-type products still existed. In the 1970s, a management consulting craze arose around a phenomenon called the learning curve. This logarithmic graph, used by industrial engineers, plots average production cost versus cumulative experience. On special graph paper the curve shows up as a straight line demonstrating that, as you gain experience doing a job, you get better at it and your cost drops by a fixed percentage. The more you do, the better you get; the better you get, the lower your costs. If you share lower costs in the form of lower prices, you can attract more customers and volume. As you attract more volume, your experience increases, your costs go down further, you lower prices further, attract more volume, build experience and—bingo!—you have a virtuous cycle that eventually leads to dominant market position. The catch? Your dominant market position exists only for goods that can be made in high volume and sold to customers attracted by low price. Something like a calculator or an electronic watch would be amenable to a learning curve type strategy. A competitor who lags in market share breaks out of this cycle by innovating; innovation is exactly how the Japanese penetrated U.S. mass markets, an opportunity created by corporate over reliance on the learning curve.

Readers interested in really understanding how the learning curve relates to the PDCA cycle of continuous improvement should look at Willard Zangwill and Paul Kantor's article in the academic journal *Management Science* (Zangwill and Kantor 1998). Nonmathematically inclined readers should be aware that the article is quite technical.

Wal-Mart's Virtuous Competitive Cycle

Retailer Wal-Mart shows how a virtuous cycle results from using competitiveness to become more and more competitive. Wal-Mart started in Arkansas, serving several small towns from one large discount store patterned on a K-Mart store. Since the rural markets served were small, no other discounter could enter profitably once Wal-Mart built its store at the outskirts of town. The first element in success was to use a store-location strategy that blocked strong competitors from entering and left only weak small town competitors.

Next, to lure customers from the local merchants in surrounding towns, Wal-Mart offered brand-name goods at lower prices. It could afford lower margins than the towns' mom-and-pop stores, because it spread fixed labor costs for each large store over greater volume than the small stores could. As Wal-Mart opened more stores in even tougher markets, the virtuous cycle of store building led to a second virtuous cycle of supplier rationalization.

As Wal-Mart built more stores, it gradually became a very important customer for some of the biggest consumer products manufacturers in the U.S. Some major consumer goods outfits (like Procter & Gamble and General Foods) were offering promotional incentives to retailers in an effort to build market share. These trade promotions gave discounts to stores that bought huge quantities of merchandise at the lower-than-normal (promotional) prices. Retailers had to build or rent extra warehouse space to store the cheaper promotional goods until demand caught up with supply. This promotional game playing by major manufacturers to improve their own market shares, drove up costs in retail distribution channels.

Wal-Mart did not want to build expensive warehouses and repeatedly fill and empty them to play along with the manufacturers' promotional games; doing so would raise its costs and cut its competitiveness. Instead, Wal-Mart wanted a steady, smooth flow of goods moving efficiently to stores with little or no expensive handling and warehousing. Wal-Mart also wanted to buy goods at the lowest prices in the market without building manufacturers' promotional expenses into Wal-Mart's cost. Using its volume buying power, Wal-Mart persuaded manufacturers to produce and deliver goods as needed to help Wal-Mart further improve efficiency. The results were dramatic. General Foods reduced its massive price promotions and found that it no longer needed to maintain plant capacity geared to pump out volume at two or three times the average sales rate of its product. Smoothing out the massive ups and downs in shipments let General Foods pass along lower prices to Wal-Mart, who in turn passed savings from more efficient flows of goods on to customers in even lower prices, every day.

Wal-Mart now is one of the largest (if not the largest) single customer for virtually all consumer brands it handles. It uses this position to set up improvement cycles among its suppliers to further strengthen Wal-Mart's relationships with its price-conscious customers and against would-be competitors.

Information-based Virtuous Cycles

A virtuous cycle can exist at the level of a firm such as Wal-Mart or at the level of a single professional. In industries that identify information as a key ingredient in success (such as the professions), virtuous cycles emerge. New technologies create higher-pay premiums for the best workers than for those thought of as "next best." For example, cellular phones, portable computers, the Internet, faxes, and airplanes let a star attorney spread time over many more cases, even though a less-equipped attorney may be more personally involved with his or her clients. It seems that many clients would rather be the thirtieth client of a star attorney than the top client of a 30th-ranked lawyer. The top performers attract more of the toughest cases. As a top-performing lawyer handles the toughest cases, he or she learns, thereby becoming even better able to handle the next tough case. Because such skill and experience increases with each success, the attractiveness to potential clients increases. You ask what is the virtuous cycle? The top performer attracts tough cases; winning tough cases builds capability and experience; clients prefer a small piece of the top performer's service to the best job that an also-ran attorney can offer and, therefore, give their serious business to the top legal guns—and so on. The fees of the top lawyers go up and up because they get better and better, attracting more and more business.

Replacing a Vicious Cycle with a Virtuous Cycle

Years ago, before foreign competition had really developed, domestic car manufacturers often found themselves short of supply on their best-selling models. Because all dealers clamored for these most popular cars, factories allocated their hot sellers to dealers by dealer sales volume. Large dealers got the lion's share; smaller dealers had to wait.

Unfortunately, at the time, the majority of auto dealers did a relatively poor job of taking care of customers. High-volume auto dealerships often grew because the allocation system encouraged them to emphasize hard selling, leaving out customer satisfaction. Allocating most of the best sellers to high-volume dealers ensured that most car buyers would experience bad dealers' unpleasant high-pressure sales and poor service. This allocation logic locked the auto companies into a vicious cycle: simply because dealers had higher sales volume, they were rewarded, even if they mistreated customers. Being rewarded, the big, bad dealers grew larger still— and treated customers worse.

At the time, foreign car companies were new to the market; they competed against entrenched U.S. brands. These foreigners spotted the evident source of customer dissatisfaction and used it to create a competitive opening; they set up a virtuous cycle to replace the domestic manufacturers' vicious cycle. The importers asked customers to rate how satisfied they were with their dealers on survey cards sent directly to new car buyers. Then the imports allocated hot-selling models to dealers best at satisfying customers—using customer satisfaction measurements by dealer, rather than sales volumes to allocate hot-selling cars. The same car allocation process, using allocation logic based on measuring satisfaction instead of sales, replaced a vicious cycle with a virtuous one. Better dealers got bigger, and bad dealers either got better at taking care of customers or went out of business.

The U.S. car companies wanted market share, so they measured and controlled immediate sales volume. Allocating cars based on dealer volume is fine to maximize market share in the short run; however, it ignores the long-run issue of treating customers right so they will come back. When foreign automakers defined the purpose of their business as satisfying customers and began measuring and controlling dealer allocations through customer satisfaction metrics, they set in motion a virtuous cycle improving customer satisfaction and retention while building long-run market share. All virtuous cycles increase your system's capability to meet its over-all purpose. This example shows that the difference between vir-tuous and vicious cycles can lie in how you define the system's purpose and choose the measures used for control.

As a cautionary footnote to the above tale about measuring cus-tomer satisfaction, some foreign dealerships have found that it is easier for salespeople to badger customers into submitting favor-able satisfaction surveys than it is to actually satisfy customers. So, if you are skeptical about virtuous cycles, your skepticism is well founded in such cases. However, when the cycle is refined to be free of manipulation it generates results; the dealers that would rather browbeat people into giving high ratings than improve unfriendly business practices will eventually suffer the competitive conse-quences, albeit slowly.

Now that you have seen a variety of cycles, you are ready to move on to the four major improvement cycles that will take your organization to excellent performance. Chapter 5 introduces four cycles that power the organizational system to generate durable high performance. The chapter also explains the first of these four cycles, the golden cycle that aligns all parts of your organization to ensure the steady, purposeful pursuit of opportunities and innova-tions that will attract and satisfy customers.

CHAPTER 5

Cycles:
Ideal and Golden

> Customer satisfaction depends both upon how well and how
> thoroughly these quality actions in the several areas of
> the business work individually and upon how well and how
> thoroughly they work together.
>
> —Armand V. Feigenbaum

High performance organizations that have won the Baldrige award
all share several characteristics. Businesses as diverse as The Ritz-
Carlton Hotel Co., to the Los Alamos National Bank have identified
and seized opportunities to excel in their chosen marketplaces in
order to generate and share wealth with all stakeholders. You may
think that it takes luck to find economic opportunity in highly competitive markets, but the examples of The Ritz-Carlton Hotel Co., and
AT&T Universal Card, among others, show that high performance
firms learn to manufacture their own luck, even against thousands
of long-established competitors. Both these firms went from startup
to market leading organizations early in their organizational life

cycles. Many other high performance firms have shown how to grow out of mediocre performance by learning how to excel.

Another characteristic these great companies share is that their top managers are leaders who create a common purpose that motivates the organization and involves its people in working out how to achieve success. Organizations do not transform overnight; they have to learn, grow and develop step by step. These organizations set about building world-class capabilities—workforce, processes, suppliers and management systems—to accomplish their plans. And finally, all these organizations make wide use of information and analyses to align performance, and balance risk and returns. In each case of organizational transformation the firms report learning specific breakthrough lessons. Reviewing these lessons learned for nearly forty Baldrige award winners shows that all the firms shared an emphasis in systematic organizational learning. They systematically increased their knowledge and understanding of the specifics that would help them progress toward their organizational purposes.

The moving parts that propelled these firms and can propel your organization to excellence are continuous, high performance value-based PDCA cycles. These cycles are simplified models of the knowledge creation process focused on critical areas in your business. They provide the knowledge that lets you develop your management system, lets your business grow, and keeps it manageable. As your organization increases its knowledge assets, its performance improves. However, all types of knowledge need not expand in unison. Only that knowledge the organization needs to move to its next level of development is important at any one time.

Each cycle focuses on one of the four major drivers of excellence—economic opportunity, plans and motivation, world-class capability and balance between risk and return. When you choose to adopt high performance values, you cannot go from where you are to instant excellence. Instead, you must learn, innovate and improve in each of the four areas to upgrade the management system and drive higher performance. The four virtuous cycles make this learning systematic and will change an organization into a high performance social system. How will cycles in your business look? How do they look in an ideal management system?

FOUR IDEALIZED SYSTEM CYCLES

Actual behavior patterns in high performance organizations focus on four major areas that collectively define high performance. Your management system must knit these four areas together into a working whole—a management system. The four cycles are idealized cycles because most management systems do not formally identify them. They are organized around the following areas:

- Economic opportunity—a golden cycle of wealth creation seeks out major market and revenue opportunities that are or could be within reach of the organization's capabilities. These opportunities, such as the development of a truly better class of luxury hotel, or of offering a reliable overnight express delivery service, create wealth by offering greater customer value to customers while innovating and improving on delivery processes. Higher value at lower production cost creates demand and profit.

- Strategic plans and motivation—a leadership and planning cycle creates a sense of shared purpose by tapping the motivation of people in the organization. This cycle sets a strategic direction, creates and reinforces a set of organizational values, and involves stakeholders in planning and executing the strategy. As in racing, this cycle includes checking on the competition now and then to see who is ahead. It also strives to improve alignment and integration so that everyone works together toward a shared mission.

- World-class capability—a capability-development cycle involves systematic process improvement, human resource development, supply chain development and management, and improvements in the management system. It generates the capability to translate strategy into operation while improving business results. The lessons learned through this cycle are about doing more and better with fewer resources. Readers may have heard that you cannot "process improve your way out of scarce resources," but this cycle exists to do just that: create more and better capability while using up less resources. Eventually capabilities attain a level at which they can successfully win customers in the most competitive markets in the world—they become world class.

- Balancing risk against reward—a risk-return cycle uses measurements and analyses to align organizational units, to promote informed risk taking, and to avoid plans and decisions based on opinions, hope and hunches. This cycle expands the analysis of data to understand and control factors that drive result measures toward goals and objectives. This fourth and last cycle produces learning about which measurements and analysis methods are most useful in driving excellence and in anticipating, avoiding or preventing poor performance. The knowledge accumulated in this cycle helps the company maximize good results with minimum bad performance from the most mundane transaction to the most critical strategic plan.

Any reader who has progressed this far in the book has a desire to learn. It will please you to know that institutionalizing a desire to learn and use practical knowledge within an organization is the source of high performance. Learning how to learn and innovate within an organization is called double loop learning. Unless the managers in the organization can learn, the management system cannot improve and change. If the management system cannot learn and change, business performance will not improve. So, a high performance organization involves individuals in these four cycles of learning and improvement as a means of upgrading the whole organization and its overall performance. The following formula expresses the relationship among the four cycles:

Sustained High Performance	=	Opportunities to Create Wealth	+	Strategy And Motivation	+	World Class Capability	+	Risk/ Return Balance

By adjusting these four factors an organization's management system sustains high performance even though opportunities may change and shifts in environment and technology render some capabilities obsolete. Many organizations perform well for a short time without rebalancing all four factors as conditions change. Firms like Wang Laboratories or Digital Equipment Corporation had world-class capability and vast market opportunities that provided them with periods of outstanding performance. However, they did not learn to learn, so inadequate learning, adaptation and innovation caused their performance to falter. They failed to correct imbalances of strategy, shifting market opportunity, or outmoded technology, which ultimately ended their periods of good performance. The integration of the four cycles takes constant monitoring and learning which chapter 9 discusses.

These four cycles tie the approach, deployment and result dimensions of the Baldrige framework together into the virtuous learning and improvement cycle—the generic PDCA cycle. The four cycles originated from a suggestion made by Solectron CEO, Dr. Ko Nishimura (Quest for Excellence 1992). Speaking at the Baldrige winner's conference, Nishimura advised his audience to turn the whole enterprise into a PDCA cycle. The author followed up on Dr. Nishimura's insight by defining the golden cycle as shown in Figure 5.1, only to realize that within most Baldrige award-winning firms this cycle resembles the system flow chart reproduced in Deming's book, *Out of the Crisis* (1989).

Deming used a simple system flow diagram to explain business as a system to Japanese CEOs in 1950. (He did not name it, but simply called it "the flow chart.") Deming's flow chart and the golden cycle omit many aspects of the performance excellence model since the golden cycle simply focused on continuous improvement and innovation to deliver ever-increasing customer value. Figure 5.1 shows a more complete version of the flow chart indicating the PDCA/I activities suggested by Dr. Nishimura. Management approaches work together to implement the PDCA steps into the way the business operates. Figure 5.1 is too high level to show all elements of a high performance management system. Many management approaches (for example, workforce development) work below the level of the organizationwide PDCA shown in Figure 5.1. To complete the system description, the author looked for other repetitive patterns of activity within high performance firms that met business excellence requirements left out of the golden cycle. Gradually patterns showed up—in how the award winners plan and motivate people, develop capabilities, and use information to manage risk in plans and decisions. This led to three underlying cycles: Plan (leadership and

Figure 5.1
The Deming/Nishimura Flow Chart

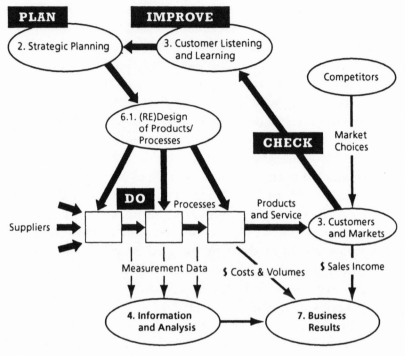

planning), Do (world-class capability development), and Check (risk-return) in support of the golden cycle (Improve/Innovate).

Because the cycles are continuous, the starting point of the organizationwide system may be shifted to the Act or Improve stage before continuing on through Plan, Do and Check stages. This approach to organizational development resembles policy deployment of many world-class firms. These firms begin by setting strategic improvement policies and targets, then negotiate plans, actions and goals with each unit in the organization to hit the overall improvement targets. Learning is embedded in policy deployment by the use of teams to research and eliminate barriers to policy deployment. So even the four idealized cycles may not be entirely new; fitting the three Baldrige requirement dimensions—approach, deployment and results—into a cycle of learning that studies and improves them is new.

Each of the four idealized cycles above is itself a PDCA cycle of learning, innovation and improvement:

- The *Plan* step of each cycle finds innovations and improvements in management approach that better meet relevant requirements of the Baldrige performance excellence business model. Each cycle concerns only a portion of the whole set of Baldrige requirements (for example, categories 1 and 2— leadership and strategic planning—fit into the leadership and planning cycle). The plan step also identifies which metrics should be included in an organizationwide measurement system and predicts which result areas should improve if the plan is successful.

- The *Do* step comprises the actions and efforts to carry out— or deploy—the approaches that will improve performance.

- The *Check* step measures and compares actual results against predicted improvements to evaluate how well the planned approaches worked out. It also investigates predicted results that did work out to gain insight for further improvements. Additionally, the check step establishes relative competitiveness and performance by comparing results to outside competitors or leading organizations, as required in the Baldrige criteria.

- Finally, the *Act* or *Improve* step systematically uses lessons learned from the three previous steps to feed new and useful knowledge forward into the next repetition of the full cycle.

These cycles continuously rebalance the high performance organization's resources and adjust its focus to maintain performance. Now, how would your organization emulate the ideal firm? As mentioned earlier, cycles function as a social system when members of an organization act on certain high performance values. Here is how the golden cycle could look in your firm.

The *golden wealth-creation cycle* links all parts of your firm into a system of continuous innovation. Your organization's cycle begins when you add the high performance values of *customer-driven excellence* and a *system view* to the usual rock solid *focus on results and creating value.* These two additional organizational values require that managers throughout the organization learn how to deliver more value to customers at increasing profit margins. *Focus on results* leads to careful measurements; the commitment to customers translates into actually measuring customer satisfaction and customer value as leading indicators of repeat purchase and buyer loyalty. The objective is to get your whole organization to work as a system following a PDCA cycle of learning and innovation to increase revenue. Once it achieves this, further progress toward high performance depends on adopting additional high performance organizational values.

Soon the organization is seeking new performance dimensions that offer greater customer value to attract more business without the need to reduce prices. This is a step toward an organizational commitment to *managing for innovation.* There can be little innovation or improvement without learning, so your organization also commits to *organizational and personal learning* in order to generate the innovations and improvements it needs to excel. Collectively these five high performance value commitments allow a cycle of learning and improvement to drive the firm onward toward major new opportunities.

The emotions underlying and driving the golden cycle are a desire to maintain good personal relationships within the organization, pride, ambition, greed, some selfishness, a healthy competitive spirit, and fear that without such a cycle growth will stop and the business may fail. In some industries, such as semiconductors, some say that the most successful firms require slightly paranoid leadership. These leaders behave like a competitive athlete who misses a workout and says to himself: "I didn't work out today; I might lose my edge to someone else who did work out today." It takes energetic people to launch a golden cycle; you do not find shrinking violets here. Sadly, many organizations adopt the golden cycle out of fear of bad performance, "a burning platform," but as the prospect of failure recedes, they revert to business as usual and complacency replaces systematic learning and improvement.

The three other virtuous cycles support your companywide golden cycle, beginning with a unified organization and direction. The *leadership and planning cycle* creates unity within your firm. For this cycle to arise, you and other leaders throughout the organization must show *focus on the future* in defining opportunities and mission. Your leadership must be based on vision, individual and organizational values, and respect for the interests of all stakeholders. (The vision, of course, is for everyone to benefit from the operation of the golden cycle of wealth creation.) Involving employees and suppliers in future planning, and helping them develop capabilities for long-term success shows that the organization *values employees and partners*. Letting employees in on planning helps them develop capabilities that improve execution. Employee participation also creates opportunities for role models to emerge, be recognized, and to assume greater responsibilities. Activities of the leadership and planning cycle also show how your firm makes *public responsibility and citizenship* important by taking responsibility for its impact on society and the environment.

The leadership and planning cycle builds organizational commitment to learn, innovate and achieve opportunities. At the emotional level, a commitment to *visionary leadership* inspires feelings of ambition, hopefulness, trust and pride in the mission: pursuing excellence for customers and other stakeholders.

To carry out plans for innovation, your firm's success depends on its capabilities. The *capability-development cycle* systematically maximizes your firm's capability to carry out plans with available resources. This cycle develops your workforce, process, supply chain and management system in support of long-term plans. The importance of *valuing partners* rests on the fact that cooperative supplier partnerships expand your firm's capability without tying up scarce resources. This cycle also asks that your organization prove that employee interests are important by training them and providing opportunities to develop their abilities and encouraging them to innovate and improve how they work. Workforce development requires knowledge of: what people want from work, what gives them pride of workmanship, joy of working, and satisfaction—all the human emotions that drive workforce capability, confidence, and high morale.

Given the opportunities, plans, and capabilities from the earlier three cycles, the last element in system performance is to understand what factors drive risks and payoffs. The *risk-return cycle* replaces gambles based on opinions and guesses with intelligent risk taking, based on understanding cause and effect. This cycle arises from acting on the high performance values of *management by fact* and *agility*. Russell Ackoff once said that business wastes a lot more money on the risks it is unprepared for than it ever wastes on preparing for risks that do not occur. The risk-return cycle begins by using measurements to align the parts of the organization with plans. Those same measurements then permit studies of variations between success and failure. Comparing planning goals and actual results invites managers to identify what factors make the difference between good and poor performance. Increasing understanding of what drives success and failure lets your firm take greater risks through informed management decisions and increased surveillance to produce more good outcomes and fewer bad results.

The risk-return cycle also embodies your people's desire to feel secure and to avoid loss and failure by replacing blame and fear with the analysis of cause and, therefore, increased understanding. This cycle elevates the human instinct of curiosity and institutionalizes systematic learning through data gathering and analysis into a powerful source of ongoing learning and knowledge creation.

Chapter 11 deals with integrating the four cycles in detail, however Figure 5.2 shows how the four cycles parallel each other. Implementing these cycles usually does not require more management planning and doing activity. Instead, these cycles usually demand increased learning in the form of checking and improvement effort—areas where many managers and therefore management systems fall short. These virtuous cycles do not require that your managers and leaders work any harder, but they may demand new interactions and behaviors, especially learning behavior.

PROGRESS TOWARD THE IDEAL

These days, most firms making rapid progress to high performance were launched on that course by their desire to avoid disaster—the old burning platform. Nothing gets managers and firms moving toward better ways of doing business than the threat of shutting the doors. However, long-term development requires more hope, commitment, and optimism than fear. Firms that begin the transformation

Figure 5.2
The Four Cycles of High Performance

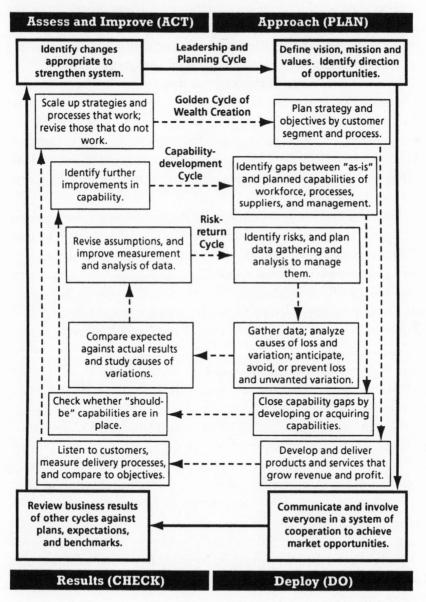

to high performance in reaction to immediate problems often find that, after a few years of moderate improvement, the wolf is no longer at the door and they stop improving. Sustained progress takes motion toward the innovative, the hopeful, the ideal—not just a reaction against what is obsolete or frightening. These propellants must come from leaders all over the organization who want the organization to grow and who realize that they need a system to manage the larger organization and maintain excellence in its performance.

There are two ways to think about improvement. One way is to think about how to work forward from the "as-is" in the direction of what would be better. The second is to work backward from a future end point (the ideal) to see what you can do now to approximate the ideal. One advantage of thinking backward from ideals is that progress toward a person's ideal is meaningful and self-motivating.

This book uses and recommends that you adopt the working backward approach to improvement. First, set the ideals and then build the closest approximation to them you can. You can reorganize your existing methods, approaches, and actions to approximate how they ideally should work. This book will present many methods and approaches used by high performance organizations. These methods are presented in the context of ideal cycles of continuously improving strategy, motivation, capability and information usage. Your challenge is to work backward from your ideals to define steps that move your management system and organization toward excellence.

You can see in Figure 5.2 how the four virtuous PDCA cycles—golden wealth-creation, leadership and planning, capability-development, and risk-return—all feed and reinforce one another in a dynamic system that improves your firm's performance. Now what? To delve deeper into the matter of moving your firm from its present status toward the ideal, it is time to look at what the four cycles offer your firm. The rest of this chapter gives you in-depth information about using the golden cycle to create wealth. Then, Part III shows how you can sustain this fundamental cycle with the three supporting cycles.

EXAMPLE: YANKEE BANK'S GOLDEN CYCLE

This story of a bank's assessment and follow-up cycles unfolded over several years, beginning with banking deregulation in the early 1980s. The events described predate the Baldrige criteria, however, the organization's assessments were built into the firm's strategic planning cycle, relying on comparisons with high performing peer banks.

Years 1, 2—Planning for a Change

Medium-sized Yankee Bank (not the name of the real bank) faced increasing severe price competition from larger, out-of-state banks that it had not previously encountered. Yankee was organized around consumer, commercial, operations and finance divisions. To ensure the bank's future viability, its board recruited a new CFO (Chief Financial Officer) with experience both on Wall Street and in management consulting. One of the CFO's initial challenges from the bank's board was to upgrade the bank's strategic planning capability, which had lagged the changes in competitiveness

After two years, the CFO's efforts with the bank's planning process included companywide assessments and comparisons to high performing peer banks. These assessments led to a senior management consensus that superior expense management achieved through productivity improvement was critical to future survival. Since bank management did not wish to reduce headcount, they concluded they had to increase business volume as they reduced expenses. They chose to work on both the income and the expense side of productivity, beginning with the issue of lender productivity: how could the bank's sales force generate greater revenue? The CFO, who agreed during the planning session to head up a "productivity issue team," attended a public seminar on process improvement. After the seminar, he went back to his bank and met with his team to outline how they would improve lender (sales force) productivity.

Year 3—A First Learning and Improvement Cycle

The bank's previous efforts to improve lender productivity had achieved only marginal success over two years. Consequently, the

CFO decided to begin with an improvement pilot project—the lender productivity effort—which he chose to lead personally. The CFO and credit executives sponsoring this effort decided to hire an outside process improvement consultant (the author) to coach them through their first effort at overhauling a critical business process. Their idea was to try for an initial success, learn from it, and go on from there. (Note the idea of feeding the pilot's results forward into future efforts represents organizational learning, a key high performance value.) The CFO pulled together a team of lenders, systems people, and retail- and credit-operations managers to work on improving the lending (sales) process. After analyzing the in-place process and measuring and analyzing data on how lenders spent their time, the team implemented seven changes in the sales process.

The new sales and lending process succeeded splendidly. Within nine months, sales productivity was up more than 80 percent, and the changes eventually raised selling productivity by 140 percent. By leading the project from initial planning through implementation, the CFO walked the first improvement around a full cycle. This involvement gave him direct, personal experience with improvement. From this initial success, the CFO brought something new into the bank's planning session for the next year: the concept of repeating the improvement process.

Year 4—Expanding on the First Cycle

In the course of the next bankwide annual planning process, senior executives again assessed the business as a whole. The second repetition of the cycle during the next year built on the lessons learned in the lending productivity pilot. More business was coming in from the improved selling process; the added volume created a need to improve several back-office processes. Bank management adopted a low-cost producer strategy based on superior processes, using expanded but frugal automation. Through planning the executives identified several major business opportunities; these depended on upgrading certain key information systems. Next, they identified the particular processes that needed to improve for the bank to realize its top priority opportunities.

The second annual cycle put three cross-functional teams to work following up on strategic opportunities—upgrading information systems in key processing areas as well as coming up with new products and services to capture revenue opportunities. Asked if the cross-functional teams had to stay within established organizational boundaries, the CFO replied, "No, they go wherever they have to. Our problems and opportunities disregard our organizational boundaries, so our efforts to solve them must disregard those boundaries as well." These three middle-management teams were modeled on the successful pilot project in the lending area. Several participants in the pilot program helped the new teams adopt the same tools and follow the same methods used to boost lending productivity: process mapping, work measurement, value analysis, nominal-group technique and brainstorming.

Year 5 and Beyond—Consolidate Gains and Dissolve Barriers

From the second year on, the bank's annual planning identified specific operational and product areas as its best future business opportunities. The CFO—who, by this time, the board had promoted to CEO (Chief Executive Officer)—assigned highest priorities to making improvements one to three years before they were needed. This forethought gave teams at the bank sufficient lead time to make process changes that boosted customer satisfaction and yielded outstanding returns, cost savings and market share gains.

As the CEO guided improvements around the annual cycle shown in Table 5.1, he ran into barriers that slowed change. Eventually he pieced together a combination of methods—planning linked to measurement, cross-functional teams, recognition and management promotions—into a system that avoided, prevented, or overcame all the barriers. Each year's annual cycle built on the lessons learned and the methods that worked in the previous cycle. During planning sessions, the bank's managers decided how to overcome barriers that had surfaced. In this way, each yearly cycle ensured that the bank delivered more and better service with less expense. The reduced costs from process improvement were used to attract new business from competing banks through lower fees. Within a few annual cycles, the bank began growing very rapidly;

Table 5.1

Evolution of Yankee Bank's Golden Cycle

Year	Plan	Do	Check	Act
1,2	• Create planning process	• Carry plans out	• Improvement was too slow	• Seek better improvement approach for Y1 cycle
3	• Identify productivity opportunity in sales	• Attend seminar • Form team • Hire consultant • Change sales process	• Review progress on process changes • Measure sales improvement	• Build process improvement into Y2 planning cycle
4	• Select further improvement process opportunities driven by higher sales	• Form more improvement teams • Select coaches from Y1 success. • Train new teams • Change to should-be processes	• Review progress on changeover to should-be processes. • Measure improved expenses and sales	• Decide to base Y3 plans on market research and cost data • Decide to form Y3 improvement teams during planning process
5	• Identify more income and cost opportunities • Target competitor's accounts to win through better service quality and lower prices	• Form improvement teams • Assign coaches from Y1 and Y2 successes • Train new team members • Change to should-be processes. • Use lower cost to attract volume from competitors	• Review team progress making changes • Measure improved expenses • Track sales growth against plans • Coach teams and identify "plate breakers."	• Allow teams to manage selves • Promote "plate breakers" into higher level positions • Standardize team process • Improve and continue annual PDCA cycles

it was attracting its competitors' most desirable customers, because its newly re-engineered processes gave those customers better, faster service while the bank passed some of its noninterest expense savings along in lower fees and prices.

While working through the first two improvement cycles, the CEO began identifying managers and others with outstanding skill in implementing their annual improvement plans. Referring to these people as "plate breakers," he began to promote them rapidly. In one case, a woman who had joined a branch as a secretary fresh out of college became a vice-president within five years. She worked on several improvement teams at her branch; after some training in information systems, she led a team that automated vital branch functions, yielding tremendous payoffs in better, faster service and sharply reduced operating cost.

The development and promotion of a secretary to a respected vice-presidency within five years—as well as promotions of many other "plate breakers"—sent powerful signals to everyone else about what type of management behavior was important.

Where they had previously used few facts and scant analysis, the CEO brought consultants in to help design systems, gather facts, and coach managers in analyzing and interpreting data to improve service and operating performance. For example, during the annual strategic-planning session, he required participants to begin using market research and internal cost studies in setting their improvement priorities. He added detailed progress assessments to the established monthly progress reviews for each unit of the bank. Every month, improvement teams reported on their progress in carrying out the action plans developed from the annual planning cycle. The CEO took great pride in the accomplishments of his teams and followed their progress closely, providing help when needed.

Over seven years, the bank grew steadily at several times the rate of growth of banking in its market; it nearly doubled in volume with no change in staff. During this growth, all measures of customer satisfaction, loan quality, productivity and service quality improved. Its profitability rose to the highest among its peers, and the CEO went on to become CEO of a much larger bank, where he launched another golden cycle, on a much larger scale.

The actions of this bank's CFO/CEO show the power of linking isolated management approaches and elements together into a system. The CFO/CEO instinctively built a management system to stimulate growth and to maintain credit and service quality and performance at high levels. The management system's purpose was to improve business results and profitability continuously by providing better service at lower cost. The system or cycle accomplished its purpose with chains of events, not by excessive personal involvement of the top manager. The event chain was: identify future market opportunities during planning, set up teams to change processes (usually through automation), boost process efficiency, reduce costs, raise customer satisfaction, offer new prospects better customer value, grow the bank, promote newly identified "plate breakers" to higher management, lift employee morale and repeat the cycle in the next year. The CFO/CEO's role became one of overseeing this system.

This banker succeeded because he persevered in the face of bumps and jolts that real improvement produces as it works its way around a firm. He personally experienced improvements in the bank's planning cycle. He captured his personal experience in an organizationwide golden cycle that—year after year—plans and improves those products, services, and processes that make the greatest difference to customers and to the bank's results.

This banker's annual improvement cycle was a resounding success. Bank performance rose beyond what any department, automation, motivation program or cost-cutting drive alone could achieve. In fact, the golden cycle at this bank orchestrated all those elements, without resting solely on any of them. Each element fit into place as it was needed, and then became part of next year's planning and improvement routine. Each year, the bank refined and improved its cycle, and the bank CEO went on to be one of the first bankers in the United States to perform a Baldrige assessment on his organization (in 1991 when Baldrige assessment was only three years old).

From active participation, the CEO's role eventually shifted to coaching the whole improvement cycle. He participated in some of the most critical early teams, and he reviewed progress of all other bank executives on their own teams. His experience led the bank to refine further its improvement process. What made him do it? The answer seems to be his personal commitment. He came with the bank to build a great organization. For whatever reason, he stuck with his improvement efforts year after year, celebrating each success and learning from every barrier and obstacle. Researcher Jim Collins, writing in the January 2001 *Harvard Business Review* refers to level-5 leaders—those who combine humility with fierce resolve (Collins 2001). This insightful article closely describes the CEO of the above bank and presents many insights into how such a transformational leader takes an organization from good to great.

One by-product of the golden cycle at Yankee Bank was to empower employees. During the first three cycles, improvement teams had to seek executive approvals for major changes. From the fourth cycle on, teams were allowed to make major operational changes in processes on their own. As each team worked out what to change, it circulated a memorandum to concerned executives summarizing what was to change and when. If there were no objections to the changes from upper management, and if the changes fit into the annual plan's objectives, the team simply made the changes without further managerial involvement. Some changes implemented this way were quite dramatic: a sweeping reorganization of the retail branch system, which cut average customer waiting time in half and cut branch labor costs by 25 percent! Empowering the improvement teams freed up senior management time for planning marketing and systems innovations and for monitoring and coaching activities.

Between annual planning sessions, the CEO held monthly and quarterly executive reviews of progress on the bank's annual improvement projects. Responsibility for projects was assigned during annual planning. The team leaders were also chosen during planning. Occasionally, a management team would hand some element of its project off to another unit—for example, to Information Systems. All of this activity was coordinated by the annual plan and frequent reviews.

Progress on implementing plans usually provides opportunities for lower level leaders to polish their skills and make themselves and their accomplishments more visible to senior managers. The emergence of new managers, comfortable with change and skilled in improving services and operations, led to promotions that reinforced the cycle's operation. The CEO's personal involvement in monthly and quarterly progress reviews guaranteed follow-up on assessment results. Another benefit of the gradual development of the bank's golden cycle was in preparing leaders for greater challenges. After several years, one of the upper middle managers of the bank was promoted to CEO of a smaller, newly acquired bank. As the new CEO, he immediately instituted the same type of annual planning and improvement management system he had learned at Yankee Bank.

Another advantage of an endless loop of improvements is that each annual cycle expands involvement. Each repetition uses and reuses know-how from previous cycles in new areas cumulating organizational learning like a snowball rolling downhill. With every completed cycle cumulative learning grows a little and rolls a little faster. The idea is to build a cycle or management system that finds out where competitors are doing a lazy job of pleasing customers, and then basing the bank's plan on what would make those customers happier. As the plan succeeded, management improved upon it, over and over and over again. Such a cycle replaces stand-alone projects that solve problems in isolation—perhaps even important problems. Isolated successes do not create the golden, endless-improvement cycle because they do not add up to a system that steadily, consistently makes the business better for customers and shareholders.

The lessons to draw from this example are:

1. Transforming an organization to excellence takes constancy of purpose or what author Jim Collins refers to as fierce resolve right at the top. The sponsor does not need to know everything about how to transform, but must be humble enough to look for answers and learn from those who have them. The sponsor must also exhibit unshakable resolve to build the best organization of its type. The sponsor in the bank described above had served both in investment banking and management consulting before taking a line management job as CFO. His vision over the years remained fixed on making Yankee Bank the most competitive and profitable firm in its class (which he accomplished).

2. Getting everyone aligned with the overall purpose takes a solid companywide planning system, as well as a balanced (more than just financial) set of metrics. Involving managers in planning helps participants feel comfortable and committed to where the organization is going.

3. Starting improvement with processes that can generate more business is important to launching a sustainable effort. If you begin transforming your organization with cost cutting to generate early successes, and add no new sales volume, you will have to cut staff to realize the savings, which will kill workforce cooperation with further improvement.

4. Involving all key executives in developing a solid, fact-based corporate planning process helps lay the political and practical foundation for a companywide cycle of learning, innovation and improvement. Setting a vital few quantitative objectives, such as doubling sales productivity, provides a basis for linking strategy to efforts throughout the organization.

5. Relying on cross-functional teams of managers to DO the plans broadens involvement and provides opportunities for people to make visible contributions and be recognized for them. People who get involved, however, must be trained in process improvement methods. The sponsoring executive needs to supervise the initial cycles of implementation very closely. The CFO above ran the first improvement cycle personally and after that held monthly reviews that scrutinized progress. By acting on what he learned through his reviews, he solved or dissolved problems and barriers as they came up.

6. Helping to carry out planned innovations and improvements should earn contributors recognition and wider leadership responsibilities quickly. Promoting those who learn and do the most to help the organization is a major lesson learned.

7. Implementing planned improvements creates a need for a fact-based process improvement approach for teams to follow. The CFO originally challenged teams to come up with 100 percent measurable improvement or show him the facts that proved 100 percent improvement was impossible. (Usually the facts pointed to opportunities for more than 100 percent improvement when you finally gathered and analyzed them.)

8. Improving the cycle is as simple as planning for and doing more of what worked each year, and improving on or replacing what did not work.

9. Achieving the first major success or two will take an investment in outside training and consulting resources to create a reliable process improvement capability in-house.

10. Pursuing opportunities wherever they lead in the organization is key to success. In the words of the CFO/CEO above, "the problems do not respect organizational boundaries so our solutions cannot either."

11. Remaining patient and committed at the top is rare. The CFO above is one that did do "whatever it takes," out of the hundreds that said they would. Top executive understanding and leadership is usually the bottleneck in the whole process.

12. Relentless resolve achieves excellence one project at a time, one success at a time, and one year at a time. It is up to the organization to accumulate the lessons learned by building them into a management system with a built-in company-wide cycle. This bank executive was one of the first in the United States to sponsor a Baldrige assessment, solely to improve his company—he had no interest at all in winning an award and never applied for one.

Even if you are convinced of the benefit, before you rush to begin an annual cycle of planned improvement and learning, there may be questions you will need to answer (would you believe there are skeptics?) about whether annual cycles of Baldrige assessment and follow-up can deliver results for your company. Even if Yankee Bank achieved high performance—how can you show that a management system patterned on the Baldrige high performance model will deliver results in your situation—especially if you are not in the banking industry? To find out how well a management system pays off in any industry, chapter 2 presents several heavyweight studies that provide specific payoff information.

THE GOLDEN CYCLE OF WEALTH CREATION

The golden cycle is the engine of growth that leads to high performance within your business. This virtuous cycle focuses your enterprise on discovering, innovating and improving how you attract and retain customers. There are two sides to the cycle, an income side and an expense side. Building customer loyalty, repeat business, and referrals by offering customer value that attracts and satisfies generates the income. Driving process improvements with an eye on cutting all costs that do not add customer value, and adding costs where customer value increases faster than the expense ensures a profitable relationship between process cost and customer value created. Together the two sides of this cycle generate profits and wealth. The golden cycle concerns business results beyond financial outcomes, as well. It concerns market share, customer satisfaction, customer value delivered, competitive position and other areas important in a competitive environment.

The basic idea of the golden cycle is to go beyond what already exists to invent products and services that offer ever more customer value and attract and satisfy more customers. Having defect-free products and services is part of the cycle, but innovation drives wealth creation, either in product and service or by innovative process. If your business exerts the leadership, planning and capability development to create its own golden cycle (even without the three supporting cycles to come) it will be able to compete against market leaders and improve financial performance against tough competition. Creating a golden cycle is your organization's starting point on the journey to high performance. One path to developing a golden cycle is by preparing for the current revision of ISO9000, but to go beyond complying with the bare bones standard. With the exception of strategic planning, a companywide cycle of process improvement that improves customer satisfaction can meet the ISO9000 standard.

The common link among all innovation activities of your firm is an imaginary "golden thread" of *information* about what really benefits customers in terms of your product and service. (See the bold arrows in Figure 5.1 that shows the golden thread tracing a cycle from customers, to listening, to planning, to implementing improvements and delivery back to the customer.) The golden thread begins with systematic listening and learning at all points of customer contact. Golden-thread data, known as "voice-of-the-customer," comprises direct, firsthand information from the market—wants, needs, feelings, trends and comparisons against competition. The golden thread also describes customers' underlying emotions and urges that drive their wants and needs. These deeper insights answer the question, "Why?" "Why do customers choose us versus them?" "Why do customers decide to leave us, and where do they go?" Understanding why your customers behave as they do can spark innovations that leapfrog incremental improvement in products or services and create major opportunities.

Value in the mind of the consumer is the *customer's view* of the benefit she gets from your goods and services. Product features, quality and service are *your view* of what you delivered to the customer. Customer value is in the mind of the customer—not on the price tag—the same way that beauty is in the eye of the beholder. Voice-of-the-customer information may be in the customer's own words. For example, GM engineers found from market research that difficulties in getting children to buckle rear seat belts was causing dissatisfaction with mothers of small children. So they wrote specifications for seatbelts that the engineers believed would be easier to use. They made a few prototypes, had mothers with children test them, and found *no* improvement. Finally, one mother said, "I want a seat belt that my three-year-old can buckle up by himself." Bingo, the engineers obtained ergonomic information about the capabilities of three-year-olds and designed a belt that got it right. Listening to the voice of the customer produces insight into what drives customer value and that concept provides the ideas for innovation.

The golden thread of customer information brings the voice of the customer into your strategic planning sessions. Raw voice-of-the-customer information undergoes aggregation and trend analysis so that plans can be based on facts about what makes customers tick. Once you develop strategies and improvement plans to attract and hold customers, the golden thread connects those plans with improvements in product, services and key processes. Again the cycle translates voice-of-the-customer data into terms appropriate for modifying products, services and processes; the way the engineers translated the physical limitations of a three-year-old into specifications for an easier-to-use seat belt. In parallel, measures of processes and results translate the golden thread into information that tracks progress and bases improvement on facts about what will please customers. Finally, as customers experience your improved products and services, the golden thread comes full circle through listening and learning from the voice of the customer. Voice-of-the-customer information represents insight into what benefits customers want and what features they do not care about; this information drives another trip around the cycle. The golden thread thus links many activities within the business into a PDCA cycle, the purpose of which is to enable your organization to win its competitive race to be the customer's best value and first choice in the market.

Learning in the golden cycle aims to understand customers, markets and what drives customer satisfaction in order to identify major revenue opportunities. IBM AS/400 Midrange Systems Division analyzed the link between customer satisfaction and its revenue. The result? A one-point increase in customer satisfaction yielded $250M per year in added revenue. For IBM Midrange Systems, improving customer satisfaction would be a better investment than hiring and training hundreds of new salespeople. As your people discover process measures and indicators that predict market success, the planning activities of the golden cycle uses a sequence of these predictors (often referred to as *line-of-sight* metrics) to ensure that innovations and improvements will please customers and make them eager for more

Figure 5.3 shows the golden cycle as a PDCA cycle. The plan stage refers to approach requirements of the Baldrige model, while the do and check stages cover deployment and result Baldrige requirements. The final, act stage involves stepping back and using knowledge learned from the check step to improve how you listen to customers and the approaches you use to deliver ever better customer value to both your old and your desired new customers.

(P) Plan—Choose Approaches to Focus on What Pleases Customers

The golden cycle's approach (plan) step, meets requirements from the strategic planning, customer and market focus, and process management categories of the *Baldrige Criteria for Performance Excellence*. The planning stage of the golden cycle takes a long view of your markets and customer relationships. Excellent companies like OMI, The Ritz-Carlton Hotel Co., and others strive to permanently keep any customers they acquire. Once you adopt a long-term view of customers and your relationship with them, the golden cycle begins when you clarify whom your firm wants to keep as long-term customers.

Figure 5.3
The Golden Cycle of Wealth Creation

P APPROACH
- Identify desired customer/market segments
- Determine satisfaction drivers ("care-abouts") in each segment
- Assess competitive offerings
- Plan products and services features to exceed customer expectations and competition
- Predict results and set targets
- Plan process and product breakthroughs

PLAN   *DO*

A IMPROVE
- Act to correct shortfalls on improvement goals
- Document and spread knowledge of new customer "care-abouts"
- Identify gaps in satisfaction versus competitors
- Seek new opportunities to further delight customers

DEPLOYMENT D
- Develop and test improved products, services, and processes
- Measure and improve processes to deliver key customer "care-abouts" consistently
- Develop and maintain pleasing customer relationships

C RESULTS
- Control processes to please customers and minimize displeasure
- Listen to and learn from customer feedback
- Gather data and analyze trends in customer buying and retention
- Gather data and analyze trends and levels of customer satisfaction/dissatisfaction versus competition

ACT   *CHECK*

The customers you have now may not be the customers you would prefer in the future, given the choice. For example, Solectron Corp., which supplies manufacturing services for makers of original electronic equipment, focuses on the size and rate of growth in cost of electronics goods sold in world markets (Quest for Excellence 1992, 1997). By looking for large, rapidly growing electronic-product segments (such as Internet routers, mobile telecom and semiconductor equipment), Solectron identifies firms that are likely to grow faster than the electronics industry as a whole. These targeted market segments contain the firm's desired future customers. Their rising sales and buying volume present the greatest future opportunities for Solectron. Of course, if their desired customers get into profit trouble all at the same time, this can pose risks for Solectron. So, attention must be paid to targeting customers for a range of future scenarios.

A firm usually begins this cycle by studying markets to understand actual and potential buying behavior and to rate the attractiveness of current and potential customer segments. In industries that can easily modify product characteristics, segmentation seeks the largest potential market for which the firm can readily tailor its products. So, for example, breakfast cereal manufacturers segment consumers along myriad dimensions in order to identify attractive niches of demand for which to develop new breakfast cereals. Using the understanding of customer behavior, and how it relates to customer value, the planning step of the cycle also predicts or forecasts the expected increase in revenue or customer base from the planned actions. For example, if you are able to improve a process so that it really wows a customer, you can predict with some confidence that the customer will come back. It is also likely that the same customer will refer others to you, saving you on marketing expense. On the other hand, if your service has problems so that customer experiences fall short of expectations, you will lose some or all of the customers who are unhappy. For a given price, offering greater customer value than the typical customer expects attracts more business; offering less customer value than expected or destroying it through poor quality drives business away. So, your predictions of sales results quantify the expected impact of changes you are making in an effort to win the race for customer dollars.

Often the experience of customers with buying and using your product or service involves factors beyond how you view that same product or service. For example, customers who are new to your product may see more benefit in your reputation for helpful customer service than they see in the specific details of your product or service, which they may not fully understand yet. They derive greater value from the feeling that if your product or service lets them down, you will do whatever it takes to make them happier than if the upset never occurred. Good reputation adds value for timid customers; even if your focus is on delivering better, more reliable products and services that do not break down. Once you have a theory of what drives customer choice by segment, the next step is to use the theory to make your business more competitive.

In technology-based industries where innovations require lengthy and expensive development, market segmentation looks for groups of potential customers that will benefit most from the next round of product innovations. How much potential revenue each market segment ultimately represents may be secondary to the buyers' immediate need. The need to fund product development as the firm builds toward larger segments as quickly as possible dictates choice of market segments. The implication is that, when innovations take large-scale research and development, being the first mover can present disadvantages. The story of the early development of the stored program electronic computer shows this disadvantage.

In the late 1940s, when Eckert and Mauchly reworked their wartime Eniac into the first commercial general purpose computer, Univac, their initial market was the U.S. Census Bureau, GE, and fewer than a dozen other firms processing huge volumes of data. Initially Univac was forced to ignore thousands of firms already using IBM punched card data processing equipment for tabulating data. Even though the potential sales in the tabulating segment were larger, only a handful of large customers who needed incredibly powerful calculating machines would spend the money that Eckert and Mauchly needed to develop a commercial version of their then astounding ENIAC. As UNIVAC succeeded, IBM, which had the cash flow from its established business, followed up to develop computers for its existing customer segments. Once IBM developed the IBM1401, computerized information-processing applications became routine in hundreds of thousands of smaller firms, enabling IBM to become the dominant supplier of general purpose computers.

Firms developing innovative products that take large investments often must segment markets by how much benefit potential customers will derive from their innovation rather than by the size of ultimate market potential. Larger firms offering soon-to-be-obsolete products to the same customers can invest some of their greater resources to protect their market base by adopting other firms' innovations. Microsoft has been highly adept at co-opting the competition to preserve their PC operating system monopoly. Adding innovations pioneered by others (such as an Internet browser) to their Windows product strengthens their operating system monopoly by shrinking the market opportunity for their most innovative competitors. One lapse, however, in which the larger, less innovative firm overlooks some novel development that appeals to its customers, may give the innovator the time it needs to evolve a bundle of features, performance and price that challenges the larger firm in its key market segments.

Learning and innovation in the marketplace leads to the development of a theory of customer behavior—why the customer makes his or her choices. You need more than a clear-eyed focus on results to generate wealth; you need a theory that lets you predict how your customers will behave as a basis for your planning. This theory, together with some creativity, will suggest breakthroughs—changes that are meaningful to markets and customers and that meet unmet or underserved customer and market needs. In its 1998 Quest for Excellence presentation, Merrill Lynch Credit Corp. (MLCC) explained how its "voice-of-the-customer" (VOC) process "distilled key client needs out of a Tower of Babel." MLCC managers involve all the firm's parts to identify key changes that will attract new customers (Quest for Excellence 1998).

As does Solectron, MLCC first analyzes trends and targets market segments that present the greatest potential opportunity. Then, within each segment, the VOC process considers inputs from vendors and partners, complaints, sales force observations, customer characteristics, benchmarking information from outside MLCC and secondary research. The approach uses these many and varied inputs to define customers' needs. It then sets priorities for satisfaction and customer value drivers—customer "care-abouts" and product needs. These "care-abouts" are considered within customer segment, as well as across all consumer-credit market segments. Next MLCC identifies which processes or work groups impact customer "care-abouts" in the highest priority segments. They analyze gaps between current services and what the market wants, and what competitors provide, to highlight the breakthroughs and innovations that respond to the voice of the customers. They also assess competitive offerings.

Comparing your offerings against the competition is important in segments where customers can choose between your competition or you. Customers make market choices that give them what they perceive as maximum benefit for their money. So, within each market segment, the golden cycle begins by understanding customer value; it asks "What did the customer get?" Customer value consists not of what you think you delivered to the customer for the money you received but what benefits the customer thinks he or she got for the price paid. What you think you did for the customer and what the customer thinks you did for her often differ significantly.

The planning stage calls for at least a few innovations and improvements strong enough for your firm to attract new customers— not just keep those that were pleased with your previous offerings. Mature, mass-market products may offer greater opportunities for improving production and delivery processes than gains from product innovation. For example, during the 1970s and 1980s the increased quality and reliability of inexpensive Japanese automobiles attracted nearly a third of the U.S. market away from less reliable U.S. models. The Japanese imports were not especially innovative automobiles. However, firms like Toyota developed profoundly innovative production processes that delivered superior quality cars at lower cost. In like manner, Ray Kroc did not invent hamburgers; he invented McDonald's, an innovative process for delivering better, faster and cheaper hamburgers (or at least better in the view of the millions that eat them, and certainly faster and cheaper).

The Merrill Lynch Credit Corp. VOC process yields a prioritized list of breakthroughs needed by process. In addition, it assesses risks, countermeasures, and types of measurement data needed to integrate each marketing opportunity with overall strategy. The list of breakthroughs includes process improvements, new products, product enhancements, strengths, weaknesses, opportunities, threats (SWOTs), a customer-oriented business plan and MLCC's critical few objectives (CFOs)—company goals in measurable form. OMI, a Baldrige award recipient for 2000, adds to this an estimate of the cost of making improvements and classifies them into **A** improvements, included in the current budget, and **B** improvements, to be funded in the next budget cycle.

Understanding the dividing line between customer value that wows customers and that which causes customers to regret their decision, sets a base line for planning and deploying improvement targets. Where you have a gap in the customer value you offer, this stage of the cycle sets improvement targets which set the stage for later reviews of how well your plan is working. The Plan stage concludes when your people convert their ideas for innovations and improvements into planned actions and innovations. The cycle then moves on to implementing those plans.

(D) Do—Deploy Approaches to Make Improvements

The deployment (Do) activities of the golden cycle pilot-tests innovations and improvements planned earlier. These tests show whether or not planned improvements really offer better customer value that will attract and please buyers. Involving real customers through field tests is like running an experiment to see how well you understood customers and their behavior during planning. Tests of innovations need to include both current and strategic future customers while your people listen to customer and prospect reactions to your improvements. Deployment goes beyond new and better offerings in the market; it may include changes in processes for making, selling or delivering your products and services.

Frequently, the deployment stage of the golden cycle involves re-engineering or improving service and delivery processes to generate better customer experience at lower production cost. Such activity meshes the golden cycle with process and workforce improvement aspects of the capability-development cycle. (Many sound market plans assume that the capability to make improvements exists in the organization; the capability-development cycle aims to convert such assumptions into actual competence.) In addition, the design of new products and services offers high leverage for creating wealth, small changes in your firm's investment can yield huge increases in return over the life of a new product or service.

Product or service design decisions that add up to only 4 percent of total life-cycle cost determine an estimated 80 percent of all costs associated with a new product or service over its useful life. The usual way to validate predictions about what will please customers is to develop a prototype of the new design and then ask real customers to evaluate that prototype. High performance businesses often use a prototyping process to build efficient, reliable new services from the best, proven elements of older systems and processes.

The deployment or Do phase of the cycle includes maintaining and improving existing customer relationships. Healthy customer relationships provide a basis for win-win cooperation between you and your customers. You learn more about what customers consider important and use this to improve your product and service delivery. The customer learns more about you, your capabilities and planned improvements that could deliver still more of what customers care about. This accumulation of working relationships and mutual understanding expands trust that leads to competitive advantages for you and benefits for your customers.

The *Do* phase of the golden cycle also includes making customer-focused measurements of work processes that deliver customer satisfaction. During the deployment stage of this cycle you need to deploy measurements along the "line of sight" from customers and the market, back to process variables that influence outputs that customers care most about. This consists of working backward to link your planning forecasts and predicted result improvements to measures of factors within your processes that move end-results in the planned direction. Measurement in the golden cycle is the single most important approach to translating voice-of-the-customer information into indicators or measures that link activity within each unit to what customers care about. Deploying such a chain of measures provides a tool that the planning stage can use for setting, and later monitoring, unit- or process-level performance against marketing and cost targets.

Now, the golden thread moves on to checking final results. So far the golden cycle has planned and deployed innovations in search of new ways to attract and please customers. The third or *Check* stage compares the results with earlier predictions to produce learning and new knowledge. Are customers really buying as planned? Or are your results different from those forecasted when you planned? And are the differences good news or bad news?

(C) Check—Learn by Comparing Results to Planning Forecasts

The Check step of the golden cycle is the point that produces learning within the cycle. Did we improve our profitability or did we not? Profitability (sometimes wrongly) is taken as a signal that things are going well. Managers of a highly profitable firm have much more freedom of action than do managers with falling profits or losses. Of course, looking at profitability numbers is just the start of checking or reviewing activity. The word *check* implies study and analysis of results beyond a simple look, see and listen. This takes drilling into detail; often you must study what customers do rather than just what they say. With planning and doing complete, in this stage you investigate whether what you did had the desired impact on customer buying, satisfaction and revenue. Checking in this context means studying what worked and what did not work.

The objective of studying is to deepen your understanding of what drives customer behavior so that you know what improvements to make to increase profitability and wealth creation. This stage investigates such questions as: "How are customers responding to our improvements in products and services?" "Were our sales forecasts or other planning predictions accurate?" and "Why did customers do that (leave for the competition, come back, increase purchases, decrease purchases or stop buying altogether)?" This step goes beyond just asking customers about their experience, it correlates changes in customer behavior with changes in features of your product and service.

Years ago, a market research firm was investigating why consumers bought various types of cereal. From focus group interviews they compiled a long list of factors that customers said were important in their choices, including, for example, how sweet the cereal tasted. Next they surveyed a random sample of cereal consumers and asked them to rate how important each of the factors was in their choice of cereal. When analyzed, the survey showed that sweetness was far down the list of characteristics that customers say are important to their choice of a morning bowl of cereal. To double check their survey findings, the firm analyzed the statistical correlation between the market shares of many brands of cereal, and data on the characteristics mentioned by customers, including the amount of sugar each contained. (Market share for cereal is a direct result of preference, since cereal is frequently purchased.) Their statistical analysis found that sugar content was the single most important predictor of cereal market share. The moral of the story is that customers may say one thing, but really do another. The only way to find out is to check actual behavior that reveals their true preference.

Checking on results also gives you feedback on how good the theory and assumptions underlying your earlier plans and predictions were. What you learn lets you revise your thinking about what might please customers. But you need a theory, otherwise results from your pilot tests of improvements are just isolated facts that do not teach. So this stage of the cycle lets you find out if you need to revise your thinking about customers' behavior. Checking on results of established products and services also alerts your business to changes in customer tastes and preference over time; customer expectations gradually escalate. Such shifts in customer expectations imply that you must continuously improve just to maintain your edge with customers. Continuous listening to your customers' voices as they react to new and existing offerings produces the knowledge you need to innovate and stay ahead of change.

Listening to your customers as they call in to help desks and hot-lines can teach you about the health of your customer relationships and provide valuable voice-of-the-customer information. Studying complaints or service incidents can alert you to changes that will reduce damage to customer relationships and prevent upsets. The check step gives you the knowledge to develop problem-solving skills and escalation ladders to recover the good will of even the most disgruntled customers. Even one customer incident can provide information that lets you prevent problems for many customers, as the following example shows.

A medical equipment maker has only a few thousand institutions that can afford its expensive medical imaging systems. Because of the large investment these machines require, reliability is a major customer hot button; too much down time can cause an institution to switch to another equipment supplier. Customers purchase field service from the manufacturer, which lets the manufacturer analyze breakdowns and equipment downtime. From the first occurrence of each type of breakdown, the company finds out how many other machines they have installed could potentially experience the same problem. Without disrupting customers, they analyze the breakdown, determine a preventive fix, prepare a service instruction and a kit of parts for every machine in the field that could experience that type of breakdown. They perform preventive maintenance during scheduled visits. Needless to say, customers experience very high reliability from this firm's machines and are extremely loyal to the firm. This shows how careful use of information from a single customer incident can help you build stronger customer relationships. Over time, this firm has become the dominant supplier in this specialized and closely-knit market segment. The acid test of customer relationships is the amount of new business that your customers place with you or refer to you.

Analyzing aggregate customer complaint data helps your organization find out which activities inflict the most "ouches" on customers, and enables you to do something about them. Then the next round of planned improvements in the golden cycle targets preventive action at the top causes of customer upset. Some innovative software firms beef up their customer relationship capabilities and listen hard to customer calls after any new software release. Such firms prove that the relationship works for the customers' own good by being easy to contact and by resolving customer problems promptly. Off line, the firms also look for patterns in data from the many customer calls to plan further product innovations and improvements.

Learning about markets and customers often means going beyond conventional market research to probe deeply and listen to why customers behave as they do. Even when customers know why they make their choices (as opposed to the cereal example above) not all market research really probes for *why*. Knowing *why* reveals underlying causes and drivers, as the following example from the automobile industry shows.

When Toyota Motor Co., began importing cars into the United States in the 1950s and 1960s, GM bought a few. GM's tests on over a hundred quality and performance measurements determined that the new Japanese imports were, by GM standards, inferior to U.S.–

built cars on virtually all counts: engine reliability, transmission performance, fuel and ignition systems reliability, etc. Having difficulty selling its products in the American market, Toyota began asking U.S. auto buyers what they liked and disliked about new cars. The number one response from car buyers was: "My new (Chevy, Toyota, _____) squeaks."

Toyota asked its engineers why the cars squeaked. The engineers found that the squeaks mainly came from rubber gaskets and grommets between the sheet-metal body of the car and other metal parts. Steel rubbing against rubber as the car went over bumps made the squeaking sounds, which customers disliked. In the spirit of root-cause analysis, where it is traditional to ask five why's, the Toyota engineers asked a second "Why?"

"Why must we put rubber pads between the metal parts?"

The answer was that the stamping process produced parts which varied in size, so the rubber was needed to make them fit together into water- and air-tight bodies.

Along came the third "Why?"

"Why do the sheet metal parts vary in size when they come out of the stamping operation?"

Answer: The stamping process clamps flat sheets of steel by their edge and hits them with a heavy drop hammer to shape them into doors, fenders and other body parts; the stamping process is very violent, so tool designers were forced to leave a little wiggle room in the dies—room that meant that each piece varied from the last.

The fourth "Why" was: "Why do we clamp the metal at its edges?"

Answer: "That is the way we do it—*that is the process.*"

Toyota set an improvement target to come up with a process that would eliminate piece-to-piece variation in stamped sheet-metal parts. Soon, engineers developed a process that punched two small locator holes in each sheet to prevent movement. After investing in new tooling, all Toyota's sheet-metal parts came out perfectly alike. The parts were so uniform that they could be welded together without any rubber. No rubber meant no noisy friction; the bodies were so strong and tight they could not squeak. Welding also meant fewer parts and less time putting everything together into a finished body, so it lowered costs. No other carmaker could match the quality and low cost of the Toyota body, because all were using the process that Toyota had left behind. In this case the innovation was a new process that conferred unique advantage, rather than a new product—say, a car with tail fins—that is easy to copy.

In the late 1980s, a reliability engineer was making a case to his company's management that priorities for product improvements should be customer-driven. To prove his point, he gathered more than twenty years of *Consumer Reports* frequency-of-repair tables on the Toyota Corolla. These tables use small circles to show whether a car has better, worse or average frequency of repairs in each part of the car. For example, a black dot next to body integrity and finish would indicate above-average rate of trouble, while an empty dot would indicate below average. He placed twenty-plus years of diagrams side-by-side on a single sheet.

When *Consumer Reports* first began publishing ratings on Toyota's product, customers gave Toyotas dismal ratings on nearly all dimensions. However, year after year, one or more of the ratings such as body fit and finish went from worse-than-average to the highest possible rating. Once Toyota improved the rating on any part of the car, it remained at the best level for the remainder of the twenty years. After fifteen or so years of steady improvement, the car had achieved the best rating in the market for every quality that customers considered important. During the time period that the engineer's analysis covered, Toyota Motor Co., went from a company with sales less than GM's net profits to a worldwide competitor that captured nearly a third of GM's car customers. This shows how repetitions of the golden cycle cumulate until a product or service can become a market leader. Of course, automobiles are stable and change is slow, but the point is to check with the customer and learn what might please the customer as a basis for driving the cycle.

The golden cycle at Toyota also developed an innovative production process that MIT experts who studied it refer to as "the machine that changed the world." Not bad for innovation and wealth creation. But the voice of the customer was the driving force behind Toyota's golden cycle; Toyota systematically found out whether its customers liked improvements that it made for them.

Finally, calling this the *Check* stage of the cycle also brings home the fact that results must be compared to an external reference or benchmark. The purpose of improvement is to become the customer's best choice in the marketplace and therefore increase your revenue. If you see a market opportunity, chances are that some other firm sees it too, and so you are always in a race. A contender in a race needs to look around at the competition to see who may be gaining or who is ahead. Comparing your results and customer evaluations of your product and service to competitors' performs the same function. To win a race you only have to be ahead by enough for the judges to see; customers and shareholders are the judges. They shop around, so you should know how you stack up against the competition for revenue and for investment.

As the Check stage of the cycle ends, the lessons learned and changes in thinking become the subject of the fourth and final stage of the golden cycle—the Improve (or *Act*) step. The Act step takes corrective actions and shares lessons learned throughout your company to speed up innovations and improvement.

(A) Act—Use Lessons Learned to Improve Future Profitability

The final Act step of the golden cycle lets your firm take short-term corrective actions, and turn lessons learned about customers and approaches that worked and ones that did not, into future strategic innovations and improvements. The wonderful thing about the golden cycle is that it improves profitability; additional profits let you invest in more improvements. So, after you have looked at your numbers in the Check step, this final step provides input and lessons learned to the next repetition of the cycle. This step also makes improvement in the golden cycle itself by upgrading how your firm:

- Listens to and learns from customers
- Deploys "the voice of the customer" to every part of your business and
- Uses "the voice of the customer" to innovate and control processes that consistently please customers and gain new ones

World-class firms such as Matshushita Electric (Panasonic, Quasar, etc.) have found that innovative products that outperform the competition by 30 percent and sell for a 30 percent lower price usually win market share even against dominant competition. Instead of just cutting prices to attract more volume, the golden cycle prompts you to increase profitability by innovating changes that boost value, and by creating more efficient production processes. Innovations that add benefits for your customers make the usual price look like a bargain; competing on customer value avoids the trap of price-cutting, so it helps maintain profit margins.

At this point you realize that the purpose of the golden cycle is to innovate beyond what is already available to customers. But, why not simply copy? The answer is that your firm then becomes a permanent follower. In the longer term, product and process innovations yield better ways of pleasing customers. Learning that leads to process innovations confers sustainable advantages when you are the first to learn. The others who learn after you must catch up while you are moving on.

Once your firm begins systematic innovation, you can spread innovation to all parts of the firm where it could pay off. This creates a need for a training and communications infrastructure that standardizes innovations and puts them into practice by revising documentation, training people in what is new, and then checking that your people follow new processes in practice. (This revision and retraining, of course, links the golden cycle with the capability-development cycle—see chapter 7.)

The idea of innovation? *To go beyond what is.* This *Act* step identifies new customer "care-abouts" (previously unrecognized wants), identifies where competitors are ahead, and defines new opportunities to delight customers beyond the current best.

Longer-term innovation tends to empower your firm's front-line employees. Expanded employee authority and responsibility often goes hand-in-hand with improvements in infrastructure, and systems that support front-line employees. The managers instituting a golden cycle need to (1) find everything that blocks each employee's ability to meet and exceed a customer's expectation on the first try and (2) engineer it out of the chain of production and delivery processes. The twenty years of Toyota improvement showed that improvement is continuous. Since it may take years to achieve all of the improvements your firm can identify, pick the ones that attract the most business first. Then, each improvement moves your business closer to the golden destination—highly satisfied and loyal customers that provide you revenue and gratitude for delivering such excellence.

The golden cycle turns your whole firm into a learning organization. It meets requirements found in several Baldrige categories:

- Customer listening and learning (category 3—customer and market focus)
- Process improvement by properly trained, empowered employees (categories 6—process management and 5—human resource focus)
- Plans and priorities (category 2—strategic planning)

Each trip around the golden cycle raises customer satisfaction, demand, market share and sales income; it leaves your firm with more marketable and competitive products and services. Each completed cycle also improves your organization's knowledge of customers and markets, while yielding process innovations that give you a more efficient and productive delivery process. In as little as two or three years, your firm's golden cycle can produce improvements that put you ahead of your competition and expands your business at the expense of slower-improving competition.

Now that you have a grasp on the companywide ideal of a golden cycle of wealth-creation, you are ready to hear about three supporting cycles: leadership and planning, capability-development, and risk-return. These supporting cycles work with the golden cycle to speed your progress toward performance excellence. The next chapter introduces the first of the three supporting cycles, and may be the toughest challenge in transforming to high performance—leading people so that they have a common purpose and direction, as well as a winning strategy.

PART III

Three Supporting Cycles and Their Interactions

We must become the changes we wish to see in the world.

—Mohandas Gandhi

This section details three more cycles that support the golden cycle of wealth-creation just described: leadership and planning, capability-development and risk-return. Your firm meshes these business cycles to create high performance at the level of your whole enterprise.

- First, a long-term, future-oriented cycle builds the management behavior needed to achieve high performance; over time, this cycle creates a leadership and planning system—vision, individual and organizational values, strategies, plans and behaviors—that gives meaning to, motivates and aligns the disparate management and improvement efforts in your firm.

- Then, your firm uses a cycle to assess and continuously develop world-class capabilities required to execute your strategy; the capability building cycle propels your whole enterprise toward its future direction.

- Next, your firm's long-term success depends on having a companywide measurement, information and analysis system that puts your firm's plans, decisions and actions on a foundation of facts. Your risk-return cycle uses quantitative analysis to control both major classes of risks: (1) strategic loss of competitive advantage and missed opportunities and (2) tactical operating losses from defects and errors as you pursue profitability.

Finally, how your firm's parts help one another is critical to achieving your firm's mission. A superior business results when you improve all its parts—*and* when those parts work together better. Likewise, your firm's improvement comes from increasing the sum of its cycles' interactions. Any system's properties—such as your firm's profitability—emerges from how the whole is designed and how the parts work together.

CHAPTER 6

Leadership and Planning Cycle

When an organization lacks committed leadership and reality-based planning, each individual, work unit or department defaults to pursuing its own objectives. It is the old story—if you don't know where you are going, any road will take you there. If the parts of your organization do not share a common purpose, then they go their own ways. This chapter deals with a systematic organizational learning cycle that answers such questions as: where will your future leaders come from, and how will you develop systems for stimulating and managing successful, profitable growth?

Author John Kotter writes that management complements leadership because management deals with organizational complexity while leadership deals with change (Kotter 1990). So management organizes, solves problems and allocates resources; leadership gets people working together to achieve a common purpose; they complement each other. Kotter's distinction between directional leadership—where to go—and managerial organization and implementation—how to get there "firstest with the mostest"—clarifies why so many well-managed companies are so poorly led and lacking in direction. Managing complexity and leading change use two different skill sets, and any one person may or may not posses both sets. Excellence in execution does not automatically confer genius in tapping motivations and setting direction; high performance demands both.

A directionless organization wastes resources and opportunities in internal conflict that could have produced higher levels of performance under effective leadership. While this waste may not be lethal, it keeps a poorly led organization from achieving its potential to grow and excel. The purpose of the leadership and planning cycle is to align all individual, unit and departmental efforts by creating a common purpose, mission and direction. Planning how to execute the desired direction connects leadership with managerial decisions about resources, and who must do what to accomplish the mission.

Figure 6.1 depicts leadership and planning as a PDCA cycle of continuous learning and improvement. This cycle creates a positive sense of future direction; it also develops the high performance organizational values, hope and commitment your organization steers by. Leadership tends to be emotional and attractive; good leaders create hope within your enterprise to justify the effort and cooperation needed to achieve ambitious plans. Managers, who may or may not be the leaders, must add pushiness to emotional intelligence and the sense to develop the talents of those they manage. Within a high performance management system, this cycle provides feedback and coaching, if needed, to improve leadership effectiveness throughout the organization. Learning and adjustment must be continuous because the competitive, technological, stakeholder and social environment is ever changing. What's more, turnover among the leaders often becomes a significant challenge to maintaining consistent and committed leadership direction.

The *Plan* step of the cycle integrates approaches from the leadership and planning categories of the Baldrige framework with three focuses. The first focus is external, on future opportunities and on making critical choices about direction and how to compete. These choices direct your business, and set and coordinate strategy across organizational units. Activities within the Plan step include

Figure 6.1
The Leadership and Planning Cycle

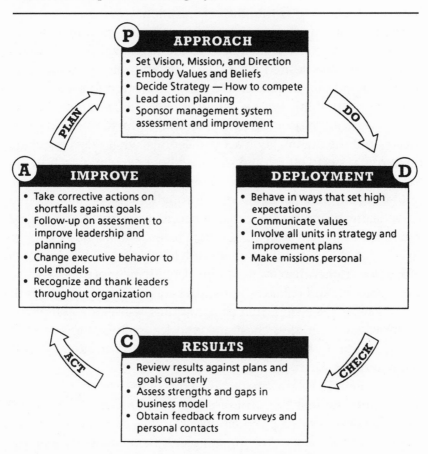

developing a vision of the future that makes the opportunity seem realistic for all stakeholders.

The second focus is on what behaviors are important to convert planning opportunities into improved performance. It seeks to ensure that rewards and recognition align with the actual behaviors needed to make progress. Often, performance assessment and promotions run contrary to what the business really needs. Just think back to the example of the utility whose people were too busy to measure customer satisfaction. The utility's rewards and performance appraisal system contradicted what common sense says that business needed most. This focus establishes the organizational values that guide how organization members work; it is also about how leaders behave within the organization.

The third and final focus considers motivation; how to obtain the best performance from members of the organization in order to work toward the desired future. Leaders and managers both seek to understand and engage employees' motivation to excel.

The *Do* step of this cycle is action oriented; it concerns what you and other leaders do. Often this amounts to how role models throughout the organization act in meetings, what they look at and do during visits to offices and sites, and how they involve individuals, teams and units in both planning and implementing plans. To put leadership into action, leaders throughout the organization involve teams of motivated, capable people from across the organization to implement plans. Often such teams will include managers chosen for their organizational knowledge and task completion capabilities rather than for their rank. Deployment of plans also creates optimism and balances individual and unit purposes with the organization's mission. Just as a conductor draws a symphonic performance from an orchestra, sound leadership aligns separate efforts so that they reinforce one another to add up to an overall, companywide focus.

The *Check* step follows up on doing by comparing actual progress and results against the progress and results you had planned. Checking or reviewing provides opportunities to encourage, thank, credit and coach those carrying out plans. Poor capability to implement plans and improvement projects is a common organizational weakness. So checking on results gives leaders many opportunities to learn where planning disconnects from doing and why; the Check step turns even these into lessons learned. One of the major byproducts of checking within the leadership cycle is that it makes emerging leaders visible and it stimulates the development of solid project and program management skills that are a building block of change, not just for this cycle, but for all changes the organization needs. Checks or progress reviews also provide opportunities to recognize contributions and create a climate of success.

Finally, the *Act* step sets up improvements in actual leadership and planning and in the methods your firm uses to lead and plan.

In this stage of the cycle, you and other leaders consciously turn what you have learned from the last cycle into improvements in *how* you plan and lead for the next cycle. Now that you have an overview of the leadership and planning cycle, the following describes management methods that high performance companies use to lead and plan.

(P) PLAN—SET DIRECTION AND PROMOTE HIGH PERFORMANCE VALUES

The Plan stage of the leadership and planning cycle answers the question of how your business will grow and prosper. Some elements of this cycle, such as spelling out vision, and perhaps mission, are "blue sky." They signify distant, hoped-for visions that lead you to aim high. Other elements of the cycle deal with very practical managerial issues, such as how to get people working together to make progress in the direction of the vision. The aim of your firm's leadership and planning cycle must be to create a unifying sense of opportunity—a brighter, more prosperous, attractive future. The most enduring opportunity is to focus on creating benefits for customers because customers always try to maximize their value—and then set up the management system to make it happen.

Spell out Vision and Mission

Leaders promise big opportunities and exciting possibilities—a computer on every desk (Apple), or controlling all of those desktops (Microsoft), or a company run for "People, Service, Profits" (FedEx)—to energize an organization. Business vision can't be pure blue sky; it must depict a believable, potentially achievable future for your entire enterprise. Such a vision has two parts:

- A potential market and product or service so valuable that it has significant, profitable and sustained demand
- A reliable process to deliver your product or service profitably and with customer satisfaction

Your firm's leadership and planning builds on both of these imperatives. It locates each stakeholder and identifies that stakeholder's roles, responsibilities and tasks within the context of your organization's overall purpose. In short, leadership and planning is about translating your ideal vision into an operational statement of purpose, usually called a mission statement—a simple, clear declaration of why your organization exists. In his book *Creating the Corporate Future*, Russell L. Ackoff defines mission as "a very general purpose that can endow everyone in an organization and everything they do with a sense of purpose." It is "a vision of something strongly desired accompanied by a commitment to its pursuit" (Ackoff 1981).

During the Middle Ages, a traveler asked two stonemasons side by side at a building site what each was doing. The first man looked up from his work and said that he was building a wall. The second man replied that he was building a cathedral to glorify God. Each worker answered the question, but the answers reflect differing hopes and attitudes toward the quality of their work. Someone trying to please the Almighty will build to last; who knows about someone just building a wall. One worker was task-oriented; he explained his function. The second worker—the one with the mission—was purpose-oriented. What will the front line workers in your business answer when they are asked what they are doing: will it be a task by rote or a purpose they pursue with enthusiasm? The answer to this question obviously makes a difference in your organization's ultimate performance.

A sound mission statement focuses on enduring customer and market requirements, rather than on specific products or services. It gives your business a constant purpose that remains stable year after year. If your firm sees its mission in terms of a specific product (buggy whip? photocopier? carburetor?) or service (ice delivery man?), you need to dig deeper to the underlying customer-focused reasons for your existence. Customers' wants and needs tend to be stable, while the advance of technology renders products and services obsolete. Consider how a narrow, product-focused mission hamstrung Xerox Corporation in years past.

In the 1970s, when Xerox Corporation was a leading copier manufacturer, it focused on paper documents. However, many Xerox research discoveries eliminated paper—the fax machine, the simulated desktop and windowed graphical user interface (GUI), the personal computer and the local-area network (LAN). Commercialization of these breakthroughs eluded Xerox managers, who were focused on a product-oriented (copier) mission. Instead of "playing to win" in the vast new markets their fantastic technology could serve, Xerox management focused on "playing not to lose" in the plain paper copier market. Eventually Xerox refocused its mission to view the firm as a "document company," as word processors, fax machines, and e-mail systems rendered documents in digital form. Xerox's change in focus sought to reorient thinking in ways that would unlock new customer value. The jury is still out on whether Xerox's strategies for dealing with electronic imaging, communication and reproduction of documents—paper or digital—will lead it to renewed profit and growth opportunities. The point is, however, that focusing on what you do (product, service) rather than on what the customer gets, can dampen innovation. Not focusing on innovations and sticking to known markets may reduce risk taking, but can wipe out future opportunities many times bigger than the immediate gains.

Have you ever wondered why many firms pursue similar visions and missions, but get different results? They differ in what they make important every day as they pursue their chosen directions; they differ in organizational values.

Embody Values and Beliefs

Organizational values or principles help everyone in your organization behave purposefully, even when facing unclear, confusing, or ambiguous situations. High performance values focus an organization on doing what is right—what will lead to excellence. High performance values stimulate creativity within the organization by freeing people to create and choose within a framework of what is important, what is right and what "we are committed to." As chapter 3 explains, when employees are faced with hard choices, ingrained organizational values pinpoint "the right thing to do when the boss isn't watching." High performance values are the foundation of your firm's leadership system and its leadership and planning cycle. (Actually high performance values are the foundations of all the cycles.)

In 1992, Solectron Corp. (Baldrige award winner for 1991 and 1997) stated that "[Our mission is] to be recognized without dispute as a world-class manufacturing company, and our drive for total customer satisfaction supports accomplishment of this mission." By 1998, this statement evolved into "Our mission is to provide world wide responsiveness to our customers by offering the highest quality, lowest total cost, customized, integrated design supply chain and manufacturing solutions through long term partnerships based on integrity and ethical business practices." Notice that the mission's focus shifted from things Solectron wanted—such as recognition—to things that customers care about, such as integrity and ethical behavior that develops trust in Solectron as their customers' manufacturing partner. This was a shift in mission toward delivering customer value.

Given a list of individual and organizational values, specific choices often raise conflicts between values. Such conflicts may pose an ethical dilemma; every alternative or choice is bad for someone or for some reason. No dominant choice may honor all values. Such ethical dilemmas call for everyone involved to think about the ramifications of what they do and try to see things from all points of view. Then, actions that place some interests ahead of others at least have explainable bases, even though some stakeholders may dislike the explanation and disagree with the action taken.

What approach do you need next to lead your firm into a prosperous future? Shift from a reactive posture to a pushy, future-oriented search for opportunity.

Bring Focus and Strategy

C. K. Prahalad of the University of Michigan in his book *Competing for the Future*, cites a 1991 EDS study that found only 40 percent of the 1970 Fortune 500 firms still alive and well in 1991 (Hamel and Prahalad 1994). To have a future, your firm's leaders need to plan now. Since your firm cannot pursue all market and customer segments at the same time, you need an approach for choosing.

Leadership and planning approaches start with a long-term awareness of what qualities will win business from competitors. Because quality creates and satisfies customer appetites, your choices of quality levels, targeted customers and prices are inherently strategic choices. Quality levels and targeted customers lead, for example, to different choices for the local McDonald's than for the dining room at the Boston Ritz-Carlton hotel.

Strategy's basic purpose is to leave your firm with a durable advantage over competition once executed (Porter 1996). Your choices among long-term alternatives weigh and balance customer, market size and competitiveness against employee, work unit, company level and environmental purposes and capabilities. Long-run plans must deal explicitly with quality as part of strategy development, integrating quality and performance planning with overall strategic and financial planning. This idea has yet to move beyond a fad or a slogan in Detroit, but appears to have taken permanent hold in Toyoda City, Japan.

In addition to considering customers and the future market, leaders need to consider the interests of other stakeholders affected by their plans and choices. The Plan stage of the cycle must work out how to involve suppliers, regulators, employees and others in providing input to plans. These stakeholders may even recommend objectives and even strategies for achieving those objectives. The idea is that plans and leadership will anticipate and address the needs of all stakeholders, thus eliminating the need for after-the-fact reaction and correction.

To reduce the risk of coming out behind competitors, strategic planning must compare benchmark information from your toughest competitors and potential competitors. These comparisons (based on facts, not impressions) compare your business's performance to the benchmark, spot competitive gaps, and stimulate planning for improvement actions to close strategically important gaps. In addition to motivating aim-high planning, benchmark comparisons link this cycle with the risk-return cycle.

Lead Action Planning

Baldrige award-winning firms for several years report that they explicitly budget for improvement initiatives and action plans. Some firms such as OMI actually set a percentage of revenue aside for business and management system improvement. Such budgeting often takes place as managers link overall plans to next year's budget allocations. However, leadership and planning also needs to consider how much time you and other resource people in the organization have available to implement improvements and action plans. Many organizations are good at planning for what must change but fail to plan for people's time to make the changes.

Rapidly improving companies like Corning, Inc., and FedEx report that top executives spend 20 to 40 percent of their time leading changes to improve quality, productivity, and competitiveness. Each senior executive takes companywide responsibility for some aspect of improvement, providing links between senior leaders and all other levels of their organizations. In a companywide role, for example, a human resources executive might sponsor a team of middle managers and others to redesign jobs to make best use of existing people resources. Or a finance executive might sponsor a team developing balanced scorecards of leading indicators to provide early warning of major moves in key result areas.

As leaders expand beyond narrow organizational responsibilities to take companywide views of issues such as human resource development, process improvement, use of information or customer focus, they help unify the whole—turning the business into a social system for high performance. Another benefit of having executives coach or lead action planning is that it gives them an opportunity to observe people they normally would not work with closely. When senior executives work with and coach people for implementation teams and action planning, it provides training and experience for participants that develops their skills and prepares them for greater responsibility.

(D) DO—COMMUNICATE AND INVOLVE AS YOU DEPLOY

Researchers George Easton and Sherri Jarrell, who have studied planning at several high performance firms say, "Formal planning systems are worthless unless they link to an existing capability to deploy or execute the plans." The companies Easton studied relied on process teams, management task forces, or quality-improvement teams for *how to* turn plans into actions. Easton says that big plans must connect to big *how-to* deployment capabilities. Newcomers to teams or task forces need to tailor plans to fit their abilities to execute; then they can expand their capabilities (Stankard 1996a).

Easton and Jarrell's research also finds that effective formal planning depends largely on networks of informal relationships and involvements: Successful executives delegate most planning activities to process owners or middle managers. Delegation in this way works because senior leaders let people throughout the firm know that they consider planning and follow-through important. Those who actually run the planning process are generally respected managers who know how to get buy-in from other key managers and build consensus. Their main tools are persuasion and good connections to top executives. The Do or deployment stage communicates and engages the whole organization in working out plans for performance (and management) excellence. Whenever plans call for going beyond more of the same, deployment is the most difficult part of the cycle. Deploying top company priorities takes major communication efforts by your firm's senior leaders. One Baldrige-winning CEO told the Quest for Excellence audience of his "seven-times/50 percent rule." He said that you could tell people what the most important priorities are seven different ways; still, only 50 percent of them get the message. His communications methods included basing bonuses on raising customer satisfaction, giving speeches, making personal contacts, and writing articles in company newsletters.

Individual and organizational values surface here once again in behaviors that do or do not align with plans. Deploying plans to turn strategy into action also gives you opportunities to reinforce high performance values and beliefs. Simply putting your organizational values, beliefs, and pursuit of quality and customer satisfaction onto planning-session agendas sends a signal that they are important. In the first one or two cycles, difficulties in deployment produce lessons learned about what you must change for the next cycle.

Involve Units in Planning

Deploying a plan throughout your whole enterprise involves participation and negotiation, rather than command and control. Each unit in your firm operationalizes the strategy as it translates strategic targets into its own action plans. The plan deployment process also must link common mission and objectives to work-unit goals throughout the organization. Asking people who must make the plans work how they can contribute to achieving common goals, engages their creativity and lets them take the initiative for progress.

One of the most effective techniques for involving units in planning involves working backward from your main strategic choices to answer the question "What do we do on Monday morning?" Managers take the overall leadership target and involve successively lower levels of your firm to work backward from ends to means, focusing on diagnosing weaknesses and removing barriers to meeting each strategic goal.

Baldrige-winner ADAC Laboratories translates its vital few strategies from its annual planning cycle into four quarterly operating "dash" plans, identified by quarter (2002-1, 2002-2, 2002-3, etc.). Each dash plan outlines who does what, when, and with what resources. The time horizon and network of goals and objectives provides the constant direction needed to align all units' behaviors between companywide annual planning efforts (Quest for Excellence 1997).

Negotiation between senior executives and middle managers over the relationship between "stretch" goals and lower-level goals is a key element in backward planning or policy deployment. Top executives set "stretch" targets for breakthrough improvements in high-level goals. They usually specify such goals for customers, employees, the management system itself, and financial performance as measured by economic value-added (profit minus cost of capital used to earn the profit). Lower-level managers analyze the goals and pass back to the higher level their plans based on the analyses. All managers and executives negotiate back and forth until all parties agree to a final set of goals, and plans to achieve those goals. This process relies on the simple insight that taking each major strategic objective and analyzing what it will take to reach that objective forms the foundation of a plan to achieve it.

As an example, top executives may choose to pursue cycle time reduction in key processes as a competitive strategy. A corporate "stretch" goal to reduce cycle time is handed over to a middle-management team and goal owner. The management team analyzes the goal, decides how to reach it, and proposes projects, action teams, and how-to plans to achieve the "stretch." They pass their analysis and estimate of the effort needed to top leadership who either commit to the plan or reduce the stretch goal to be consistent with the actions to achieve it. Some middle managers supplement annual strategic improvement and learning cycles with quarterly cycles to deploy improvement policy. Departments may even coordinate their own monthly cycles to solve problems quickly and efficiently. So deployment of plans can follow annual, quarterly and even monthly cycles.

Dana Commercial Credit uses a negotiation process to anticipate, avoid and prevent risks by analyzing uncontrollable external trends that may arise in finance, market, society, economics and technology (Quest for Excellence 1997). Inputs from customers and competitors ensure that the organization stays at the forefront in emerging business-opportunity areas. Dana's goal is to minimize risk by ensuring a stable, broad base of core businesses while driving product development and expanding the company's level of expertise. A second strengths, weaknesses, opportunities, threats (SWOT) analysis identifies factors for success or problems that will interfere.

Leading firms report that sound backward planning or policy deployment allows them to hit 90 percent or more of their breakthrough targets. To control risk, the approach requires everyone to bring factual data into planning sessions: for example, if the goal is to raise customer satisfaction from 20 percent very-satisfied to 50 percent very-satisfied, factual inputs should include surveys, compliant logs, sales reports and other information about factors that boost or destroy customer satisfaction. These data along with factual analysis lead to effective plans and actions.

The final step in deploying your firm's leadership and planning cycle is to create a financial plan and budget that answers the question, "How are we going to make money in the next year as we implement our strategies and action plans?" In addition to financial results, improvement targets eventually tie to day-to-day measurements in each of your firm's units. Tools such as strategic scorecards translate strategic, system-level plans into goals and objectives for every process, department and stakeholder class.

The key insight in deployment is to recognize that goals and targets should help everyone in your firm contribute to overall success, the true definition of productivity in the work place. Involving all of your organization in linking their goals and targets to strategy widens the commitment to achieve or exceed those goals. One 3M Dental Division executive described deployment as "lots of empowered employees telling leadership what they must do." Executives see facts that normally would be invisible to them, while middle managers buy into the plans that they have developed with their own facts, analyses and insights.

Make Missions Personal

In his book *Emotional Intelligence*, Daniel Goleman says that the degree of internal harmony that lets a group take advantage of each members' full potential is the single most important driver of excellence of that group's product (Goleman 1995). Dana Commercial Credit communicates its plan and reviews its strategy with all people in its organization. About 10 percent are involved personally in strategic planning; an additional 70 percent gather customer data and provide suggestions. Finally, 100 percent set personal targets and generate ideas for achieving them.

Personalizing your firm's mission spreads strategic thinking throughout your whole organization—encouraging leadership behavior at all levels. These leaders make your firm's mission or purpose real, immediate and shared. Horst Schulze often uses the example of leadership in the dishwashing department of one of the Ritz-Carlton's hotels. When asked what their mission is, the dishwashers say "they want to be the best." When asked to be more specific, they set goals—for cleanliness and sanitation, for breakage, for efficiency. Schulze proclaims that top managers could not set any more stringent goals in this unit than the unit sets for itself because it takes its mission personally.

Reality and immediacy of mission come from setting goals in terms of measurable performance. Where linkages to strategy are unmeasurable, they use common sense relationships. As you and others work to spread performance leadership across the organization, management jobs must shift to emphasize removing roadblocks that block progress.

Another help in personalizing strategy for top executives is to learn from firms that are further along on achieving excellence. Many executives prefer to learn from their peers by benchmarking top managers of other excellent firms and Baldrige award-winning companies. For example, leaders at Xerox studied Fuji-Xerox; those at Milliken studied their Japanese competition; leaders at Ritz-Carlton hotels studied Motorola and Milliken, and so on (Quest for Excellence 1990).

Leaders of excellent firms also make a personal commitment to the well-being and satisfaction of those they lead. They treat their employees and associates as internal customers and seek to reduce dissatisfaction, and to raise satisfaction and loyalty as they would with a paying customer. Integrating human resource plans with overall business planning considers how strategy impacts people, just as it considers how strategy impacts financial results. Reflecting employee satisfaction concerns in planning activities generates hope and motivation, and encourages people to upgrade their personal capabilities through education, training and leading activities outside your workplace.

Helping people see how their business is a system is another way to help people see how they fit into the whole. Ideally, before planning, managers and key suppliers will flow chart processes from supplier input to final customer. This helps each employee or functional manager see how his or her personal responsibility fits into the whole "value-adding chain of processes." Such a flow chart should clarify "here is how your job fits into making a profit." When the flow chart also shows feedback loops and learning approaches, it becomes a system diagram. This helps people identify where they need to go to get feedback. Often, parts of an organization are isolated from each other, or worse, they contend with each other. Breakdowns of working relationships among the parts of the organization wipe out the performance advantage of the system.

Cycle-Time Reduction Helps Deploy Improvement

One of the most powerful forces for deploying improvement in an organization is to reduce cycle times. Fast cycle times—ranging from time needed to respond to customers' complaints, to the lead time to launch new, improved products—are a hallmark of excellent firms. Customers implicitly put a price on their time, especially when you waste it by keeping them waiting. Cycle-time reductions that save customers' time act like price decreases, so selecting which processes to target should reflect the urgency of customers' needs. Striving to reduce cycle time impels your people to find the problems and bottlenecks that cause delays. Their search helps them see what they must do to speed delivery of process results. Cycle-time reduction usually saves money as well because it drives effort to avoid or prevent problems that cause delay—and cost— before they occur. Consequently, emphasizing cycle-time reduction in deployment of plans offers a win-win for your business and its customers.

At Solectron, leaders measure times-to: -market, -quality (presumably zero defects), -volume, and -distribution for new products. In a single case, Solectron's product development system cut four months from the customer's planned time-to-market. During the four months saved for this customer, this one product generated $200 million of revenue and, because of early introduction, secured the customer's position as market leader (Quest for Excellence 1997). Process cycle-time reductions by factors of ten to fifty are often attainable once people determine what is needed to do real work—without delays, interruptions, and dead time that adds cycle time but not customer value.

Leaders in high performance firms deploy plans by expecting people to "Do as I do," rather than telling them to "Do as I say." Their visibility inside and outside their firms makes them "missionaries"—visible examples of the behavior they seek in others. As leaders all over your organization work to deploy its vision, mission, strategies and plans (or when they review progress and results), they are walking advertisements for organizational values. They orchestrate and balance involvement so that all people and units work together as a system. Any job that promotes the vision, mission, organizational values and goals of your firm does important work; those doing important work are productive. So deploying plans ensures that everyone is productive.

(C) CHECK—REVIEW RESULTS AND FEEDBACK

The Check step provides a forum for solving problems and removing barriers that arise when an organization tries to do something new. During the planning phase of the cycle, each initiative identifies a set of result measures that the initiative will move in a desired direction. Factual information on results compared to planning goals provides essential input to effective reviews. Such factual information is an output of the Check stages of the capability-development cycle (chapter 7) and the risk-return cycle (chapter 8). Shortly after the start of deployment on any initiative, progress reviews begin checking progress. Executives and managers review data on measures related to plans, as well as progress on specific tasks and responsibilities defined during planning.

Reviews of progress and performance also constantly remind members throughout your organization about its fundamental purpose and high performance values. Executive involvement in business reviews provides opportunities to showcase high performance values to the organization by discussing issues raised in reviews in terms of those values. Even leaders who worked side-by-side coaching people on plans constantly check progress. Formal executive reviews usually occur quarterly. Monthly and more frequent lower-level reviews escalate problems or delays up to higher-level reviews. So opportunities to live the values and refocus on organizational mission come up often.

Progress reviews often reveal cases in which individual values conflict with organizational, high performance values. For example, individuals who do not consider personal accountability important soon become visible through their alibis, excuses and broken promises. The reviews from the first one or two iterations of the leadership and planning cycle provide opportunities to see where individual and organizational values reinforce each other and where they inherently conflict. Some individual values are character traits and changes of personnel may be necessary.

In organizations with a history of difficulties executing strategy, sponsors of action plans sometimes demand weekly one line e-mails from each participant in implementation. The single sentence states how many hours were spent and what was accomplished—something as simple as "Four hours spent this week; ten strategic metrics defined and accepted for the unit-level balanced scorecard." Tracking and acting on dozens of small weekly feedback signals such as this can be enough to keep even a massive program of change and implementation on schedule. (Falsifying these weekly one-liners, of course, shows disrespect for others and lack of integrity, which are both individual value gaps inconsistent with high performance.)

Whatever their format, reviews check progress and performance against plans, expectations, and goals set earlier in the leadership and planning cycle. People implementing plans and improvements in an organization almost always run into barriers that impede progress. Reviews that turn up barriers, issues and other problems blocking progress must not degenerate into excuse-making and blaming. The bad example ruins much of your earlier work on approach and deployment.

Barriers that turn up during reviews trigger an immediate jump ahead to the action stage of the leadership and planning cycle. Findings such as unfinished tasks, faltering attendance on action teams, urgent daily priorities crowding out work on strategic initiatives, and too many routine problems to work on improving the management system call for corrective action. Unless corrected immediately, early problems and implementation delays cumulate into major delays or even failure of the whole strategy or action plan. At first, corrective actions on barriers arise case-by-case. However, repetitive problems soon signal systemic roadblocks to implementing plans.

One major benefit that emerges from the leadership and planning cycle is that within a year, or two at most, the organization learns the discipline it needs to execute plans and manage improvement projects. Solutions to systemic problems in deploying plans and improvement actions remove their root causes from the organization and management system. Finding cause takes more fact gathering and analysis than can fit into a monthly two-hour progress review. Usually one or two people accept a data gathering and analysis subtask, work on it between reviews, and report their findings back at the next review. Once the root cause is identified, permanent, constructive, non-punitive actions readily deal with those root causes.

Reviews also provide feedback on the effectiveness of your organization's planning and leadership. Many companies now inventory the critical behaviors needed for excellence, and evaluate manager performance on these behaviors. (This could also occur as

part of the capability-development cycle.) Retailer Sears has identified all managerial behaviors critical to implementing its main
strategies (Rucci, Kirn and Quinn 1998). Sears' leaders encourage
these behaviors through training, role modeling, performance assessment and feedback. Involving your senior leaders as coaches
during reviews lets them identify natural leaders and clear up con-
fusions over organizational capabilities, roles, and responsibilities.
Reviews also give senior leaders direct information on capabilities
and firsthand insight into how effectively they have communicated
organizational values needed to achieve high performance.

Most high performance firms check leadership behavior by gathering facts. They survey organization members on the adequacy of
their immediate and overall corporate leadership. Sears in the above
example asks those who have worked with an individual to rate his
or her performance on various leadership behaviors. Other leadership surveys cover issues such as clarity of mission, ownership of
key organizational values, the level of cooperation among work
units and indicators of effective leadership. Data from such surveys
check clarity of direction and whether organization members see
those in leadership roles as good examples to follow. Survey information on ownership of high performance values—what the organization considers really important—is especially helpful in giving
feedback to senior leadership.

Planning Reviews Include Assessments

Making organizationwide assessments part of annual planning
and budgeting cycles is also becoming an accepted part of planning and leadership, says University of North Carolina's Professor John Evans; he recently finished the first year of a two-year
study of how American Express, Henry Ford Health Systems,
IBM Credit, Johnson & Johnson, Procter & Gamble and others
conduct organizational assessments. Managers at firms studied
say they first pursued three to five specific goals for several
years—for example, defect reduction, process re-engineering or
raising customer satisfaction—before getting into assessments.
"Once firms respond to any immediate crisis, if a crisis occurs,
they look for comprehensive ways to improve," says Evans. This

shows that assessment and follow-up are part of a transition from reactive to proactive leadership.

An emerging best practice (demonstrated by Solectron) is to have your senior executives directly conduct a Baldrige assessment of each of your firm's units. For example, Solectron's CEO and more than twenty of his senior executives are trained as Baldrige examiners; each year they personally assess the management systems of the business units they lead. The process gives them deep insights into the capabilities and needs of the units they direct. It also lets them guide improvements at the whole-company level. Solectron combines the Baldrige model with process documentation and with an ISO9000-based internal auditing model.

(A) ACT—IMPROVE BY BUILDING ON LESSONS LEARNED

The *Act* or *Improve* stage of the leadership and planning cycle builds improvements into your next PDCA cycle based on lessons learned. Usually, the leadership team itself, occasionally with some staff support, reviews the results of last year's planning cycle. Instead of after-the-fact fault-finding attitudes, high performance firms treat their own managers as customers of the leadership and planning process. They ask how well planning met current needs, seeking continuously to improve these internal customers' levels of satisfaction. Information from regular reviews also sheds light on where the prior year's leadership and planning activities ran into trouble or need improvement. At this point, high performance firms usually consider feedback from employee surveys about their leadership.

To make improvements during this stage of the cycle, the executive team usually analyzes insights gained from the earlier Check stage, and identifies the top two or three priorities for improving the leadership and planning systems. As a team they work out the actions and improvements that they will make during the next cycle of leadership and planning. These executives also work out the personal commitments they will make to improve their own personal leadership behavior. Thus, every complete cycle improves leadership and planning effectiveness and speeds up progress.

Although organizational issues have not specifically been addressed up to this point in the leadership and planning cycle, improvements in organization structure (in contrast to work design) fit into this stage of the cycle. One accelerator of organizational improvement is to promote those who contributed the most to the organization's successes during the previous cycle. This puts those who excel at getting things done into position to do even more. Sorting out the players with values consistent with the organization's mission and its drive for excellence also signals to the rest of the organization what is important, providing tremendous leverage for change in your firm. As natural leaders reveal themselves by building and improving the management system, you promote them and the personal and organizational values they represent. Promoting people with values that align with high performance becomes a self-reinforcing cycle that develops future leaders and strengthens your organization's management.

Several Baldrige award winners report that efforts to transform organizational culture stalled until top leaders began assessing actual management behavior to see which managers were role models for the rest of the organization. Linking eligibility for promotion to whether a person's subordinates and peers rate him or her as a role model of leadership behaviors reinforces key behaviors. Participation in leadership or planning initiatives is an excellent training ground for maturing future leaders and promising management talent.

In this "Improve" step of the leadership and planning cycle you and your organization's leaders and management may decide to generate and evaluate alternative organizational structures tailored to your firm's mission. Organization structure usually refers to formal authority—"power over," who reports to whom, and assignment of managerial responsibilities. However, leaders are more concerned with capability—that is, "power to." Organizational boundaries and chains of command of an organization chart rarely increase the flow of information and cooperation between individuals or units in the organization. In contrast, improvement within the leadership and planning cycle considers how to improve your firm's working relations and maximize cooperation to achieve overall goals (increase the "power to" in the organization). For example, if organizationwide performance depends on developing new, innovative products and processes rapidly, management must decide whether marketing, or development or research units should be centralized, or whether a team drawn from individual departments would be preferable. Should some or even all development work be outsourced? Such decisions provide input to organizational innovation in succeeding repetitions of the cycle.

Improve Your Firm's Planning Payoff

Planning for improvement does not automatically lead to improvement, any more than the ritual dance leads to rain. Improvements happen not so much because they were planned, but because planning built the necessary commitments to make improvements. Researcher George Easton has found that high performance firms do not allow the subversion of planning into a justification system for what the top people want (Stankard 1996d). Planning should be a fact-based, objective, and forward look at what your company should do. Since many senior executives leave most planning details to others, plans in some firms focus on building a factual case for what top managers *want* to do. Sometimes, it is difficult to tell whether a plan simply justifies the intuition of a few managers or if it presents the results of a careful analysis of options.

For your firm's planning to be worth the effort, it must connect to realities: data on market trends and technological opportunities, understanding of cause and effect in key business areas, and internal networks of managers willing and able to put action behind plans that move your company forward. Basing plans on anything less is like accounting with debits and credits that do not have to balance.

Easton also finds that excellence in management comes from knowing how to surround formal, controlled planning processes with informal systems that build consensus about how to make the formal plans work. Successful firms artfully combine multiple planning systems to seek improvement and better business results: for example, strategic planning, business or financial planning, project planning and service or quality planning can operate in parallel. Planning is often highly distributed, involving many people from widely scattered locations and contexts. Easton says that the art consists of integrating all that planning into operational excellence.

You have seen in this chapter the approaches that top performing firms use to set direction, create common purpose and motivate action. Once the ends are clear, the next step is to create the means to achieve the ends. In the final analysis, it is not enough to have a winning competitive strategy and top leadership commitment to execute it; your firm also needs the execution capability it takes to make your strategy happen. Your organization needs to develop the world-class processes, workforce, work designs and supplier capabilities within a system of management. The next chapter covers this need to build the capability to execute strategy.

CHAPTER 7

Capability-Development Cycle

Ordinary people can do extraordinary things in the right environment.

—Dr. Ko Nishimura, Solectron Corp.

If your strategy talks about what the business will do, then capability development addresses the question of what the business needs in order to do it. Once leadership and planning have set direction and strategy, capability—your firm's ability to repeatedly deliver good results—is what gives your firm the capacity to meet the challenges of competition. When your organization learns to attract new customers, invent new products, improve processes, empower creative employees, and make customers happy, it is building capability in terms of repeatable performances. Capabilities that create customer value and provide durable competitive advantage are expensive or hard to acquire. Guided by strategy, your organization's capabilities make your plans a reality and improve your competitive position.

Ambitious, "aim-high" objectives stretch your organization to be better, faster and cheaper. Your firm's strategic direction puts new requirements on your workforce, product and service designs, operating processes, supply chain and management system. The capability-development cycle helps do what your firm plans *and* expands the range of what you can plan to do. That is, capability includes two kinds of change: (1) incremental improvements in technology or processes that make a good operation better, and (2) innovations that render some existing capabilities obsolete. New or expanded capabilities then feed forward into planning, creating a round of new possibilities.

Once strategy is set, organizational capability must match your plan's intention. When capabilities are inadequate to achieve goals and future directions, performance becomes inconsistent and unpredictable. However, last year's organizational strengths do not guarantee success with this year's environment. Shifting competitive, technological or other challenges·can render your organization's strong capabilities inadequate even if your strategy does not change. The dynamics of strategy, technology and process development demand that your organization anticipate and develop capabilities before weaknesses can slow down progress. The capability-development cycle is your mechanism for matching planning aspirations with necessary capability.

Planning and leadership provide a multiyear context within which you evaluate, plan, and manage your organization's capabilities. For example, your long-term strategy may be to become the low-cost producer and gain a pricing advantage over your competition. This will take leaps and bounds in productivity. To accomplish these strides you need a flexible, well-trained workforce; you need high quality, efficient suppliers, and you need to be able to re-engineer processes to deliver more customer value for less cost. The lack of any of these capabilities increases the likelihood that your organization's low-cost producer strategy will fail. Yet, developing any of these capabilities that you lack can take several years. So, long-term strategic success requires that your organization anticipate capability needs for several years into the future. Failure to have the means when you need them will undermine your long-term strategy of being the low-cost, high-profit provider. The cycle described in this chapter puts the above logic to work systematically.

The capability-development cycle integrates approaches drawn from the strategic planning, human resource focus, and process management categories of the Baldrige framework. Required capabilities usually fall into one of four major areas:

Workforce capabilities—skills to excel at jobs and to improve the design of work; process-improvement and -innovation skills

Process capabilities—technology, flows, and capacities of work and support processes, cycle times, and efficiencies, as well as quality and productivity management

Supply-chain capabilities—external competencies required for strategic success; win/win arrangements with strong suppliers of purchased products and services that yield competitive advantage

Management capabilities—upgrades in management approaches that amplify performance

Figure 7.1 shows the cycle's four phases. The (P) *Plan* stage identifies capability changes needed to ensure that the organization's strategic plan is feasible and its strategic objectives can be reached. It identifies where plans for excellence stretch present (as-is) capabilities and works out how best to acquire should-be capabilities needed for overall company plans. The second stage of the cycle— the (D) *Do* stage provides—acquires or develops—needed capabilities. During this stage, your firm adjusts and trains its workforce, upgrades or improves key processes, adjusts suppliers and supplier-management practices, enlists partners, and improves its management approaches to keep capability in line with strategy. The (C) *Check* stage compares actual capabilities against planned requirements to spot needed adjustments and improvements to continue on plan. This stage's activities usually coordinate with leadership and planning reviews in the Check stage of the leadership and planning cycle (see chapter 9). Finally, the fourth stage— the (A) *Act* or *Improve stage*—distills lessons learned earlier in the cycle to improve the next round of capability development; it also reviews and improves the capability-development process itself before the cycle's next repetition.

Figure 7.1
The Capability-Development Cycle

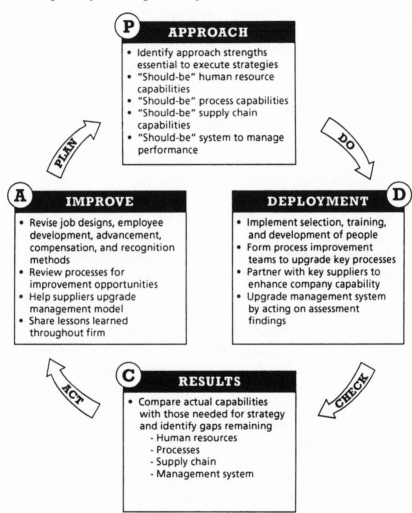

For a capability-development cycle to take hold within your organization, your firm needs to incorporate several high performance values into its culture. *Visionary leadership* and *focus on the future* create the willingness to invest longer term. These investments may be in research and development, improved productive capacity, and in workforce and organizational development. The return on investments in capability may be in the near future, rather than immediate. *Personal and organizational learning* and *managing for innovation* turn capability development into an ongoing PDCA cycle. Without these organizational values, your efforts may result in one-shot developments or gap-fillers as the needs arise, rather than anticipatory investment. Also, innovation in processes and work design can enhance capabilities at lower cost than simple expansion or scaling up of existing methods. *Valuing employees and partners* leads to involving your people in working out what capabilities they need for success. Working with supplier partners ensures that excellent outside-supplier capabilities mesh with execution of your enterprise's plans.

Here are the detailed stages of the capability-development cycle—starting with the Plan stage of the PDCA/I model.

(P) PLAN—DECIDE WHAT CAPABILITIES TO BUILD

Any goal or strategy that relies only on your organization's strong capabilities probably can succeed without major change. To check their organization's capabilities to execute plans, planning teams often prepare a matrix that shows how key processes, or capabilities (in the rows) align with strategies and goals (in the columns). Table matrix entries show how each capability (row) impacts attainment of each strategic goal (column.) A plus sign in a row and column shows that the capability (row) represents strength in implementing that strategic goal (column). Similarly a minus sign indicates that the capability concerned represents weakness with respect to the strategic goal and failure is likely without some action. If your organization's strategy depends on capabilities where you lead your competitors, they will have difficulty copying your strategy, which widens your advantage.

State-of-the-art requirements planning uses problem-solving approaches to close gaps between what capabilities you have and what you need. When aim high planning targets imply that you must have higher performance than you can achieve with present capability, the planning stage of this cycle treats these performance gaps as problems (or challenges if you prefer a positive word). Planning teams of managers tackle each gap as a problem or challenge to be met, or as a research and development challenge if the gap requires new knowledge. For problems, managers may do a formal cause-and-effect analysis to identify root causes of each capability gap. As team members identify root causes, they invent or create action plans to eliminate each root cause and close the performance gap.

The following discussion of approaches found in the planning stage of this cycle offers examples from all four areas of capability planning: workforces, processes, supply chain and management system. The first of these is workforce development.

Should-be Workforce Capabilities

A high-performance workforce achieves more and better results than an equal-sized conventional workforce can. Job descriptions that define the workforce need to answer several basic questions: what is the purpose of each job, what skills are needed to do it, how does the jobholder know whether his or her work is of good quality, and what does the jobholder do if he or she runs into trouble? The answers to these questions serve as a basis first for selecting and training new members of the workforce and then as expectations for evaluating performance. They also provide a framework for assessing hiring and training needs.

The starting point for building a high performance workforce is to assemble all elements of human resource management into a system that strives toward that goal. There is no one magic bullet. Incentives, training, communication, motivation and selection are all elements that have their place within a human resources management system.

Working for the National Science Foundation, two researchers on Human Resource Management (HRM)—Carnegie-Mellon University's Kathryn Shaw and Stacey Ichniowski—studied HRM practices in forty-five separate steel industry operations, all doing essentially the same work (Stankard 1996c). They looked at how "progressive" or "participatory" HRM practices relate to productivity and quality. The research found that changing one HRM practice at a time yields no measurable quality or productivity improvement; however, moving to a complete, up-to-date system of practices yields 13 percent higher quality and 7.5 percent higher productivity than traditional methods.

Shaw and Ichniowski measured performance, talked to workers and managers, and recorded HR practices. Their analysis tracked all changes in HR management. The researchers found four basic combinations of HRM systems practices:

Traditional: strict work rules, narrow jobs, incentives paid on quantity, not on quality—no problem-solving teams, little or no screening of new employees, little information-sharing and job training

Communication: some sharing of financial information or costs, but minimal training, narrow jobs, incentives based only on quantity, little screening, and low participation in formal teams

High Teamwork: ongoing skill training, regular participation in problem-solving teams, some progress in areas like flexible assignments, selective hiring, ensuring job security, and broad-based incentive pay

High Performance: jobs broadly defined with flexibility in job assignments, reasonable job security, carefully selected workforce, extensive use of problem-solving teams, intensive skill training, plenty of communication between workers and management, and a multiattribute pay-for-performance plan

Shaw says gains in both quality and productivity occurred without new investment in equipment. For example, workers and managers in a traditional workforce run into problems, they correct them, and go back to work. In high performance systems, they go on to discuss ways to prevent those problems from reoccurring; often, they hit on simple ways to spot things going wrong before real damage occurs.

High workforce performance requires a system of Human Resource Management that builds trust and cooperation. Table 7.1 quantifies how HRM practices affect both productivity and quality. On raising performance, Shaw made additional observations:

- Innovations that add just one "progressive" practice to an existing HRM system have no measurable effect on performance.
- Highest performing companies add extensive employee screening and selection to ensure new hires will work well in team

Table 7.1

Common Patterns of Human Resource Practices

Specific HRM Practice	Tradi-tional	Communi-cations	High Team-work	High Per-formance
1. Incentive pay	No	No	Sometimes	Yes
2. Very extensive pre-hire screening	No	No	No	Yes
3. Job-assignment flexibility	No	No	Sometimes	Yes
4. High participation in teams	No	No	Yes	Yes
5. Some teamwork practice	No	Yes	Yes	Yes
6. Employment-security pledge	No	Sometimes	Sometimes	Yes
7. Information-sharing or meetings	No	Yes	Yes	Yes
Productivity gain	0%	2%	3.5%	7.5%
Quality gain	0%	4%	4%	13%

activities, respond to training, and want to use the skills they acquire.

- Most successful firms build in broadly focused incentive pay, using formulas that combine quantity, quality, safety and profitability measures that workers can control.

The Carnegie-Mellon research shows that high performance HRM systems work because they build trust between the workforce and management. By involving workers in raising productivity and quality, your company can make credible promises of job security as well as obtain performance improvements.

One more element is needed to achieve true high performance in a workforce—simple rules that guide decisions when upsets occur. For example in Ritz-Carlton's lateral service workforce model, any employee that needs help serving a customer may request the assistance of any other employee who is not immediately occupied with his or her own customer. The employee receiving the request is trained and obligated to comply in assisting the customer. Anyone who has stayed in a Ritz-Carlton hotel and experienced the action of this simple rule will attest that it produces amazing performances in unexpected situations.

Should-be Process Capabilities

In parallel with workforce capabilities, you should ask, "How does our workforce do its work?" Now, you are looking at processes—the technological recipes that your organization follows to turn inputs into products and services. Your organization's processes (technological recipes), and the skills and tools used in following them, inherently limit business results. Poor processes get poor results even when talented people work very hard in them; great processes get great results from the practiced efforts of appropriate people.

A flow chart of your business as a system would show a chain of processes from demand creation at the beginning to after-sale service at the end. One or more of the processes in this chain must be a bottleneck; otherwise there would be no limit on your business's capacity. The golden cycle, which sets customer-driven priorities for products and services, gives you a basis for deciding whether your firm's actual processes fulfill the demands of profit-making. The starting point for deciding what your process capabilities should be is a framework for measuring processes.

The American Productivity and Quality Center has developed a family of measures that bracket all key elements of process performance (Christopher and Thor 1993). As used by the insurer USAA, these measures assess process capability along five performance dimensions:

- *Quantity requirements*: measures of process capacity and cost such as total output per time period, dollars per unit of product or service completed, and/or productivity levels. Nearly all firms count quantities like units processed or customers served.

- *Quality requirements*: defect or error rates (so many defects per unit of output) or defects relative to numbers of opportunities for defects (a process that directs attention to market damage). Motorola uses a proprietary measurement known as six-sigma quality to measure quality consistently across a variety of processes. A process capable of six-sigma performance generates as few as 3.4 defects per million defect opportunities.

- *Satisfaction rates*: the percentage of customers satisfied at some level (from low to high) with the results of a process. Satisfaction measures, to be meaningful, must relate to a behavioral scale that predicts whether a customer will or will not return for more of the same from a given process.

- *Timeliness*: how long it takes from the start of the process to the complete satisfaction of all the customer requirements of the process (cycle time). Alternatively, process capabilities may be expressed in a response ratio—the process cycle time divided by the total value-adding time spent in the process. Leaving a car with a repair shop for one day to do a one-hour repair is an example of a 24 to 1 response ratio. High performance response ratios usually fall in the range of 1 to 3.

- *Customer Value*: the perceived worth of what your process produces relative to its cost, or price charged. The difference between the worth of the product's benefits and the price paid gauges whole-process effectiveness.

Widely used measurement systems often cover only one or two of the more complete family of five measures above. For example, the famous Motorola six-sigma measurement is a statistical index of frequencies of defect and therefore measures quality but says nothing about quantity, timeliness, satisfaction or customer value. Other process measures such as quality or defect rates look at what customers want and need from the process (or how often the process fails to deliver what they want).

Federal Express defines customer satisfaction from the customer's point of view, using a weighted index of numbers of each day's defects—such as missed delivery deadlines or wrong addresses (Quest for Excellence 1991). Using weights derived from customer surveys, FedEx calculates a weighted index of all defect types that occurred in a day. FedEx's final customer service index (CSI) then provides an overall measure of how its pickup and delivery system is running. FedEx uses its index to estimate how many customers experience poor service, providing a basis for improving processes.

Planning for process capabilities needs to consider the absolute size of gap between present capabilities and those needed for strategic success. Each gap between what is and what is needed must be closed. Usually, these gaps are turned into improvement or innovation priorities, which are fed into the next leadership and planning cycle. For example, you may discover that customers find that your order entry, administration and billing processes waste their time and cause them to prefer dealing with your competition. If your organization has a low cost strategy, forcing customers who buy from you to waste time and money coping with unfriendly administrative processes undermines your strategy. Clearly, a customer-friendly order process that makes it easy for customers to do business with you will support the success of your competitive strategy.

High performance firms use an approach known as process benchmarking to estimate the size of gap between your as-is process and world-class, or at least to competitive levels needed for success. Process benchmarking consists of finding a process similar to yours in some other company and exchanging information on performance with the process owners. A search of relevant industry, technical and quality literature can identify candidates to benchmark. After contacting benchmark process owners, you often can arrange a sharing of information and even a site visit to see the process in action. High performance firms that have won the Baldrige award share benchmark information publicly through the annual Quest for Excellence conference and other means. Unfortunately, some high performance firms now restrict benchmarking exchanges to their customers and their suppliers. So, your own suppliers and major customers may provide a starting point for benchmarking excellent processes.

When done properly, benchmarking reveals how the leader achieves outstanding process results. Benchmarking can also provide lessons about factors that enable outstanding process performance. Understanding enablers, for example an unusually loyal workforce, is essential for your success in upgrading process capabilities. Enablers are often as important for success as the specifics of a process.

When benchmarking or improvement efforts fail to bridge process and technology capability gaps, the remaining alternative is to invest in research and development. In some industries, such as molecular biology and computer science, the research and development is guided more by the commercial opportunities identified through the golden cycle than by shortcomings in existing products and processes. However, the very high returns on investments in corporate research and development (estimated at over 30 percent per year) suggest that research and development either drives future market opportunities or yields process breakthroughs that increase competitiveness in present markets.

Once you have plans for should-be workforce and process capabilities, this stage of the capability-development cycle moves on to consider how you approach your supplier base.

Should-be Supply-chain Capabilities

Typically, your business relies on strengths and capabilities of key suppliers and other partners (such as distributors, dealers or retailers). Managing suppliers' performance can be as important as managing their expense. Both cost and operating capabilities of your firm's supply chain influence your long-term flexibility and competitiveness. Your supply chain can confer competitive advantage two ways—lower total cost of doing business, or unique contributions beyond competitive pricing and ease of doing business.

When your strategy assumes certain supplier/partner capabilities, including them in your planning builds their capabilities into your system and replaces assumptions with commitments. The main question suppliers and partners need to answer for you is: "What capabilities can we offer that help ensure your strategic success?" While suppliers need not be privy to all your planning, involving them early lets them propose unique or innovative solutions that you might not have asked for. They may find unique designs or new ways to distribute or package existing designs to help lower your cost. Suppliers that fit their innovations and unique capabilities into your plans give you the jump on competitors that rely on less-tailored, more mundane supplier solutions.

To build a high performance supply chain, firms like STM Microelectronics, North America, developed a supplier quality management cycle (Quest for Excellence 1999). This cycle begins with defining what your strategy demands from the supplier, then sets specifications, selects, qualifies and enters into a contract with a supplier. Once the business relationship begins, STM monitors the supplier's performance, compares it with benchmarks and plans improvement projects with the supplier. As suppliers and their customers work toward improvement they often move through several stages:

- *Approved suppliers* sell your firm goods of acceptable quality at the lowest purchasing cost or the most favorable terms, with no advantage over competitive firms.
- *Preferred suppliers* take full responsibility for managing price and quality to become the lowest total-cost suppliers meeting all your firm's requirements. They search out unique ways to meet your firm's needs, using two-way communication to promote capabilities and receive feedback. Customer and supplier firms form teams to engage in process improvement.
- *Supplier partners* invent new ways in which your joint relationship helps both firms fulfill their strategic missions. This level of organization-to-organization cooperation goes beyond goods and services that can be purchased in the open market. Partnering removes routine barriers so operating people can work together as a network, thus boosting your own organization's capacity to create customer value through your partner's added capabilities. The basic idea of partnering goes beyond purchasing inputs; it embraces working together for a common measurable goal, via sharing of information technology. Firms such as e-Bay, Charles Schwab, Palm and Cisco show that networking with supplier partners gain flexibility and capabilities unavailable on the market; your supplier partners gain steady, consistent flows of business and a sharing of risks across many partners. The best partnerships develop a "challenge everything" environment that seeks radically new actions; then, whatever is learned can be spread to other suppliers.

Capability planning often leads to important decisions about retaining capabilities in-house or relying on outside partners. Capital-intensive activities with low return can be outsourced to spread the large investment over many customers. This frees up capital that might be better invested in developing product breakthroughs to expand market share. Facing these realities, many firms seek to outsource to a company like Solectron, who then becomes their manufacturing partner. Solectron buys and runs their customers' former manufacturing plants and increases its utilization by loading it with business from a dozen or more clients. This revs up Solectron's return on investment, frees up its customers' investment, and reduces the customers' manufacturing cost.

Leadership and planning interact with capability-development in deciding whether your firm and its supplier partners represent a more effective system than your own business without partnering. For partnering to succeed, smaller organizations prefer suppliers with well-developed, customer-oriented research and development capabilities. Many firms find that large suppliers willingly perform research and development on new products or technical processes to help smaller customers. The reward for the customer is innovation without investing in research and development, and the pay-off for the supplier is expanded businesses with that customer and with other businesses that might have a similar need.

Should-be Management Capability

Having planned for workforce, process and supplier capabilities as they are needed to support your strategy, the capability-development cycle now plans needed improvements in your firm's capability to manage. Assessing your firm's current management is part of the Check step in the leadership and planning cycle; and chapter 10 describes the assessment process in detail. However, it is critical to make the best use of all management talent in order to meet the demands of high performance. To do this, high performance firms seek to understand managerial employees better than those employees may understand themselves.

Butler and Waldroop state that people have deeply rooted life interests, themes that show up in work situations they find personally gratifying (Butler and Waldroop 1999). Butler and Waldroop list eight such life interests, for example, using technology, conceptual thinking, managing people, enterprise control, teaching and mentoring; people who perform best and derive the most satisfaction from their work use their dominant two or three themes in daily work. Even though people may have ability in many areas, only work in the areas of life interest is deeply satisfying. Part of the gain in performance achieved by the management system arises from putting managers and professionals in the jobs at which they will excel. Then your management system earns its keep by expanding cooperation and alignment of those high performers.

Each year or two, the capability-development cycle assesses your firm's management system against the high performance business model, identifies weaknesses and selects the vital few actions to improve your management capability. Following up on these actions upgrades your organization's key management methods, moving them closer to the standards of excellence of the high performance business model. Often, assessment discovers that the bottlenecks to improved management performance are behavioral rather than in specific management methods. Many organizations find out from their assessment that they have all the parts of a system. They just do not understand or even behave in ways that let those parts work as a system. Either way, eliminating roadblocks by changing methods or by changing organizational values and behaviors ties new and existing methods into a more effective system for pursuing the organization's mission, whatever its challenges.

Once all agree on the should-be capabilities to implement your firm's overall strategic plan, some portion of the overall plan and its capability requirements becomes the coming year's operating plan. You have concluded the *Plan* (Approach) step of the capability-development cycle; now, the cycle moves to *Do* or deploy your planned approaches to upgrade your firm's capabilities.

(D) DO—DEPLOY CAPABILITIES

Most doing, in terms of capability development, fits right into the daily operation of the business. Consequently the Do or deployment stage of this cycle consists of the daily effort to execute the operating plan, which itself links back to strategy. Actions that deploy capabilities within work units of the organization are simply scheduled and completed. At least that is the theory. In practice, failure to execute planned actions does more unintended damage to businesses than their competitors can inflict intentionally. This defines a major challenge confronting the leadership and planning cycle. You, and other leaders in your organization, must do the teaching, coaching, reviewing and cheerleading that disciplined execution of carefully laid plans demands. (This will come up in the Check step of this cycle.)

Deploying capabilities across organizational boundaries presents special challenges. Most organizationwide capability improvements rely on cross-functional teams to make needed change. Often, the same cross-functional team that planned what to do, simply shifts into project-management mode and carries out its own plan. Changes in workforce capability might improve selection, orientation and training of people, or re-engineering work processes. Teams take on the task of developing new product or service delivery capability, or upgrading capabilities to serve customers in new ways, such as via the Internet. Some teams may attack the actual design of work and deploy work designs that raise productivity, improve job satisfaction, or both. Still others may be concerned with the deployment of planning and information systems throughout the whole organization. (Chapter 11, on getting results from an assessment cycle, details the process of deploying improvements in a management system.)

Select, Train and Develop People

Virtually all high performance organizations have identified personnel selection as a high-leverage variable when it comes to performance. Workforce turnover can either slow or speed capability development, depending on how well strategy and the hiring process are linked. Leading firms ensure that new hires build workforce capability in areas dictated by strategy and future direction. Firms like Solectron share a hiring philosophy "Hire for traits, train for skills." They use some combination of behavioral and character assessments to hire new members of their workforce with skill profiles and work capabilities needed for future plans and directions. Here is an example of how hard one high performance firm works to gain leverage from personnel selection.

In a typical year, Southwest Airlines receives about 150,000 employment applications. Of these, it interviews 30,000 to 40,000 applicants to fill only 4,000 to 5,000 openings in its high performance workforce (a 30 to 1 selection ratio). Attracting and retaining high-quality personnel is a critical first step in building your firm's workforce capability to what it should be. In *Fortune* magazine Geoffrey Colvin says that the three most important steps in developing a creative, innovative work force are: (1) Stop crushing creativity and innovation by blaming people for failures, (2) look for people for whom creativity and innovation come naturally, and (3) make employees feel safe and secure, since fight or flight are normal human reactions to fear, and neither leads to innovation or requires creativity (Colvin 1998).

In a speech before the American Society for Training and Development (ASTD), Ritz-Carlton president, Horst Schulze, characterized the state of employee selection and hiring practice in much of the hospitality industry in the 1980s as follows: the old waiter, who had been on the job for a few months, is asked to train the new waiter. The new waiter's qualification for being hired is that he stays sober enough to walk from kitchen to dining room without stumbling. For a few days, the new waiter follows his mentor, learning his job as best he can. At some point during training, the old waiter turns to his trainee and whispers confidentially, "This place is the worst." With this, the new waiter is oriented to the company and now represents the company to its customers.

Schulze is not trying to knock hiring and training practices that existed in the hospitality industry. His point is that new employee selection and orientation in a service organization is too important to be left to chance. He and the executives who report to him personally orient all employees in new Ritz-Carlton hotels. They explain to new hires that they're important and that the hotel can't run without them. They also explain the objective of the company and of the employees' work in the hotel—"to be the best in giving genuine care and comfort" to the hotel's guests. Of course, Ritz-Carlton's formal orientation involves much more; however, this initial briefing introduces new employees to the heart of the organization—its values and beliefs—and sets expectations for performance (Schulze 1993).

Most Baldrige award-winning firms use character-trait-based employee selection, profiling star employees and selecting new ones with similar characteristics. Other firms hire as they please and then try to obtain outstanding performance by training, paying incentives and rewarding performance. This variation in practice raises the question, should you try to obtain improved work performance through selection or through compensation?

Gerry Bush, formerly of Brandeis University, who is an expert on selection, reward and recognition, says that most compensation decisions are tactical, unrelated to overall performance. Firms need to clarify compensation's message. Is it "we love you?" Or does your firm use dollars to send a "wake-up call?" (A big no-no, says Bush.) He maintains that selection is more important than compensation to determine overall performance, saying that the right balance is 90 percent emphasis on getting workers to do work for which they're best fitted and 10 percent emphasis on compensation—an equity (fairness), not a performance (motivation) issue (Stankard 1994b).

Beyond selection and initial orientation of new employees to their mission, on-going workforce development creates new work attitudes and cooperation skills. Putting the parts of an organization together without training them in tools that help them work together effectively undermines performance. When your firm has chosen the right people for jobs, capability development usually entails new tools, skills and responsibilities—all areas that call for training. The final issue in selection is ensuring that the workforce will learn quickly and efficiently—the best basis for this is workforce education.

Education and Workforce Performance

A Wharton School/U.S. Census study sampling more than 3,000 firms, demonstrated that increases in workforce educational levels raise company output more than twice as fast as comparable increases in capital investment (Cappelli 1995). Dr. Peter Cappelli, Director of Wharton's Center for Human Resources, described this link in "The Other Shoe: Education's Contribution to the Productivity of Establishments." Just a few of the study's conclusions make the point:

- Controlling for all other factors, education has a higher ROI than competing investments. Nonmanufacturing firms adding 10 percent in equipment and capital assets averaged a 3.9 percent increase in output; nonmanufacturing firms averaging a 10 percent increase in all employees' average education (just over a year of schooling) generated an added 11 percent in output. For all firms, adding 10 percent in capital investment yielded 3.4 percent; adding 10 percent in training yielded 8.6 percent.

- Worker compensation rises at 8 percent per year of schooling. A 10 percent increase in employees' education raises firm productivity by 11 percent and wages by only 8 percent; the difference equals increased profitability.

- Service firms that use employees' school grades to screen new hires average significantly higher levels of productivity.

However and wherever your employees have been educated, your plans will call on them to master new capabilities. This raises the issue of how you deploy new skills throughout the organization through some form of training.

Train to Develop Your Workforce

Training benefits the organization at two levels. The individual undergoing training acquires new skills and adds knowledge. As each individual employee develops to meet career goals through training, it fulfills the requirement of a social system that it develop the capabilities of those working within it. Training associates in problem solving and quality improvement tools, in listening, in delegating and in working on teams, helps employee empowerment pay off by ensuring that empowered employees know the right way to do whatever they are empowered to do.

Training also benefits the whole organization at the level of the workforce. Cross-training to broaden job skills, to share process knowledge and best practices, to create a common purpose and to foster teamwork expands the workforce's capability to meet organizational goals. The role of supervisors as coaches and trainers cannot be emphasized too strongly. A significant portion of every supervisor's time in high performance operations is spent in training and coaching.

John Bishop, of Cornell University's Center for Advanced Human Resources Studies, says, "Worker training pays off because it's designed to pay off—it fits your business's needs." New employees, new products, new management systems (re-engineered processes, TQM or Just-in-Time, for example) all drive training needs, so the more innovation and change your strategy calls for, the more education and training your employees will need. Here are some highlights of Bishop's findings from a study of what firms are doing in training (Stankard 1995a).

Bishop found that levels of education and school performance are among the best employee-selection indicators. For a national policy study, he reviewed and summarized 200 studies of the payoff on worker training; he found (among other facts) that:

- Employee training is one of a company's best investments. ROI is between 20 percent and 40 percent for the first 100 hours of training of a new hire; productivity gains of 17 percent to 40 percent continue for new employees' first two years. Wages go up, too, but at less than half the rate of productivity improvement.

- Particular job factors raise training needs: high-value-added work (high risk of loss from poorly trained workers), complex thinking (professional, technical, managerial), sales jobs requiring knowledge of complex, customized products, high capital intensity, and reliance on job- or company-specific skills not taught outside the company.

- About 10 percent of training is formally designed—that is, the survey says, "someone has thought through what they are teaching." Formal training saves big firms money because size saves on course development and administration; big firms also report higher productivity improvements from training than do small firms. The remaining 90 percent of training is informal; it comes from working with others, being shown, and doing the job in an expert's presence (coaching). In all but large firms, supervisory training, training by peers, or even self-training from computers or CD-ROMs yields better benefits for cost than formal classroom training.

A better trained workforce can produce a cost advantage because less time goes into inspecting and supervising the workforce. To achieve this advantage, high performance firms have found they must push authority and responsibility down in the organization as low as possible. Training in delegation and coaching skills is a key part in empowering front-line personnel.

Workforce Self-management

Once your firm's executives view their employees as "internal customers," managers adopt the roles of coaches and teachers (not bosses or superiors). In these roles they try to discover and provide whatever employees need to excel in fulfilling and satisfying jobs—to remove the barriers to excelling. Self-management, employee development and clarity of goals or alignment all work together. It is no use to allow people to manage their own work if they lack the understanding and skills to do a good job managing. It is also no use to allow people to innovate if they do not know where the organization most needs innovation, and if the people have not developed their capacity to think creatively. High performance demands that innovation in an empowered work unit must go far beyond calling for more staff when they are busy.

Firms like Solectron and others link goals "by line of sight" to individual employees' actions. They have found that when people understand how their performance is being measured and linked to overall strategic goals, they are empowered to excel. Employee and supervisor usually negotiate developmental goals and link them to training—strategic career planning at the individual level. This creates a focus for empowerment and creates a zone of individual entrepreneurship for each employee.

High performance values or principles play an important part in empowering a workforce. Property and casualty insurer, USAA, teaches ten behavioral principles as they develop every employee's capability to exceed his or her career enhancement goals (Stankard 1996e). The program, known as PRIDE, began with customer satisfaction and expanded over several years to include work performance and workplace satisfaction. The empowerment vehicle consists of a set of linked goals and communications so that each person understands: "I own my job as a business," "I own my behavior," "I am accountable for my own behavior." And "It is up to me to stay relevant to the business objective."

Documenting responsibilities for each work task in a process is a key element in process management and improvement. This includes clarifying exactly how much authority people working in the processes have when upsets occur. A workforce cannot deliver high performance without adequate processes; they may turn in stellar performances, but they will use ten times the resources to do so because of poor process. Instead each person merely resorts to doing his or her best and the overall system breaks down into isolated individual performances, much the way a symphony orchestra's music would deteriorate if every orchestra member simply did his or her best to hit all the notes. Doing one's best is insufficient; harmony demands hitting each note on the music score at the right time, not when each player feels like it. Consequently, deploying self-management in an organization means integrating job training with process development, documentation and deployment (another aspect of capability development).

Individual accountability for performance and for development is a basic building block for workforce high performance. The more authority and capabilities employees have to make decisions, solve problems and recover from upsets, the more they can contribute to overall performance. However, firms like USAA have found that employee empowerment goes hand in hand with employee involvement and communication. USAA PRIDE communications teams parallel the property and casualty unit's formal organization structure from senior leaders to work units. This structure provides immediate feedback to managers on how their decisions impact employee and customer satisfaction.

Now that your firm has trained and empowered its people, how are you going to deploy new and improved processes? Virtually all firms that upgrade process capability rely on teams that understand the processes in question from end to end. Teams are almost always used for new product or process development. And most high performance firms rely on teams to design improved ways to deliver goods and services externally. Finally, internal improvement teams are useful in upgrading how your organization supplies internal business functions.

Deploy Process Improvement Teams

All work should be managed as processes to achieve high performance. For example, OMI, a Baldrige winner, has identified over 150 processes that link into a network for accomplishing the firm's business (Quest for Excellence 2001). The many processes are grouped into three links of a value-adding chain: acquire business (contracts to manage and operate waste treatment plants), carry out contracts and renew existing contracts. All processes fit within or support one of these three links in the chain. Each process has an owner who completes standardized documentation on the process, defines and monitors key metrics to track the health of the process, and gathers user or customer input on a survey that is deployed across all processes.

Most firms that have identified their processes review them frequently and assign each process to one of three states:

- Capable of meeting relevant strategic goals
- Incapable of meeting strategic goals for one or more dimensions and being improved
- Not yet in operation and in need of design and development to meet relevant goals

Process management deals with all three states. For processes that run as they should, you have to exert control. For processes that are incapable of fulfilling strategic requirements, you must find the bottleneck elements and improve or remove them. (Note that improving a process is not a one-shot operation; on a highway, it's common to get past one bottleneck, only to find another just down the road.) Process capacity also obeys the same law: no process can produce more output than gets through its tightest bottleneck. Strategic goals for which you have no adequate process present a third possibility—you need to develop and deploy a completely new process or capability. Training and supporting teams of employees to take responsibility for processes is the most common approach to process management.

A spokesperson for Baldrige award-winning Eastman Chemical, speaking at the Quest for Excellence, told how a Baldrige examiner during their site visit asked management to show evidence that process-improvement teams had contributed to Eastman's financial performance (Quest for Excellence 1994). Eastman management had never previously looked at the data from that perspective. However, they hastily retrieved two graphs—profitability and process-team activity—that revealed a striking relationship: the data showed that the year that Eastman formed its first process-improvement teams, financial performance stood about average for peer companies. As process-improvement teams' activities picked up, so did financial performance. Several years later, when Eastman won the Baldrige award, its profitability had risen to number one among its peer group of chemical companies, with the number two firm far behind. Financial results improved because of better processes; processes improved because team efforts focused on specific improvements needed to execute Eastman's strategy.

Process-improvement teams give empowered employees a magnificent opportunity to put ingenuity and a spirit of progress back into your workplace. Typically, teams check a process by measuring its performance (both in-process and at end-of-process) against standards set up during planning. Once they have measures, they need criteria for determining when a process has deviated from normal, acceptable performance standards. Generally the standards derive from customer satisfaction research. For each process measure, the standard is set at or above the threshold level that correlates to customer satisfaction.

Using statistical data from a process to determine how it's running offers the most effective basis for controlling processes. However, statistical measures are not sufficient for improving most processes. To improve a process, your teams must learn how to analyze variations in process data. By stratifying examples of good and bad variations, your team can determine and validate causes of good and bad performance. Then they can innovate in ways that produce more good and fewer bad variations.

Ideally, process teams possess all of the skills needed to Plan, Do, Check, and Act on their processes, so they can integrate prevention, correction, and improvement with their daily jobs of working *in* the process and of working *on* (managing) the process. Wainwright Industries, a Baldrige award winner in 1994, reported generating fifty-four process improvements per employee per year. Wainwright is the American benchmark for the most implemented process improvements per capita (Quest for Excellence 1995).

Once the easy opportunities for improvement are captured, process-improvement teams need simple, powerful tools in addition to their job knowledge to maintain a steady rate of improvement. In addition to process-mapping, they may learn how to

- Brainstorm improvements as a team
- Use affinity diagramming to link related ideas
- Gather and analyze data by turning numbers into pictures such as run diagrams or Pareto charts
- Perform root-cause analysis
- Manage projects and more

Teams also benefit from a curiosity about how others achieve excellent results with the same or comparable processes. When used thoughtfully, process benchmarking can reduce risk and speed up performance improvements. Process-improvement teams can often adopt lessons learned outside of their own industry to improve their processes. For example, Southwest Airlines is said to have benchmarked how Indianapolis Speedway pit crews make major mechanical repairs on racecars in minutes instead of hours. Southwest studied the principles they found in the pit crews' work designs and translated them into new capabilities required to reduce aircraft time on the ground, increase seat miles flown per aircraft, and raise operating profit in the process.

Some service firms have found that a marketing strategy of guaranteeing service levels can drive rapid improvement in key processes. Delta Dental Plan of Massachusetts is a managed-care, not-for-profit dental-insurance company that serves 300,000 group-insurance subscribers. In 1989, says former senior vice-president Tom Raffio, Delta adopted a seven-point service guarantee—satisfaction or your money back (Stankard 1994c).

Point 2 of Delta's guarantee promised no-hassle customer relations: "Delta will either resolve your question immediately, on the phone, or will guarantee an initial update within one business day and continuous follow-up through to resolution. Failure to live up to this guarantee promises a $50 refund to the group or individual hassled by each occurrence."

To support this marketing move, Delta formed an internal cross-functional team to redesign its customer-service processes. Initially, the design team found that customer-contact people accessed four out of five possible computer screens during an average five-minute customer call to question benefits or claim payments. They estimated that putting all data to handle customer questions onto one screen would halve time per call on 90 percent of the calls; it would also improve service quality.

Delta's team benchmarked Fidelity Investments, AT&T Universal Card Service, and Federal Express, learning that these leaders had

- Dropped customer-service "assembly lines" in favor of teams able to handle all customer needs on first contact
- Given each team the supporting information resources needed to excel

Raffio says the design team identified two major areas of change needed to achieve no-hassle customer relations: (1) job design, training, and behavioral change to implement teams and (2) improved information systems and support.

Here's how Delta achieved affordable quality—service plus productivity. Teams of customer-service reps report to a customer-service manager. New, low-walled office cubicles let members see each other face-to-face. Teams have no supervisors, but they have developed quality metrics (e.g., percentage of calls answered within three rings) and displayed them for all to see.

Delta assigned a full-time trainer to the department manager (with 700 plan designs, 5 dental networks, and constant product innovation, retraining is nonstop). The firm trains associates for three months before they go on the phones. The dedicated customer-service trainer also monitors calls as an educational and coaching tool—not for appraisals. Delta also formed an auxiliary customer-service team from noncustomer-contact personnel (six people from Claims, Operations, etc., who had service orientation and phone skills) and trained them in customer service. During workload peaks, the Automatic Call Director (ACD) routes calls to this auxiliary team to maintain short customer waiting times.

A systems analyst identified items used for typical calls and distilled the most critical onto one prototype screen so the designers could combine five customer-service screens into one. Now, associates use only that single screen on 70 percent of the calls. Tracking and categorizing calls showed:

- Many customers could not understand explanations of benefits; Delta created user-friendly narratives, in words that subscribers often use when they call, and thereby prevented many calls.

- Numerical codes to explain benefits or reasons for denial of benefits bothered customers; Delta now uses simple explanations developed by a cross-functional marketing committee.

Delta's thirty-five customer-service associates and six auxiliaries handle 200,000 calls per year. Abandonment rates went from 15 percent at peak down to 5 percent. Calls answered in three rings went up from 42 percent to 80 percent+. Busy signals at peak went from 10 percent to fewer than 5 percent. Calls resolved on first contact went from 91 percent to 97 percent. Customer-service staff turnover has been more than cut in half. In two years, only thirty payments were made on the promise to pay $50 to hassled customers.

The common thread through the above companies and thousands more is to give employees plenty of practice working as a team—handling disagreements, learning to gather and use facts, making presentations and selling proposals on their merits. All these skills let your teams perform a complete PDCA cycle on their work processes and occasionally to join larger cross-functional process-improvement teams. The objective is for employees to in-novate their work in ways that maximize customer value as well as worker satisfaction on the job.

Ensure Process Integrity

The simplest reason for you to ensure process integrity is so that your firm's top management can sleep soundly at night, freed of worry about haphazard performance and upset or angry custom-ers. Eventually, many organizations discover that ensuring the integrity of their processes is a core capability of performance ex-cellence. The ISO9000 standard offers a model that can be directly implemented as a golden cycle. Thus, achieving third-party certi-fication under a process management system standard can be a powerful first step toward deploying excellence in your organiza-tion. You can use pursuit of ISO9000 certification as the foundation of a high performance management system as long as you under-stand the broader competitive and innovation issues which this book outlines, but which the international standard ignores.

Most high performance manufacturing firms and a growing mi-nority of excellent service organizations ensure process integrity by adopting the discipline of third-party process certification. Between recertification audits by independent registrars, teams of trained internal auditors systematically audit processes, identify areas in need of improvement and initiate corrective action or improvement. Some outstanding firms such as Motorola and Corning, Inc., insist on having all key processes certifiable to obtain the benefits of for-mal process management. They train teams of internal auditors to audit processes and ensure integrity. However, they may stop short of hiring outside auditors to certify their processes and manage-ment systems, relying solely on internal audits or system reviews. In the service sector, organizations such as Manpower, Inc., and FedEx have decided to seek the "good housekeeping seal of ap-proval" by hiring third parties to certify their processes or facilities to relevant ISO standards.

Usually, teams prepare for certification by mapping best practices found in the work place into a best-documented process. For ex-ample, The Ritz-Carlton Hotel Co., had teams of their top-performing employees from each of dozens of hospitality processes identify their best practices and draft work instructions, operating procedures, quality checks and performance measures. This documentation becomes training materials from which new work team members can be trained in best practices.

By deploying a process management system, The Ritz-Carlton Hotel Co., ensures that a guest staying in a Cancun hotel will experience the same consistently enticing service he or she encountered at the Boston, Atlanta or Tyson's Corner Ritz-Carlton. Process documentation also serves as detailed training and operating instructions to ensure the integrity of each repetition of a key process—like having a written recipe for a favorite cake ensures that the cake will come out the same each time no matter who bakes it.

Identifying and deploying the best way of doing each job eliminates many specialized work methods, which increases staff flexibility. Of course, when documented practices depart from how people were really doing their jobs, you need to retrain people in following documented practices. Once trained, documented processes let people go home at night knowing that they did their jobs right. The documentation and training ensure that they know what elements of their work are negotiable, and which are nonnegotiable.

Ensuring process integrity also dictates that you set up a corrective action system. Such a system lets those working in each process flag upsets in their process and provides a feedback loop to those responsible for taking immediate corrective action. Corrective action is followed up with preventive action that removes or blocks the cause of that type of upset permanently. When the corrective action loop includes a rigorous analysis of the root cause for upsets, the system leads to reduced defect levels and improved process cost.

A corrective action system can also proactively stimulate improvements by identifying opportunities and suggestions instead of focusing only on upsets and problems. For example, before instituting process management, work often arises because of hidden system glitches that people devise ways to work around. With a corrective action capability in place, people on the job have a way to red flag previously invisible time wasters and annoyances that only they can see. Then a process-improvement team can make the problem go away permanently. When the problem goes away, so does the effort wasted in working around the problem and the process gets more work done with the same or less effort.

Most third-party process standards (ISO9000, QS9000, TL9000, AS9000, etc.) call for internal audits to ensure that all preventive measures and quality system responsibilities work as intended. Often these internal audits turn up gaps in systems, training and implementation resulting in corrective action requests and lead to improvements. These corrective actions drive a cycle of revisions or improvements in the process, documentation and practices. Many organizations need several cycles of audit and revision before processes and practices stabilize and quality management responsibilities are fully deployed. Eventually designing, testing, documenting, training and certifying people's skills and processes becomes the way people work.

The hardest part of instituting process integrity is getting people who are already proficient in previous work methods to see the benefit of adopting new common processes and working within the process management system to take corrective actions. After working in and on their processes for years, push-back against change is natural. Deploying best practices across a workforce makes your business scalable so that you can expand workforce capacity as needed to handle more volume. Also, continuous improvement increases throughput by some percentage each year, which improves productivity and reduces unit cost, which helps profitability.

Finally, management reviews of the quality and other performance measurements of the management system are important in verifying process integrity. These reviews of the effectiveness of the process management system can highlight areas where capabilities need improvement. Reviews should focus on the effectiveness of follow-up on corrective actions, as well as the results from preventive and improvement efforts. For example, some organizations create a waiver (approved after the fact) when process changes depart from documented procedures for a good business reason. Analyses of these waivers show which processes are not responsive enough to customer requirements. These can then be re-engineered to make sudden process changes or workarounds for unusual customer requests unnecessary. Executive reviews of process management system performance also offer opportunities for recognizing outstanding innovations and contributions to process improvement and integrity.

The ISO standards for process management or quality management systems were originally designed to facilitate customer-supplier relationships without the need of excessive auditing of suppliers. This introduces the subject of upgrading supplier capabilities to what is needed for strategic success.

Manage Your Supplier Base

In deploying supplier-partnering and management approaches, your firm goes far beyond just shopping for the lowest-cost supplier; for example, you may conduct supplier audits and assessments and form joint customer-supplier teams. Some automotive companies have excelled in supplier management, as the following example from Chrysler shows.

Chrysler's SCORE program (Supplier COst Reduction Effort) is an outstanding example of continuous improvement in a partnership framework. In 1997 alone, the program had saved Chrysler $1.2 billion, with more than a quarter of the savings in immediate, direct costs and the balance to be realized as new models sell. Total savings since the program was implemented in 1989 exceed $3.7 billion. These savings accumulated from ideas and proposals submitted by Chrysler suppliers. In all, suppliers have offered Chrysler more than 25,000 proposed improvements since SCORE's inception. Thomas Stallkamp, formerly executive vice-president of procurement and supply says that Chrysler shares costs savings realized with suppliers who pursue quality, efficiency and affordability without eroding supplier profit margins (Struebing 1997).

Supplier-partnering arrangements need not be exclusive. Firms like Motorola select a main partner supplier and a backup supplier. Rather than relying on bargaining power to hammer prices down, your firm works with each supplier-partner, finding unique ways for them to add customer value. You may even cut costs to levels below market prices—a process that takes close cooperation between partners, often to the extent of finding ways to help your company help itself. For example, your supplier may develop a new product for your company that uses that supplier's products and expands your firm's sales.

So far, deploying capabilities has involved improving your firm's workforce, processes and suppliers. As important as each of these is, the final capability the cycle must upgrade is your firm's context for improving all other capabilities: your firm's own management system.

Upgrade How You Manage

During the Plan step of this cycle, your firm identified improvements to your management system. Note that "upgrading management" does not necessarily equal trying harder, hiring smarter managers, or reorganizing (the perennial favorite). Upgrading management involves upgrading methods and processes that your managers actually use to get results. Selecting which management approaches to upgrade depends on how closely those approaches relate to achieving your firm's overall mission.

During deployment, the capability-development cycle activity asks your firm's leaders to integrate management system changes into how the business works. The stimulus for deployment comes from your organization's needs for better methods to achieve performance expectations of top management and stakeholders. Since top executives own and control your organization's management system, they must champion this integration of new methods, behavior and processes into the existing system. Deployment of new management methods requires that executives allocate resources— especially time. You and other leaders throughout the organization also train, coach, recognize and give feedback to teams of middle managers that actually change the methods and processes to deploy better management. You have to fit new management methods into your ongoing management activities. Here's the secret: since middle-management workload will increase temporarily, *only* management approaches directly useful in fulfilling your annual operating plans obtain top priority. Next, the *Check* step of the cycle determines whether your firm has succeeded in putting in place the capabilities to meet your strategic requirements.

(C) CHECK—REVIEW RESULTS AND FEED FORWARD

The timing of strategic change drives capability development and checking. Your strategy dictates what your organization's high leverage capabilities are, and therefore drives checking of such elements as:

- Operational effectiveness of key business and support processes
- Capacity, compatibility and capability of suppliers to fit into your firm's strategy
- Resources, capabilities and capacities of key computer systems, offices and facilities
- Workforce readiness—size, skill levels and capabilities
- Managerial and workforce morale—rates of employee volunteerism, participation, cooperation, unwanted turnover, lost-time accidents and absenteeism
- Types and effectiveness of education and training
- Financial resources

Checking highlights strengths, performance gaps and improvement potential. When your checking identifies accomplishments and strengths, you can celebrate team and individual achievements and recognize the people who set good examples for others to follow. You can expand on the successes by sharing lessons learned throughout the organization in the next stage of this cycle. Honest reviews of capabilities are critical for high performance. Sustained excellence is not an accident; it takes a system. To excel, your organization needs the management and process capability to produce excellent results—so checking capabilities must be a regular part of your firm's management system to have consistent performance.

In capability checking, you and your firm's leaders also study and explain examples of excellence as references or benchmarks for strategically important capabilities. Benchmarks compare your firm's capabilities with competitors' or with examples of excellence; you want to find out where you stand. Benchmark comparisons can open minds to new ideas and approaches, just as open windows can let in fresh air.

Occasionally, benchmarks achieve mind-opening results through their "shock value." For example, the CFO of Yankee Bank that created its golden cycle had found out that peer banks in other parts of the country were already doing twice the volume of business per lender than his bank's lenders; he used this information to set aim-high targets and to shock his people into taking a new look at sales productivity. From checking capabilities and the results of upgrading them, the capability-development cycle now comes to the final Act or Improve stage, which uses lessons learned from studying the results of deploying approaches to improve your whole business.

(A) ACT—BUILD IMPROVEMENTS ON LESSONS LEARNED

The Improve step of the capability-development cycle improves the *process* of getting better by expanding on what has worked for you and replacing what failed. Sharing lessons learned in this cycle is key to getting them to pay off across the whole organization. After decades of comfortable living with older methods, each victory needs to be studied for all it is worth in order to use its lessons to retrain your whole enterprise. Sharing each discovery throughout the firm maximizes the payoff from your investments in learning and improvement.

To share knowledge, your firm must encourage people to interact and spread information. Some larger firms, like Baldrige winners Armstrong Building Products and Solectron, set up international councils of subject-matter experts by function or process; members meet in person two to four times per year to share lessons learned of interest or potential use to other parts of the company. Between council meetings, members stay in contact electronically, making expertise in any site immediately available to all other sites. Some firms give these internal experts travel budgets to get help from others or to give it; this internal-consulting approach reduces the need to transfer and relocate a company's experts.

Organizationwide databases of best practices are another rapidly growing way to share improvement lessons across your organization. For years, leading firms have used common databases to share lessons learned by process-improvement teams. Moreover, recently developed intranet capabilities allow firms to make best practices available online. Most firms that embark on this type of sharing begin with sharing information on customers. What they really seek, however, is to leverage the company's whole knowledge base by earning returns in four or five places from discoveries made in one place. Any discovery made in one location can earn a payoff in every location that uses it.

Finally, some firms like Solectron train and involve top executives in periodic assessments of each unit's management system. Their assessment process requires a team of executives to visit each site and evaluate its strengths and areas for improvement. At Solectron, and other firms, the visiting assessment team also recommends actions to upgrade capabilities. When visiting executives share their direct experience of what is working elsewhere in the organization, they kindle the enthusiasm of those who must change to improve. They also have the opportunity to learn from the unit they are assessing and can bring new ideas, contacts and methods back to their own parts of the organization.

The preceding cycles have started your firm on the path to learning and increased competence in crafting winning competitive strategy, organizational commitment, and ongoing development of capabilities to execute that strategy. What is left? Change creates risk as it tries to fulfill promise. The last element in a complete high performance management system organizes data and analysis to manage the ongoing balance of risk and return that inevitably accompanies high performance.

Chapter 8 relates the growing use of factual information in planning, deciding and controlling to lower business risk and to increase financial return in high performance organizations. That infamous philosopher Murphy said that anything that can go wrong, will go wrong, usually at the worst possible time and place; variation in a wrong direction from what you expected is risk. Chapter 8 shows how measurements and data provide feedback on variations to confirm what is working and to signal what is not working in time to do something to avoid unpleasant consequences. The cycle of risk-return is a departure from judging organizational performance based on how the CEO feels today. Leading firms are creating a more factual understanding of business results and using it to manage risk and return.

CHAPTER 8

Risk-Return Cycle

Risk recedes as knowledge grows, and as knowledge grows,
so does the firm's capacity to move forward.

—Gary Hamel and C. K. Prahalad, *Competing for the Future*

Daring to innovate brings with it the possibility of failure. Organizations often manage their risks by sticking to what they know best. They automatically have the information they need to evaluate their risks. However, innovation beyond what the organization already knows takes knowledge beyond what is familiar and convenient, which is harder to obtain. When information is hard to obtain, the overwhelming temptation is to develop plans for which there is information, and either shy away from areas with less information, or replace missing facts with opinions or guesses. This subjects the organization to the greatest risk of all, the risk of lost opportunities to invent, to innovate and ultimately to survive.

The purpose of the risk-return cycle is to enable your business to play to win by taking greater risks, especially the right risks. Lack of sound analysis and information causes many organizations to play conservatively—so as not to lose. The challenge that the risk-return cycle addresses is to integrate forecasts, data and analysis systematically into planning and management approaches to maximize financial returns for taking risk. Risk is not bad, per se; it comes with your firm's need to earn financial return. "Nothing ventured, nothing gained," as the old saying goes. Since high performance produces a higher return, your high performance business must be commensurately better at taking risks than the average. Surprisingly, the vast majority of management *opinions* about business performance are found to be untrue when tested against hard data. This disturbing fact arises from the nature of unplanned learning in a business. An entrepreneur who starts a successful business often has a fundamentally deeper understanding of the business than a manager who later takes over a running business to manage it. The successful entrepreneur has hit on a combination of factors that collectively make the business successful; these factors are collectively sufficient for business success. However, the manager, who has not had to experiment to find out which combinations of factors drive success, learns from failures and upsets. Knowing everything about what can go wrong is different from knowing what drives business success, as the following example helps to clarify.

Suppose you run a bakery, baking bread by the thousands of loaves per day. Naturally you would not take a bite out of each finished loaf to see how it tastes; instead you control oven temperatures, baking times, measurements of input ingredients and follow a recipe. You rely on a process to turn out good bread instead of the 100 percent inspection, taste test approach. Now suppose that an upset occurs in your process and salt, called for in the recipe, is omitted. Soon customers complain that the bread does not taste right. As manager, you investigate and find that, sure enough, salt was left out. Corrective action is called for and taken, and you have learned a lesson; salt is important. At a later time when thinking about improvements in the process, you hit on an idea; salt is important because customers complain when it is omitted, so why not triple the amount of salt in the recipe? Why not indeed, salt is necessary for good tasting bread, but not sufficient for better taste. Tripling the salt makes no sense to us because we understand the baking process. However, most real business processes are harder to understand.

Much managerial understanding of what is important in managing a business or its processes arises from such unplanned experiments—most of the lessons learned are about necessary conditions—factors that, like the salt, ruin the result when omitted. But, necessary factors do not guarantee good results when present. Planned trials, pilot tests, and experiments are essential to learning what factors drive good performance. Also, studying the competition is another source of understanding what works. As you execute your plans and strategies, competitors adjust, causing predictions and forecasts to change dynamically. All of these factors make it important for you to understand cause and effect in dynamic competitive environments.

Business success is based on discovering both what factors are necessary and what combination of those factors is sufficient to generate excellent results. Basing decisions and plans on up-to-date, valid information and reliable analyses is the antidote to risk. Just as knowing that saltier bread will not sell well, understanding the underlying causes of success makes actions based on that understanding less risky. Better understanding improves the success rate on innovation at the cost of learning from careful plans that fail. Leadership, planning and capability cycles deploy freedom and capacity for action throughout your work force. They mass-produce potential opportunities, some of them for new revenue, and some of them for reduced cost. However, not all of these opportunities offer risk-free rewards. They are all experiments with differing degrees of potential for return and risk of loss.

Empowering and motivating your work force need not necessarily increase your firm's total risk; expanding employee use of data, analysis and information to understand potential outcomes can and must offset the increased risks. The risk-return cycle creates a companywide system that provides information and analysis to manage your organization's plans, decisions, and actions by facts. Where the organization identifies a success factor at risk, the cycle seeks information that can put your evaluation of risk and return on a factual or analytical basis.

Figure 8.1 shows how a PDCA continuous improvement cycle deploys data and analysis to support effective risk-taking and financial reward seeking. The cycle's Plan (approach) step identifies the issues or factors that drive your firm's risk of loss, error and defect. These issues usually come to the risk-return cycle from the other cycles. Examples of risk drivers include plans for change,

Figure 8.1
The Risk-Return Cycle

P APPROACH
- Identify issues driving risks in strategic planning
- Align measures with what is important and deploy measures to all units
- Forecast ranges of outcomes
- Set standards, limits, and countermeasures on risks of failure
    - Customer-level risks
    - Process/product-level risks
    - Individual risks
    - Financial risks

A IMPROVE
- Take corrective action where indicated
- Identify and replace invalid planning or business assumptions
- Improve data/analysis
- Improve forecasting approaches to flag risks
- Assess prevention and avoidance measures
- Learn from outside benchmarks

DEPLOYMENT D
- Gather data
- Monitor risks
- Communicate standards
- Analyze data to find leading indicators of risk (loss)
- Use countermeasures to anticipate, avoid, prevent risks (losses)

C RESULTS
- Compare operating results against standards
- Compare progress against plans to find shortfalls
- Compare actual results against forecasts and study significant variances
- Compare results against outside benchmarks and peers

PLAN   DO

ACT   CHECK

significant variations in capability, upset stakeholders, roadblocks to company strategy, or violations of important organizational or individual values (such as public responsibility and citizenship or ethical behavior.) Risk-return also considers allowable limits on risk and defines the information and analyses needed to monitor plans and risks.

Next, the Do (deployment) step gathers and analyzes data pertaining to the risk-producing issues so that people in your organization can make informed decisions as needed. This step of the process includes information systems, communications technology, software and training in analytical tools useful for prediction, forecasting, analysis and process control.

The Check (result) step of the risk-return cycle compares your firm's actual outcomes and returns against predictions and forecasts. These comparisons may simply show that your original forecasts were off, in which case you need a better method of forecasting. Since actual results vary favorably or unfavorably, systematic analysis of variations is part of this step. By building an understanding of which factors cause results to vary, you improve the accuracy of forecasts and therefore the success rate of your plans. Once you understand what factors drive performance variation, you are in a position to manage those factors to skew variation toward the good direction and away from the bad.

Lessons learned about causes of deviations between actual and planned results lead into the Act stage of the risk-return cycle. This stage of the cycle uses constructive criticism of decision making and planning to highlight opportunities to improve information needs and use. By investigating significant deviations your people can revise incorrect assumptions and theories. During the Check stage they asked, "Why did things not work out as expected?" In this stage, what they learned drives improvement in information use, risk taking and factual decision making.

There is tremendous room for improvement in using information to boost return in the face of risk in modern organizations. Firms that deploy balanced scorecard measurement systems (a good start on building a risk-return cycle) often find that their information systems omit data on over half the factors that can potentially cause their strategy to fail. Involving those closest to the issues in finding existing data is an efficient way to close gaps in your information and to encourage use of data in reviews and decisions.

Now that you have an overview of the four stages of the risk-return cycle, the following describes what high performing companies do in each stage of the cycle.

(P) PLAN—RELATE INFORMATION TO RISK AND FINANCIAL RETURN

Leadership, planning and capability development all raise risk issues that can threaten the success of your strategies and action plans. These issues become input to the risk-return cycle, which translates them into measures, expectations and reviews to detect and manage risk. Usually, people in organizations want to stay out of trouble. So their involvement in defining risk-driving issues and in deciding how to measure risk factors and results addresses their concerns and also helps them accept measures that help keep them out of trouble.

As your firm plans how to manage its risks of poor performance, you are seeking hard facts: How can you measure performance? What issues drive your firm's strategic risks? What data do you need to get a handle on the key issues? Aligning all decision, plans and units with overall mission, strategy and high performance values is the top consideration. Lack of alignment risks loss of organizationwide effectiveness as units optimize tactical or local performance. Solectron shows one approach to reducing the risk of poor performance.

Align Measures to Whatever Is Important

Solectron Corp. aligns its performance measures directly with its mission and vision, but it also quantifies performance against its list of corporate beliefs (Quest for Excellence 1998). For each belief, such as "customer first," Solectron identifies business drivers. In the case of Solectron's customer first belief, they identify a single business driver, customer satisfaction. (They use the term "business driver" instead of the word, "issue," to describe a factor that causes good or bad performance.) Next they link this driver with key processes and process-level performance measurements. For example, their key processes for sustaining customer satisfaction are their processes for

- Market and customer requirements determination
- Annual customer survey
- Customer satisfaction assurance process

Finally, by deriving performance measures directly from the operation of the relevant processes, Solectron can monitor and control operating process performance using their measures. For the customer satisfaction driver they list four performance measures:

- Overall evaluation of Solectron
- Customer satisfaction index (a weekly numeric score based on customer grading of Solectron performance)
- Customer return rate
- Market share

Solectron communicates and reviews these measures frequently at the local level and rolls them up into a quarterly scorecard by site.

Organizations measure whatever they consider really important, which is a key to deciding on where information will help your firm understand risk. Profitability is really important, if not to managers then to shareholders and tax collectors, so all businesses measure their revenues and expenses that make up profitability. Because employee satisfaction was and is really important at Federal Express in order to maintain a nonunion workforce, it chose employee survey methods to gather and analyze data needed to reduce the risk of employee dissatisfaction. A business that really makes all eleven high performance values of the Baldrige business model important would probably have a set of measures similar to those listed in Table 8.1. Because information gathering begins with what is really important, your organization's values, vision and mission are the starting point for information gathering, measurement and analysis.

Thomas Mackin, Training Director of Merrill Lynch Credit Corp., explains that his firm manages information and sets priorities "in

Table 8.1

Relationship of Values to Performance Measures

Values	Issue Generating Risk	Performance Measures
Visionary Leadership	• Organizational effectiveness	• Employee opinion survey results • Employee turnover and quality of new hires • Employee performance results • Independent assessment results
Customer-Driven Excellence	• Customer loyalty and referral	• Customer satisfaction by segment • Customer retention and loyalty • Rate of customer referral • Market share
Organizational and Personal Learning	• Competitiveness	• Trends and levels of improvement in planned measures • Performance relative to benchmarks • Rate of successful new product introductions
Valuing Employees and Partners	• Employee satisfaction, morale, and motivation • Supply-chain quality	• Education and training level of workforce • Trends and levels of employee/partner satisfaction • Trends, levels of employee involvement • Number of supplier-partners • Incoming quality levels • Supplier-generated cost savings • Fraction of buying from partners
Agility	• Customer satisfaction • Flexibility	• Cycle times on all key processes • Time to market • Time to break-even • Time to profit
Focus on The Future	• Economic opportunity • Economic value added • Research investment • Proprietary Technology	• Economic value added (profit minus cost of invested capital) • Corporate growth rate • Patents and patentable trade secrets • Rate of innovation
Managing for Innovation	• Product/Service competitiveness • Process/Technology development	• Percentage of sales from new products, market segments, and technologies • Pace of adopting relevant new technology • Rate of product obsolescence
Management by Fact	• Reliability, validity, and availability of information and analyses	• Information system user satisfaction • Forecasting error rates
Public Responsibility and Citizenship	• Corporate reputation • Customer trust • Community confidence	• Image survey results • Customer likelihood of referring others to firm • Time spent in community/professional service efforts • Recognition and favorable press mentions
Focus on Results and Creating Value	• Stockholder satisfaction • Investor satisfaction	• Performance of stock • Earnings performance • Return on investment
Systems Perspective	• Overall organizational effectiveness	• Economic Value Added, ROI • Stakeholder satisfaction

accordance with what information supports its vision—finding out what the right things are first" (Quest for Excellence 1998). As Table 8.2 shows, MLCC's P-Q-M sequence of measures forms an interlocking chain of measures. Its P-metrics in the work processes (where workers can influence them) link to Q-metrics at the end of each process; several Q-metrics for each process may predict a strategic M-level metric (M for Mission). Furthermore, several processes may simultaneously influence a single M-level metric.

Table 8.2
Merrill Lynch Credit Corp.'s P-Q-M Metrics

Type of Metric	Measurement Purpose	Example Measure
P	Early-warning indicators, based on data gathered from within each process, that predict how well Q metrics will turn out	• Cycle time for each processing step (How long does each take? Is there "dead" time?) • Capacity of each processing step. • Backlogs of work waiting at each processing step. • Opportunities for error in each step • Error rate of each processing step
Q	End-of-process measures defined so that they "roll up" to the M metrics	• Total transaction-cycle time (Customers want orders processed quickly.) • Quality levels, error or defect rates (Customers want accurate service.)
M	14 key measures of firm's health—such as client and employee satisfaction, financial measures—with targets set in business planning process	• Customer satisfaction (Customers want fast accurate service.)

MLCC reported at the Quest for Excellence conference that about 80 percent of its measurements were P-metrics, which people use to manage end-of-process results measured by Q-metrics. The 20 percent balance goes into measuring results. This ratio of four process measures (leading indicators) to each result measure (lagging indicator) directs attention to what you must do to achieve the result; in-process leading indicators ensure that prevention activities happen well before results deteriorate. The key to effective risk control is ensuring that the P-metrics or leading indicators are very timely and directly lead to preventive measures. Prevention is the surest way to avoid risk of bad results. The "P" for process metrics could just as well be "P" for *prevention* metrics. During the plan stage of the risk-return cycle, the emphasis is on developing timely leading indicators that people in the organization can use to maximize reward and avoid or prevent loss and risk.

Within your business, each process interacts with others in a chain of internal customer/supplier relationships. Because processes link within the system, losses in any process can ripple throughout your whole system, growing as they touch other processes. Big things like competitive strategies and market share depend on small things such as diligence, consistency and honesty in executing each process detail. Both strategy and execution play their parts in your firm's overall success—neither alone is sufficient.

Once your firm establishes M-level measurements that relate to strategic advantage, you need to identify and control the risk that these measures might move in the wrong direction. You cannot afford to wait until you are in strategic trouble to take action, so you must cascade the strategic measures down to end-of-process result measures (Q-metrics, in Merrill Lynch's terms), and then back up from the end-of-process measures to identify high-leverage in-process measures that serve as leading indicators.

Balanced measurement systems or scorecards are but one version of a set of metrics that relate strategic financial and marketplace results with internal processes and their performance. The real issue is to find and use measures that really link operational causes to strategic effects.

Unfortunately, balanced scorecards one sees in practice too often create as much risk as they prevent because they contain untested managerial hypotheses and opinions about factors that drive strategic results. (Remember, most managerial opinion about what it takes to be successful is incomplete because it mistakes necessary factors for sufficient success drivers.) The first few years of using a balanced scorecard type of system involves replacing managerial opinions with empirically proven factors that drive success. This means that standards for selecting scorecard measures need to include validating cause-and-effect relationships before relying on these measures for planning and forecasting.

During the planning stage of this cycle, strategic measures, end-of-process measures and in-process measures all need to be aligned. In Merrill Lynch terms, P-Q-M metrics all need to be linked, and targets and ranges of variation established. Once your management information passes the following acid test it is relatively complete. Can the metrics you use to run the business all look good, and still produce bad results for some stakeholders? If the answer is yes, you have at least one gap in your measurements. If you answer no, you have a reasonable set of information for managing risk and return with respect to business results. Organizations often measure performance and quality to show how they are doing, but still have unhappy customers. If your performance and quality numbers are good, but some customers are unhappy, what is wrong with your measurement system?

The implication for your organization is that it needs to learn to analyze data, turn it into information on what is happening and why. Risks and benefits in many situations, such as investments in new technology, or decisions to outsource critical service functions, go far beyond what you can obtain quantitative data on. When intangible factors drive future benefits or financial risk for an investment, instead of trying to measure inherently fuzzy benefits, using indices or ratings lets you model the importance and relative impact of qualitative factors in making fact-based decisions.

Another lesson from high performance firms, which the risk-return cycle must build on, is that simply deploying measurements of important variables without teaching managers how to interpret data is dangerous. The next aspect of planning for risk-return is to set the range of variation allowed for each measure based on an understanding of statistical variation.

Set Limits on Variations to Identify Risks

In the planning stage, managers need to understand how to set limits that signal when to intervene in some business process. It is equally important to know when not to intervene because some variability in measurements is to be expected. Actions taken in response to random fluctuations waste effort and increase risk. Planning activities in the risk-return cycle set standards or limits on expected and allowable variation of important measures from target or forecast. The targets are set to win the competitive race for market dollars. So, if customers prefer cars with fewer defects, the auto firm that sets targets for defect rates that yield cars with the fewest defects for the cost wins the race for customer dollars. An auto company that turns out a mix of high-quality cars and lemons will lose market share to one that turns out more quality vehicles and no lemons.

Setting limits on how far any measurement should be allowed to vary from forecast or target depends on the size of loss in relation to variation. For example, if a Firestone Wilderness AT tire on a Ford Explorer is designed for a target inflation pressure of 28 pounds per square inch of pressure (PSI), will underinflating the tire by two pounds to 26 PSI cause a loss? If the tire runs one-tenth of a pound under target pressure, losses will probably be small; however, they grow rapidly as deviation from the target widens. Unfortunately it turned out that running a heavily-loaded Ford Explorer on four such tires with a 26 PSI inflation pressure overburdened at least some of them, producing life-threatening consequences. So far, Ford has publicly stated its losses at over $1 billion due to deviations from tire inflation limits, and ended a 100-year-old customer-supplier partnership that Henry Ford and Harvey Firestone began personally.

Setting limits on measures for controlling risk and return takes an understanding of variation and loss, usually referred to under a label such as statistical process control. The basic idea is very simple. When you take measurements from any repetitive process, the data tend to cluster around a typical value—the average, for example. Not every repetition of the process produces exactly the same result, however. There is variation around the average. Variations further away from the average are much less likely than small variations close to the average, so any process defines a pattern of likely (near the average) and unlikely (large departures from the average) outcomes. This range of likely and unlikely process results lets organizations create measurement-based control tools to put workers in charge of processes. As long as the process measurements fall in the likely region, the variation is usual for the process. However, when measurements turn up in the unlikely region, this signals that something has changed. Measurement variation has exceeded the usual variation by drifting unusually far from the average. Such an unlikely result from the process means that it is time to see what is going on.

Variations in process outcomes are inevitable. However, not all variations in results impose the same loss. For example driving an

SUV on a Firestone Wilderness AT tire, at a tire pressure one-half pound below design target might increase tire wear slightly. But the deviation from typical tire performance would impose no life-threatening consequences. However, as deviation from the design target pressure of 28 PSI grows, the potential economic loss grows. So running the tire at 26 PSI, two pounds below target pressure, can incur losses that are a lot worse than tire wear—the tire can fail and the vehicle roll over. Without knowing the range of inevitable random variation, and how loss varies by size of deviation, managers usually react to what are actually meaningless random fluctuations, changing processes even when no change is needed. This is called tampering and causes tremendous waste and loss as the following example shows.

Unnecessary interference in processes has devastating impact when processes interconnect as they do in most businesses. A group of American steel company managers visited Japanese steel mills back in the 1980s when Japanese steel makers were beating their American competition in U.S. markets. The visiting American steel makers wanted to discover why their Japanese competitors had such high quality and low cost.

As the story goes, the visiting American steel executives were standing in the Japanese mill's control room just as one shift was quitting for the day and the new shift was arriving. The managers watched as each outgoing employee walked around the control room with his or her replacement. They discussed each control and went over operating logs of how the process had been running during the shift that was ending. No one touched any of the controls; the change of shift process consisted of the outgoing shift presenting a careful review of how the process was running for the incoming shift, and nothing more.

Later as the Americans informally discussed what they had seen, one remarked how different the Japanese shift change procedure was from the way shifts changed at his plant back in the United States. When shifts change at his mill in the United States, the outgoing operators would exchange places with the new crew, and as soon as the outgoing shift left the control room, the incoming technicians would begin resetting their controls to targets they felt more comfortable with. Could it be, asked the visiting American, that allowing plant operators to reset process controls at will injected extra random variation into the steel-making process?

When the American steel executive returned to his plant, he pilot tested a shift change procedure similar to what he saw in Japan. No operator changed any control unless the measurement related to that control had become unpredictable and drifted beyond desired settings by an amount known as a control limit. In other words, the operators were taught how to determine when a control needed action to return it to predictable performance. Otherwise they were taught to leave the process alone and monitor the measurements further. This simple change immediately reduced scrap 40 percent and raised quality significantly. It turned out that all of the efforts of the operators to smooth out the operation of their process were unnecessary responses to random fluctuations of the steel-making process. They were working hard to make good steel, but their tampering destroyed the predictability of the process, making it even harder to control.

The point of the Japanese steel mill story is that variation at the end of a critical process can add up to strategically significant consequences at the mission level. The variation in end-of-process quality came about because managers allowed operators to change process-level controls (P-metrics) in response to random fluctuations in the process. These fluctuations were within the likely range of variation for the process, so they signified nothing. The process controllers' unnecessary adjustments reverberated through the steps of the process causing still more variation and reaction at other stages. As a result, the self-inflicted variations (process tampering) made the U.S. mills uncompetitive, even though they used the same production technology as their Japanese competition. The solution, of course, is to train the operators to think about their measurements and controls from a simple, but valid statistical point of view.

The key to setting measurement limits to ensure that you detect upsets in a process and not just random variation is as simple as charting process measurements. First you must get everyone to stop tampering with the process. But once the process stabilizes the fluctuations on your graph will show what pattern of result variation is natural for the process—often called the process's capability.

When actual results vary randomly within that pattern (and no nonrandom patterns or trends appear), leave the process alone.

When a process performance is inadequate to your needs, however, it must be improved. First you select the improved target level for business reasons. Then it is necessary to change the process, not to control its output to the new level, but to actually change the process's inherent performance to a new level where it can achieve the improvement target naturally.

Now that you have planned measures to align performance in all units, and provided limits or standards that let them separate random noise from meaningful variation, the next step is to actually gather data on the measures and use them to maintain and improve performance.

(D) DO—GATHER AND ANALYZE INFORMATION

One of your main leadership challenges is to spread the use of factual data and analysis throughout the whole organization to every point of risk. The Do (deployment) step of the risk-return cycle links data, analysis and better-informed decisions to yield more return for a given level of risk. The reward maximization and risk prevention approach is simple. Your daily operations generate data on the process level (P-level) leading indicators. Based on control limits, standards and targets, those who work in the processes act when their process measures signal a need for action. Timely action ensures desirable end-of-process results (Q-metrics). As mentioned above, all unwanted variation in results (Q-metrics), however small, imposes a loss, which grows rapidly as size of variation increases.

Managing risk and return at the operational level involves looking at data in the process that is relevant to its future results. Analysis of data is the most efficient way to discover causes of both good and poor performance within your organization. Spears and Bowen say that the mystery behind the success of the Toyota organization is its total, unconscious reliance on the scientific method for seeking improvement (Spears and Bowen 1999). At Toyota, pervasive use of the scientific method emerges from four simple questions that Toyota asks about all it does. These are: (1) How do people learn their work process? (2) How do they know they are following the process correctly? (3) How do they know if the product their process produces is defect free? and (4) What must they do when they run into a problem? As people dig more deeply into the facts of their work processes to answer these four probes, they encounter problems and eventually make discoveries. What emerges is an organizationwide practice of answering questions and solving problems that make the workplace more manageable and productive. Toyota shows how powerful consequences emerge from applying simple rules throughout an organization.

The bulk of the information you need to manage risk and return comes from operational systems, either directly or as byproducts of other work. Systems for order processing, customer servicing, billing and the like all can provide data that has great power in detecting and avoiding costly process upsets and competitive moves. For example Toyota gives each worker an indication of the time available to do each step of a job, even though the time may only be seconds. Their simple method is to paint time marks on the floor next to the assembly line. As the work moves along, the marks indicate when each step of the work task at that workstation should be complete. By looking at the marks, each worker knows within a second or two if he or she is getting into trouble on his or her task. That worker stops the line and seeks help before inserting a defect into the car they are working on. It sounds backward, to stop the line if someone gets into trouble. However, it is a powerful method for controlling risk, because this rule forces managers and supervisors to take responsibility for keeping all work and workers out of trouble. This, of course, is an extremely valuable use of expensive management time, and pays off in world-class high quality at world-class low cost.

AT&T Universal Card Services has its customer service people enter comments by customers into a customer listening data base. Once a week a customer listening team classifies the comments and generates a graph showing the volume of each type of comments by week. This graph, called a "hot topic" report, alerts the company to competitive moves and offers, as well as to upsets in its marketing and service delivery processes. Other firms that have benchmarked this practice of AT&T report having been able to reduce market research expenses by having customer service personnel listen to customers and record customer comments. Data on competitors is often difficult to obtain and obtaining it from customers often gives you the first indication that a competitor has figured out some way to counter your market strategy.

The point of gathering and analyzing information is not to produce data and charts for their own sake, but to answer the four basic questions that Toyota asks of its work. As leaders continue asking these questions, they induce the use of better methods and tools for making sense out of facts. This drives a need for education and training in the workplace.

Analyzing Information

Strategic changes are like companywide experiments; managing risk and return at the strategic level takes two types of analysis. The first is a prediction of trends in important factors such as market growth, customer requirements, customer choice behavior, changes in technology, supplier capability, your competitors' capabilities and the like. These predictions help you to develop strategy; each prediction should be accompanied by some estimate of the margin of error so the strategy can be robust—not sensitive to prediction error. The word prediction means that you pre (before) dict (say) what will happen based on understanding cause and effect in your measurements. Prediction differs from a forecast, which mechanically "casts" past trends ("fore" ward) into the future. A forecast need not involve understanding cause and effect. Forecasting is what led to the 2000-2001 Internet bubble. Prediction is what led to IBM's comparative success in expanding its e-business and services initiatives during the same period.

The second type of analysis considers robustness and stability if the environment changes. Firms like OMI systematically seek out the issues driving overall risk and subject their plans to a careful "what-if" analysis of likely outcomes under a range of scenarios. This type of scenario analysis backs up planning and alerts you to decisions, or combinations of factors that can upset your business or results. The mere fact that analysis can reveal potential upsets provides a basis for anticipating, avoiding or hedging such "bet the company" types of strategic risk.

At the operational level, measurements tell nothing by themselves; however, grouping and analyzing data tells you a story or reveals patterns. Graphing measurements from a process can reveal how your process is running. Teaching your workforce the statistical insights they need to understand and evaluate measurement variations lets them manage the risk of defects, delays, errors and other factors that harm performance. The following examples show how two leading firms gave their workforces the authority to act on measurement information.

Empowerment and Risk Taking

In 1990, Globe Metallurgical used a what-if analysis of problems to bridge the trust gap between supervisors and lower-level employees (Stankard 1990). Globe wanted to give control of complex workflows to self-managing work teams. At first, supervisors did not trust worker teams acting on their own to fix occasional serious problems. To overcome these fears and build trust, Globe leadership had supervisor and worker teams use Failure Mode Effect Analysis (FMEA) to work out what-if scenarios for each possible problem.

Teams of workers and supervisors flowcharted their work processes, identified things that could go wrong, assessed the risk of each and figured out the best way to prevent or handle each type of failure. As management and the workforce agreed on what-if actions the supervisors trained the work team in carrying out their contingency plans. As each work team showed it was qualified, that team took over process management responsibility from the supervisor. Although this approach took a lot of work to empower the work teams, after they were trained things ran smoothly without supervisory intervention.

Once employees master the skills of informed risk taking, they do not perceive their actions as particularly risky—an attitude that reduces the fear factor. The following story shows how one financial services firm let its employees control the risk of processing error and upset.

Pioneering Services Corporation, a winner of the Massachusetts Quality Award, once relied on 100 percent checking of all financial transactions to minimize the risk of error and to ensure accuracy (Stankard 1994d). Inspections added about 30 percent to operating cost, slowed processing and became a crutch. People knew that if they made mistakes, someone else would probably catch the error.

Pioneering's quality staff got line operations (accounting and clerical units) to change to statistical sampling, dropped 100 percent inspection and improved error rates, timeliness and morale. Per-employee productivity went from 2,600 to 3,400 accounts per full-time equivalent employee. Pioneering let its people control the pace of change when they

1. eliminated the "quality" (checking) unit inspecting all work by reorganizing all checking staff into production positions. Pioneering kept 100 percent checking temporarily while quality management started statistical sampling of clerical work on top of 100 percent inspection;

2. announced that management wanted to eliminate 100 percent checking and make each person responsible for doing his or her own work right;

3. set up a test in a department doing the most demanding work—the legal processing unit—with quality management and departmental staff planning the change. One of four legal processing teams served as a test unit; each member put his or her completed work in one of two "out" baskets—100 percent inspection (as before) or statistical sampling to estimate departmental, but not individual, quality;

4. reported sampling results daily to the department, and calculated the statistical accuracy rate for the test unit, plotting its accuracy rate from sampling versus the 100 percent inspection results for the rest;

5. gained confidence in sampling and put less work into the 100 percent inspection basket. Test-group accuracy rose over the rest. Also, as the amount of work put into the inspection basket declined, productivity rose. Eventually, Pioneering improved productivity more than 30 percent;

6. held open, weekly quality meetings to review each unit's sample results. Attendees spend up to 40 minutes assessing

root causes of problems, which volunteers then tackle between
meetings.

The switch to sampling focused weekly quality meetings on facts
and let staffers feel in control and in the know about what was going on. The meetings and discussions of problems revealed by
statistical sampling provided teaching opportunities and helped
Pioneering quality management people spread the lessons
learned.To be worth gathering, data must be widely deployed and
accessible to users who know what to do with them. Few developments have more potential than communication technology to
expand your firm's wealth-generating capability. Enterprisewide
software systems such as Lotus Notes, SAP, Baan, Oracle and
Peoplesoft® free firms like yours from rigid patterns of information
collection and usage.

Enterprisewide information and analysis tools make data available wherever they are needed as the following example of a worldwide high-tech firm shows. One of the firm's financial analysts had
tried unsuccessfully for years to obtain an accurate picture of car
rental charges from thousands of sales and technical people traveling on business. Soon after deploying enterprisewide accounting
and administrative software, the analyst used the new information
system to analyze rental car expenses from all over the company.
His findings led to new agreements with car rental suppliers that
provided better service to staff while saving several million dollars
per year. The firm's traveling employees got much better terms and
car availability, and the firm got huge cost savings—win-win. This
is but one big example of how an empowered employee with good
information can boost returns. There are as many more similar potential success stories in your organization as there are employees.

Communications technology: e-mail, 800 numbers, Internet,
intranets and even video conferencing make it possible to link all
parts of your enterprise (as well as customers, suppliers and even
competitors) so you can obtain new information and share what's
known. The development of desktop computers with profoundly
capable analysis tools such as SPSS, Lotus 1-2-3 and Excel let trained
workers turn raw facts into charts, graphs, spreadsheets and other
analyses that reduce risks.

Information and communication technologies pay off when they increase internal cooperation to reduce risk and raise return. The high-tech financial analyst that negotiated better worldwide corporate rates from car rental suppliers translated the savings into nearly pure profit. The computer already had the travel cost data in its files and the software was able to retrieve it and present it in a fashion that let the analyst take action.

Informal communication in person or by phone with friends who see and understand parts of the system that are not visible to you, also gathers data effectively. Reaching out in person to gather information gives you decision information earlier than through regular reporting channels. Being forewarned lets you prepare for events and prevent or avoid undesirable consequences. Learning by walking around needs to be balanced consciously by more formal information gathering and analysis—a straightforward task now because electronic networks connect information systems in your firm's workplace.

Regular communication with others in your organization—in team meetings, review sessions, planning sessions, problem-solving sessions and other forums— gives your people the information they need to take greater risk with safety. Integrating or correlating information from many different sources also is effective in reducing risk. Comparing information from multiple independent sources helps validate it and confirm when something significant has changed. Inconsistencies among several sources of data may flag a risk in the making. After your firm has deployed information and analysis to the point of use, the next task for you and other leaders is to review results so you can manage risk and learn lessons that will help improve your risk taking.

(C) CHECK—REVIEW RESULTS

If you were to sit in on a staff meeting at a high performance organization and observe data being presented and discussed, you would usually spot four leading indicators of performance for every lagging or result indicator discussed. In Merrill Lynch's P-Q-M model, most of the effort would be on looking at P-metrics and the Q- and M-metrics would be checked occasionally to see that plans and processes are working as expected. The discussion would focus on what can be done to improve future outcomes, what can be done to anticipate, avoid or prevent shortfalls in sales, rises in cost or error rates before they have hurt performance. Leading indicators give you the lead time in which to think and act effectively to change outcomes for the better.

If you were a fly on the wall while executives of a poorly performing organization reviewed performance, you would find that most reports cover results that have already happened. When the news is good, fine; everyone is happy. But when things go wrong, discussion turns to damage control and the organization's best firefighters have another opportunity to be heroes. Everyone is so busy that no one has time to work on preventing history from repeating itself before the next staff meeting. Why do organizations that perform poorly restrict their information to results, often just financial results? Are their people blind to data on factors that move the results toward better performance?

To determine firmwide health, you aggregate or roll up your firm's own detailed measures. Mr. Thomas Mackin, Training Manager at Merrill Lynch Credit Corp., explained how his firm uses information to review results (Quest for Excellence 1998). Each workforce group in MLCC uses a monthly management report (MMR) to report progress. A key analytical tool for tracking strategic progress, MMRs are also diagnostic tools that spot gaps between where plans say the company should be and where it really is. In monthly meetings with the CEO, MLCC's leaders review MMRs; they use gap analysis to identify shortfalls and then analyze root causes of shortfalls or rapid advances ahead of targets.

Involving all leaders in monthly reviews of MLCC's performance measures gives each person a comprehensive view of the whole firm's performance. Then, within their own groups, individual leaders decide on actions that fit within the context of the whole organization. After this senior executive review, MLCC "rolls down" reviews through all company areas. Each area then sets priorities for its own actions to get back on plan (or to revise the business plan and its performance targets). Finally, the whole workforce obtains feedback from top management in quarterly meetings, at which leaders review how well MLCC is doing against its plan for all hands.

Every process- or outcome-level measurement that can signal losses needs to be measured, analyzed and controlled by the person most able to act upon unwanted variations. When your firm installs control points that pinpoint potential upsets, your workforce can self-manage processes to stay out of trouble and avoid losses. Most firms do not leave the identification of sources of information up to the workforce; instead, specialists often help define the metrics to use and set criteria for separating problems from random variations that should be ignored.

At any level, your firm's information reviews need to avoid four common traps that waste time and accomplish nothing; when checking results against plans or forecasts your people should avoid:

- *The trap of looking for a cause for every variation.* Treating every measured change as if it had a cause wastes valuable management time. Once a process works, about 95 percent of variations have no cause—they are simply built into the process activities—normal variation. Your firm needs to investigate only *significant* variations—the 5 percent or less that signal a real departure from normal.

- *The trap of citing improvement trends or deteriorations when none exist.* Your managers need training to know the difference. With random variation in any measure, each point must be either above or below the point before; in fact, there is a 50 percent chance that the second of two points improves on the first; a 25 percent chance that three points head in the same direction, and a 13 percent chance that four go the same direction. All of these "trends" are nothing more than runs of luck from random variation in a measure.

- *The trap of setting arbitrary cutoffs for deciding when things have gone wrong.* Most managers use exception reports to focus on items needing attention. Management-by-exception can be effective when managers understand that the variation inherent in a process—not management—determines what is exceptional. Using an arbitrary percentage without studying the normal variation of a process just invites tampering with a process that is just varying normally.

- *The trap of setting arbitrary improvement targets without having an improvement method capable of making the improvement.* This method is backward: Your organization cannot achieve an improvement target when you do not know how to improve performance. The only improvement you can make is the one you possess the know-how to make. Developing improvement know-how—understanding what causes good performance— logically comes before target setting, if your targets are to have any meaning.

You and other leaders throughout the organization may be able to coach an organization into the discipline of gathering and analyzing facts. All it takes is a meeting rule like: "No data, and we postpone the meeting until the presenters gather and analyze facts." Analysis need not be sophisticated; it merely has to turn numbers into a picture or a graph that shows a pattern that answers an important question. One organization formed a team to look at customer installation problems. The team members all agreed that the root cause of the problem was with a supplier that was not doing the job. The team presented this view to its sponsor who insisted on facts. She told the team to take a sample of 40 failed installations, and research each one down to the source data, job tickets, e-mails and any other hard facts that proved beyond doubt why the installation failed. The team did the data gathering and analysis as homework, and a month later reported back with a bar chart showing all the reasons for failure. When the heights of the bars were added up, over 60 percent of the failure causes were in the team's own work processes. Less than a third of the failures were due to the supplier's performance. That sponsor's demand for facts took a team that was sure to fail or even make matters worse, and put it on the road to success and better results. It took an insistence on facts and analyses rather than opinion.

Reality Checking with Outside Information: Benchmarking

Do managers in your firm cling to the idea that if they hit all their targets your firm will stay out of competitive trouble? Simply trying to better your own past performance will not keep you competitive if you have set the wrong targets. You could find out too late that some other firm has outperformed yours. The risk lies in believing and acting as though your firm is ahead when, in fact, it lags behind. If your firm fails to look carefully to see what others are achieving, you may slip behind your competition without realizing your mistake. How do you know whether or not your firm's setting the right targets?

At Merrill Lynch Credit Corp., applications specialists have put a ten-step benchmarking process into a common "toolbox" binder of flow charts and documentation. They ensure that benchmarks are linked to company strategy and process-level metrics and also that internal benchmarks are measured against best-in-class firms. In a quarterly report, MLCC updates senior managers on all benchmarking efforts and recommends additional projects.

All high performance firms benchmark the best in class inside and outside their industries. These firms learn where they stand; they also study benchmarks for insights into best practices they can use to achieve excellent results. Outside information from firms that achieve excellent results can be used to set aim-high goals. The knowledge that the benchmark firm has already achieved that goal removes arbitrariness that can drive people to cheat. Knowing that someone else figured out how to achieve a significant improvement spurs people to try to discover or invent their own approach that will outperform the previous best.

To pay off, benchmarking must be well organized and conducted with respect, gratitude, tact and willingness to share. Much of your work is done at home, studying and measuring your own firm's processes and practices to understand their limitations and problems; then you study the benchmark for insights that lead to performance breakthroughs at home. To be sustainable, benchmarking must be a two-way street: The firm asking questions must be willing to teach the benchmark company something it wants to know if the requesting company wishes the benchmark to share its knowledge; each side wins by exchanging new and useful information that the other lacked, making them both better off.

From planning and disseminating risk information and analysis capability throughout your organization, and reviewing progress to prevent loss and maintain performance, we next move on to improving the results from your corporate risk taking.

(A) ACT—IMPROVE

This step closes the loop on your use of information to maximize returns from the risks your business takes. It is amazing how much information most companies amass. Yet, when you ask managers on what basis they decided to take some action, few ever point to any analysis of data as the source of their action. What this means is that these companies have not closed the loop on the risk-return PDCA cycle. Without closing the loop and comparing data to projections they are missing out on opportunities to learn.

Each significant loss or deviation from plan or projection becomes an opportunity for your organization to learn, if it simply investigates why the deviation occurred. Anything unexpected presents opportunity to gain knowledge. When unexpected results do damage, investigating why lets your firm fashion preventive measures to lower the risk of reoccurrence. When unexpected results are favorable, investigating why can make the favorable result happen more often. One key to improving the use of information to reduce risk lies in asking better designed questions as the following illustrates.

Imagine that your organization has an ideal information system, which looks like a crystal ball. The user informs the crystal ball about what his or her decision or plan is. The information system responds, not with information, but with the most powerful question to ask in the situation. The answer to the most powerful question provides the user with the greatest possible insight into the risks and rewards of the decision or plan. The user then may pose the question to the system, which answers with factual information. With that answer, if the user is still unable to decide on the proper decision, he or she repeats the process until the right action becomes clear.

Does your firm have a crystal ball? The idea of using one illustrates three aspects of managing risk and return by fact: First, you and all your co-workers in the organization need to develop an appetite for data and information—people must be trained and encouraged to ask questions. Most organizations already collect the facts needed to answer their most important questions, but too few people are asking the questions and looking at the facts.

Second, your firm needs a framework that sorts out the most critical questions. In this risk-return cycle, your organizational mission, your purpose and your key organizational values help spotlight issues, assumptions and information relevant to risks. The questions arise from reviewing your firm's assumptions and other elements and asking "why?" The more people thinking systematically about your firm, the greater will be the demand for factual information to answer such questions.

The third aspect of the crystal-ball ideal is the need to set up measurements and capture data at key points, aggregate those data into information, and deliver it to every person in the organization whose decisions have risk or reward consequences. This aspect relies heavily on newer forms of information and communications technology as well as informal communication methods.

The most important questions often revolve around the potential to lose customers or market opportunities to competitors. Focusing on the market damage and customer attrition that could result if the firm does not invest in improvements guides information gathering and thinking. However, high performance firms focus more on opportunities: future revenue or potential business that the firm can realistically achieve. The greatest losses most organizations experience are opportunity losses—the rewards they did not reap because they knew too little, or failed to act.

In a *Harvard Business Review* article, Hammond, Keeney and Raiffa report that people are risk-averse when a risky decision is posed in terms of gains (Hammond et al. 1998). However, these people are risk-takers when the same situation is posed as a choice of avoiding losses. High performing firms focus on opportunity loss, which makes them more willing to bear risk in pursuit of customer satisfaction. Average performers, by looking at investments as ways to gain profits, behave more conservatively. This framing phenomenon seems to explain differing attitudes toward risk and return in many organizational situations. If staying the same threatens to produce major loss, people risk making improvements. However, if staying the same and not improving seems to sacrifice only a small margin of profit, people will avoid the risk and settle for the lower profit as long as there is no clear challenge to their success. This human risk-taking phenomenon is the greatest enemy of expanding excellence in the U.S. economy. Only when a firm risks its future in trying to compete against a high performance peer will it venture to upgrade its management system.

The whole PDCA cycle of risk-return has come full-circle. In the Plan stage, you and other leaders of your organization identified risk drivers and discussed approaches to bring information to where it can raise returns and reduce risk. Then, in the Do stage, you deployed those approaches. During the Check stage, your people measured the risk/reward results looking for places where losses occurred. Finally, your firm (during the Act stage) used the lessons learned to improve risk taking, to drive management by opinion and hunch out of the system and to seek better management of information and analysis in your firm's next planning and capability development cycles.

In chapter 6, 7, and 8, you have considered separately the three supporting cycles—leadership and planning, capability-development, and risk-return. The performance of the whole system of wealth production improves by improving how its parts work together as a whole. Chapter 9 introduces the surprising means for integrating the three supporting cycles into a whole system.

CHAPTER 9

Interacting Cycles Generate High Performance

The more developed individuals, organizations, or societies becomes the less they depend on resources and the more they can do with whatever resources they have.

—Russell L. Ackoff, *The Democratic Corporation*

Thus far you have seen the idealized cycles of a high performance management system as full Plan, Do, Check, Act cycles. However, most of the effort of the four cycles is in coming up with approaches (Plan) and deploying them (Do). Integrating the four cycles is more about coordinating reviews (Check) and rebalancing resources or priorities among them (Act/Improve). An ideal organization would coordinate the four cycles seamlessly so that excellent performance would emerge. However, no annual planning and review approach exists that seamlessly meshes all the moving parts into organizational excellence. The realities are often too messy, or unfolding events leave too little time, making tight synchronization infeasible. High performance is a long-running, occasionally wobbly balancing act, punctuated with occasional brilliant steps forward. The major focus of the four cycles of high performance is on approach and deployment (planning and doing.) This chapter changes the subject to checking and acting (learning and innovating.)

Innovations that win new markets depend on flexibility and agility in the face of shifts in the organization's needs and business environment. A shared vision of future opportunity from the golden cycle holds the parts of your organization together while feedback and learning maintains balance so that overall performance never crashes. Progress results as the organization becomes more effective at learning from and acting on feedback. Leadership helps the integration process by creating a culture that rewards people who learn and improve. As researcher Jim Collins says, the leaders who build organizational greatness do so through a triumph of personal humility and unshakable resolve (Collins 2001). The humility ensures that corrective feedback is received, and the resolve ensures that it is used to transform performance.

When managers jump directly from doing back into planning, they short circuit feedback and learning which suspends organizational learning. Organizations can become so busy planning and doing there is no time left to check, learn, and innovate. They become so busy that they never close the loop. Eventually when performance falls too far, unlucky organizations abandon planning and simply lock into doing, doing, doing until they are sold or they fail. A management system that just cycles between *planning* and *doing* contains too little feedback and learning to sustain performance over time. Building in *checking* and *acting on* lessons learned closes the feedback loop to complete the learning and innovation cycle to raise performance.

Here again, individual and organizational values come into play by reducing the fear factor so you can have an honest dialog. Individual commitments to honesty and integrity, and the organizational value of accepting feedback as a contribution to learning are essential for reviews to surface problems. Receiving and acting on feedback demands unafraid plain talk about what is really going on. It is ironic that when organizational and individual values make honest, constructive conversations possible, bad news drives improvement. Unfortunately many organizations have very little bad news because it triggers blaming, finding fault and threats. When people fear criticism, they suppress bad news, the lack of timely, honest information on upsets and threats hurts performance and prevents the management system from progressing (see Argyris 2000).

The Check and Act steps of each cycle provide feedback to planning in all cycles and integrates all elements into the management system. The four cycles play four different roles in deriving performance from the business. The golden cycle unifies all parts of the organization into a system for finding bigger and better market opportunities. The leadership and planning cycle mobilizes and empowers the organization through a common mission, vision and organizational values; it also develops and acts on strategies that capture the business's best profit opportunities. The capability-development cycle continuously improves the cost-effectiveness of the organization's means to execute business strategy. And finally, the risk-return cycle expands understanding of how things really work (cause and effect) as a basis for maximizing profit while minimizing unpleasant surprises and delays.

The golden cycle parallels life itself: leadership and planning is like thinking, capability-development is like moving and doing and risk-return is like looking and listening; taken together they add up to living and learning. While life is more than thinking, moving, and sensing, life is either impossible or less desirable without each of them. Each cycle interacts with the others to produce complex or even unanticipated behavior. In business as in life, thinking precedes moving and doing, and sensing provides feedback that improves both thinking and doing, all in the interest of a better business or a better life.

Integrating these four cycles into overall organizational performance is a little like the original design of the U.S. federal government—a fragmented system connected by internal checks and balances with occasional outside corrective actions in the form of elections. Integration of your management system's learning and improvement cycles within your organization is not bureaucratic or formal, however. It is just the opposite, as you will see later in this chapter. In place of corrective action by public elections, your organization faces corrective action when customers cast dollar votes for or against your products and services or investors increase or sell off their stakes in your business. Comparing what you do and how well you are doing with outside benchmarks also provides feedback useful for corrective action. But the basic integrating methods stress reviews and improvement actions to create checks and balances within and across the four cycles.

INTEGRATION THROUGH LEADERSHIP

Few organizations achieve sustained high performance with leaders who are not trusted, and members of an organization must really know their leaders to trust them. The leaders who achieve organizational excellence are deeply committed to a general direction; they eagerly translate that commitment into adaptation of many, seemingly small opportunities to move in the right direction. Excellence accumulates learning from small failures and small successes; it cuts the failures short as soon as recognized and expands successes into major victories. Excellence is, in fact, opportunistic within the context of its direction. Trusted leaders have a general, unshakable direction at the heart of their opportunism that deserves and inspires trust and attracts commitments from those they lead.

Leaders throughout the organization ignite constructive change by checking and reviewing activity scattered throughout the organization and synthesizing it into a whole. They have changed their behavior from one of knowing and just giving orders (during planning and doing activity) to emphasize probing, listening, learning, diagnosing, coaching and problem solving. They link those in the organization whose work could complement each other (during checking and act/improving activities). The leaders are the ones who take the high performance values out of hiding, dust them off, and put them into action. They receive new information and send signals by how they actually behave.

Real individual and organizational values strongly influence the pace of your firm's evolution toward excellence. You do not need lip service values, the values that companies print on posters hung around the workplace and then ignore. Real values come from leaders all across the organization that coach, teach, develop and empower people and energize change. They bring integrity and commitment to what is important—the direction of excellence. Such leaders inspire trust, an essential ingredient in asking people to change how they work, behave or think. By guiding people to the right choices, individual and high performance values tell what is important, what to ignore and what to avoid. Because real values rule, processes that shape culture and behavior through the four Ps (pay, promotion, privilege and punishment) are vitally important. Reward, recognition, budgeting, succession planning and other human-resource processes that shaped your organization's culture may now limit or constrain leaders all over your organization from doing what common sense and the needs of your business dictate. Therefore, both your leadership and capability-development cycles have to *Check* frequently to ensure that your business culture—its organizational values and standards of behavior—are consistent with your opportunities and your golden cycle.

Leaders stimulate cooperation that keeps the organization focused on the right direction as environmental upsets and internal imbalances among the cycles disrupt progress. Then leadership within the organization pulls parts of the organization together, stimulates cooperation, corrects imbalances, overcomes upsets and closes the next golden cycle. For example, in its early years, Microsoft was a small software shop with capabilities it needed to sell BASIC and other languages to hobbyists. However, as soon as Bill Gates and company spotted the opportunity to deliver operating systems for the IBM PC, closing this capability gap became the key to a golden opportunity. The acquisition of a piece of software (by purchasing a reverse-engineered version of CP/M—the leading control program for microprocessors) successfully corrected an imbalance between the IBM opportunity and Microsoft's software capability.

Just as scientists arrange meetings for dialog about their latest research and theories, leaders from all levels of an organization need to meet and talk about their progress and challenges. During planning, the balance of messages shifts toward communication from leaders as a group out to the rest of the organization; during deployment, checking and improving, the balance reverses with leaders as a group mainly receiving messages back from the rest of the organization. Leadership has to consciously manage its flow of information in and out from the rest of the organization; otherwise a monotonous monolog replaces two-way dialog and gets ignored. Communication flows within an organization are important to maintaining performance and autonomy as the following story shows.

In the late 1970s when office automation and "the office of the future" was a management fad, one of the largest firms in the Fortune 500 launched a project to convert its executive headquarters into a paperless environment. Early in the project, they retained consultants to measure the flow of communications within headquarters and between headquarters and every point outside headquarters. The measurements astounded the consulting study team; over 95 percent of all headquarters communication (whatever the mode) began and ended within headquarters. Communication between headquarters and the rest of its organizational world was tiny by comparison with the volume of internal dialog. The amazing finding that the top managers of this organization talked mainly among themselves, led the consulting team to observe privately that headquarters (where most of the planning was done) was out of touch with its operating units (where doing occurred). Unfortunately, the client took no interest in this observation; it lay beyond the scope of the consultants' charter. Within ten years of the study, this company, once one of the largest and most respected U.S. industrial corporations, was acquired and dismembered.

You and other leaders for excellence in your organization need to devise and encourage activities that successfully cause interchange of information and understanding among all four cycles. You need to get people who know the facts and trends in your markets and the opportunities they present, face to face with others in the organization who can allocate resources to realize the opportunities. These interactions generate new proposals, hash out conflicting views and lead to better understanding of your opportunities for new products, services, and processes. The emphasis in the dialogue is on asking the right "what if" questions about the realities and future trends in your organizational learning and improvement cycles.

Richard Rainwater, a self-made billionaire with training in both science and business equates business to science because of their common objective: "discovery of the unknown" (Helyar 2001). Rainwater made over a billion dollars from published analyses of population and resource usage trends. He tells the story of his business success in a matter-of-fact manner reminiscent of how a scientist might announce a new discovery. Says Rainwater, when a businessperson's predictions work out as theorized, wealth results; when a scientist's published prediction turns out right, praise results. In Rainwater's case his conversations about investment opportunities involved academic experts who published studies of supply and demand trends, Wall Street analysts, and the best thinkers in the industries he was about to invest in. He gets the big picture right, even though the details may differ in the short run from his long-term predictions. Developing an overall understanding is critical to fit the workings of all cycles together; analyzing fragmented parts must give way to synthesizing those very elements into a whole new pattern.

SYNTHESIZING THE WHOLE FROM PARTS

Opportunities for higher performance arise when leaders from all over the organization ask each other "what if" questions; their answers help to verify the soundness of overall direction and lead to speculation on new possibilities for progress. The organization's overall mission provides an organizing theme just as the desire to advance human knowledge drives scientific conversation. Synthesis looks at and understands an organization and its performance as a whole relative to its mission. It puts simple parts together into a more complex whole that transcends the properties of its original parts the way you can ride a bicycle but none of its parts.

Synthesis leads to high performance in your organization by conscious checking (reviewing) and acting (innovating) within the context of much larger and tangible planning and doing activities that consume most management resources. Synthesis is to the organization what imagination is to innovation and problem solving. There are two basic modes through which synthesis causes the cycles to interact. The first is to detect and correct contradictions and inconsistencies among the cycles; the second is driven more by invention and imagination of what could be.

Continuously reviewing the consistency of opportunities, strategies, capabilities and risk is the first approach to synthesizing better organizational performance. Exploiting imbalances and inconsistencies among the four cycles has a powerful influence on overall performance. Creative rebalancing of strengths and weaknesses by innovative combinations of organizational resources creates new, non–zero sum opportunities during each trip around the golden cycle. Haves meet have-nots, share ideas, opportunities, resources and rewards and invent higher performing plans in a synthesis that seeks ways to make the most glaring weaknesses irrelevant and makes the strengths into your organization's greatest opportunities. The result is sharing and cooperation in which each part of the whole enhances every other part in pursuit of overall purpose. The price of this form of synthesis is internal cooperation among all parties to the synthesis. Increasingly such cooperation must arise around and in spite of formal organizational units because problems seem to accumulate between units that block formal cooperation.

The second way to exploit synthesis is to use what has been learned from reviews within each of the four cycles to synthesize whole new combinations of what is being planned and deployed. The idea is to link the Act or Improve activities across all four cycles into an internal system for generating innovations that empower the business to pursue its mission more effectively. This goes beyond working with what is, to include innovation on what is not, but should be. Such a synthesis involves much more than just a research and development capability, it draws on the innovativeness of all members of the organization. Lessons learned supply a springboard to fresh ideas and innovations that build a better business, a more powerful management system and a more developed organization. The price of this form of synthesis is overcoming conflict between managers who must deliver on what is and leaders who are inventing what must replace it, a clear instance of institutionalizing Schumpeter's creative destruction concept within the management system. (Schumpeter, the economist, first observed that economic progress creates new structures out of resources made available by the dismantling of outmoded structures, for example, creative destruction.)

REVIEWING AND ADJUSTING IMBALANCES ACROSS CYCLES

When your organization plans for its future, presumably it plans for a bright future. If results turn out otherwise the first step is to find out why. Checking and reviewing activity in each supporting cycle seeks imbalances between what was expected and what actually happened. For example, a strategy based on a new product technology may be failing due to weak sales capability. Once a review identifies this weakness it stimulates plans and cooperation to upgrade sales capability. Those who agree to develop a new selling process either succeed or fail. If they succeed the new sales process becomes part of the business and its management system and performance improves as planned. On the other hand, if commitments to upgrade sales were not kept, or task assignments were not completed, the need for another round of follow-up becomes obvious. When an improved sales capability is in place, it augments the success of the new product technology strategy and corrects imbalances that yield long-term performance gains.

Putting a new capability in place creates risks, so leadership and planning need to set up status checks, measurements and reviews to monitor progress and anticipate, avoid and prevent disasters. These checks seek to create and focus internal cooperation on removing the greatest imbalances or barriers to performance. Each initiative or action plan improves the management system in some lasting way. As a further benefit, those who took the risks of making the strategy work grow in their organizational skills and influence. Their experience of working through changes adds to their development and shows that they can be relied upon. So individuals that develop the management system also develop themselves.

Imbalances that affect performance can also arise outside of firms, say in markets or as the result of new technology. For example, in the 1960s Corning, Inc., invented glass fiber optics, which led to incredible increases in the amount of information that telecommunications firms could transmit per dollar. In the 1990s, the Internet created torrents of data and video traffic to carry over the new telecommunications capacity. Finally, Internet equipment manufacturers such as Cisco, Lucent and Nortel began outsourcing portions of their manufacturing to firms like Solectron, Jabil Circuits, and Flextronics. The Internet equipment suppliers wanted to allocate their resources to marketing and design activities that created competitive advantage. Unfortunately, commodious new fiber optic capacity led telecommunications carriers to cut price in an effort to attract customers. These price cuts depressed their profitability, which reduced their returns on telecommunications equipment investments. Lower paybacks on investments depressed spending on more equipment from Lucent, Cisco and Nortel, collapsing demand at manufacturing service firms like Solectron. One hears much about supply chain management, but for many of the firms in the above history, customer chain management (or at least review) would have been useful. Searching reviews of supply and demand balances beyond the organization needs to be a part of your organization's checking for imbalances. Such a forward look calls for understanding your customers' customers; you may need to construct a system's view of your customer chain forward to ultimate final demand.

The golden cycle is the open loop that lets customers into your organization to satisfy their needs and, at the same time, stretch you to improve your firm's profitability. This overall "business model"—the golden cycle—creates a business context within which the three supporting cycles operate. It defines the profit opportunity that the supporting cycles seek to maximize. The golden cycle builds current and future customers into your organizational system. As your organization becomes better at serving new markets and customers, the customers become more familiar and satisfied with what you do for them. In a sense, the golden cycle co-develops your organization's relationship with its customers in a win-win synergy.

INNOVATING WITHIN THE MANAGEMENT SYSTEM

In recent years, Baldrige award winners have used internal dialogs about corporate objectives as a means for integrating all parts of the business into an effective system. To be of benefit, dialogs must have focus. One CEO abandoned a successful companywide suggestion system because over half the suggestions received had nothing to do with top company priorities. This CEO did not believe that better communication about plans and priorities would elicit more suggestions focused on those top priorities. Synthesis in this case would have arisen from focusing on ideals and working backward to what is, rather than working from what is to what could be.

Once your organizational objectives are set, dialogs about new opportunities bring about synthesis and integration. Such dialogs bring grass roots information together with those who foresee long-term opportunities and understand the firm's capabilities both as they are and as they need to be. Corporate objectives are usually relatively stable from year to year, but constant change is the rule for the relative importance of such issues as customer and other stakeholder needs, shareholder value, employee and process needs, leadership and potential for risk and profit. People involved in integration dialogs should represent all stakeholder points of view, not just by function and location but also by role, stake and attitude. Such wide involvement ensures that what is good overall is also good for every participant in the system.

If your organization is in transition from a tight functional hierarchy to a more process- and flow-oriented management system that emphasizes cross-functional cooperation, leaders within top management may need to engage in searching discussions with anxious department managers who are proud to be running tight departments. These difficult conversations are about how to live with the dilution of their previously inviolable functional management authority. You will be well advised to pay attention to how those around you feel about all of the changes and make sure of the answers to the "what's in it for me" questions. Without building a broad base of understanding (if not acceptance) your synthesis might omit one or more stakeholders with adverse long-term consequences. They will overtly or covertly undermine the very initiatives that help to secure the organization's future. Those involved in the integration dialogs should be motivated by the opportunity to lead, to participate in doing something exciting for the joy of it. Leaders of the future must be loyal, persistent, and hard working because the biggest opportunities take a long time.

Russell L. Ackoff has put forth one of the more practical dialoguing methods for generating new opportunities from a straw man (Ackoff 1981). Ackoff's idealized design involves a group in discussions to come up with an ideal or straw man, from which to work back to reality. The ideal must be operationally feasible, self-sufficient and improvable. Usually the ideal shows a new way to create customer value that will attract revenue. Often it is compelling enough to attract resources and support from across the organization or even from outside backers. The challenge then becomes to design, evaluate and implement feasible approximations to the ideal. This challenge stimulates creativity and lets people play with new possibilities for the organization. Working backward from an ideal is more powerful than simply trying to develop a new business one step forward at a time. It brings together more points of view and more resources; the single ideal focuses thinking.

With Internet technology allowing seamless publishing, every unit in the firm could share its most wanted list (of ideals) with others to spark dialog and sharing. Such a dialog would also cover political links about possible entrepreneurial combinations and configurations (as a purely hypothetical example, marketing and production actually finding ways to cooperate). The participants may stop short of an action plan, but the framework for developing an action plan (in terms of requirements on the supporting cycles) needs to be clear. New working relationships among parts of the organization expand possibilities just the way that ultrastrong minimagnets in a research lab led to hi-fi headsets to go along with existing tape-recorder technology to create Sony Walkmans and billions of dollars in new sales.

Your organization's dialogs must cross boundaries to maximize contrasts and generate creative tension. Within each cycle, you will find few complements. The dialogs must share information and work out implications for new possibilities. Opportunities will most likely be improvisational—linking together elements that already exist into new combinations that show promise. The overall order that creates cycles must also create and empower sharing, entrepreneurial events, and occasions when your firm's experts discuss their visions of what could be done with what they have or know, or what they could have or could know.

E-mail and groupware technology such as Lotus Notes are allowing dozens or hundreds of people to join and be understood in ongoing brainstorming and planning discussions. The new technology of short messages, wide distribution, multiple eyes looking for something new and interesting, multiplies possibilities and interactions exponentially. Simple e-mail and Lotus Notes based systems have already increased organizational sharing of tactical data within many firms, and sharing of organizationwide strategy will be the encore. Increasingly firms cannot function effectively without discussing issues and opportunities through long, threaded sequences of e-mail among the discussants; the future will bring more of this type of collaboration.

In an online publicity stunt that also previews future possibilities, over 50,000 IBM employees participated in a four-day–long virtual gathering called WorldJam (Reuters, Limited 2001). The session, which took over nine months to plan, involved IBM's Intranet, web sites, online bulletin boards and e-mails. The session was an electronic version of a popular internal recruiting and sharing SummerJam conference that IBM held a year earlier. The electronic WorldJam involved nearly thirty times more participants than the previous SummerJam meeting and generated thousands of employee relations and recruiting ideas. WorldJam participants then voted on the ideas; finalists in the voting actually attracted a number of volunteers willing to test the ideas generated. IBM is researching participant experiences in this enormous online bash to identify which tools were utilized most effectively. Quick, interactive organizationwide collaboration without the need to bring all collaborators to a central forum promises to become a wellspring of important new possibilities.

Another advantage of internal e-mail dialogs about the data, information, knowledge and understanding inside your firm is that it lets authors of the best ideas and practices associate their names with their ideas. Status and esteem become the reward for those who give wisdom and commitment to action. (Of course bonuses are usually paid to those who made a great idea happen, rather than those who first had the idea.) Baldrige award-winner OMI evolved their companywide system for communicating best practices and innovations to offer internal "patents" on strategically significant accomplishments. Patent holders automatically become eligible for highly prestigious Presidential Teamwork awards. One question for you to consider: should ideas be named for those who originate them (patent holders), or be named after those ("licensees") who first use them to make the organization better off? Why not both?

People who excel at generating internal business plans usually are "loose cannons" or "plate breakers" who engage often in the ad hoc, sporadic, opportunistic and entrepreneurial activity of seeking and creating opportunities to have a big impact. Such people usually have to work in the "white space" between boxes on the organization chart. They move where they must to synthesize all four cycles into a whole—perhaps something very different from what is making money this year. They often use their influence rather than their political power.

Successful dialogs across your firm's cycles must eventually lead to formal business proposals to exploit new opportunities for input to the golden cycle or to the leadership and planning cycle. Each proposal states the opportunity (golden cycle), discusses the strategy to be followed (leadership and planning cycle), the capabilities needed (capability-development cycle), and analyzes the success factors, major cause-and-effect linkages and trends (risk-return cycle) that produce wealth. These plans consider not just each cycle, but also the trends in each cycle and their rates of change. Encouraging your people to create these proposals cuts the time your organization needs to create linkages, act and either speed up successes or learn from failures.

To ensure that quantity or authority does not drive out quality, you must build in some form of quality control on your firm's dialogs. Peer review and comment on the dialogue—much the way that scientific journals assess and ensure the quality of articles published—is one basis on which to build commitments. However, in business as in science, facts, reliance on data and predictions that can be tested, must be the acid test of whether someone knows what he or she is talking about. The bursting of the Internet bubble in 2000 shows the danger of making major business commitments on the basis of entrepreneurial speeches rather than successful pilot demonstrations of performance superiority. *Ultimately, each potential opportunity must be assembled into a business plan with assumptions clearly spelled out, with the opportunities quantified for examination and assessment by others.* Such a plan should address each of the key cycles: Where is the profit- and wealth-creating opportunity? What is our strategy for realizing the opportunity and who will lead in its execution? What are our capabilities or what should they be to make the strategy a success; what are the assumptions and issues driving risk, and what information must be gathered and analyzed to maximize return for a given level of risk? *There is little difference between a financial projection in a business plan and a set of predictions that a scientist develops from a new theory. Both are statements about the unknown and subject to test. The sooner such plans make testable forecasts of cost, revenue and profit, the more likely they are to be made workable.*

As your organization tries out or tests business plans resulting from dialogs among its cycles, it obtains feedback. Things actually turn out either better or worse than you or others envisioned. Some feedback strengthens relationships that fit the market opportunity. Feedback on what is not working stimulates improvements in those relationships. This testing and learning strengthens your business and how you manage it.

PACE, COORDINATION AND DEVELOPING A PROGRESSIVE CULTURE

Your organization's rate of growth depends on how effectively you maintain learning and improve integration within your organization to match evolution of your customers and markets. If supporting cycles simply react to gaps and disconnects, performance improves slowly. Slow is not necessarily bad; in fact it was how Yankee Bank ran through its first major golden cycle. However, in subsequent years, the bank built on what it learned in all areas, and developed capabilities and analytical methods in anticipation of its future market opportunities. Over time, this anticipation and coordination enabled the bank to program its growth and competitiveness, product by product, market by market, year after year. If you had talked to that bank's CEO at the time he would have been happy to tell you about the future profit opportunities that his organization was working on all the time. The time it takes your firm to complete a full golden cycle by bringing to market a superior product or service determines the potential wealth your business can produce. The supporting cycles of strategy, capability and risk-return either speed up or slow down wealth production, depending on how well they coordinate and integrate with the golden cycle.

The need for feedback and adjustment to keep a system or an organization on track makes completing each cycle more important than coordinating the cycles perfectly. No rigid, inflexible links exist among the cycles. Instead, their connections are fuzzy—discussions during planning sessions, excellence summits, chance meetings in hallways, cross-functional teams "working in the white space," informal e-mail discussion groups, managerial reviews of projects or progress on plans, bright ideas that come up when traveling with a companion from another part of the organization and the like. What really matters is an organizational culture, a firmly planted set of habits that make organizational and personal learning and development important. These habits must replace the fear factor with honest feedback. Be on the lookout for blamers and excuse-makers looking to shift blame. They never find causes, they only find fault, their actions spread fear and destroy organizational excellence.

Stranding capability within a culture that does not appreciate it, or care to see it used, squanders opportunity. In the 1970s and 1980s, researchers at Xerox's Palo Alto Research Center (PARC) invented the graphical user interface (GUI) and the Ethernet networking technology—large pieces of what is now the Internet. Yet this capability existed within a culture that stressed selling more Xerox copiers to companies processing information on paper. Why were the voices that saw the opportunities not listened to? Xerox's whole golden cycle revolved around customers making more and more copies on paper with Xerox's photocopying machines.

Capitalizing on one of the single largest lost business opportunities ever, Jobs, Wozniak, Metcalf, Gates and others founded companies on technological capabilities hamstrung within the Xerox culture. People with vision, ambition and the willingness to work sixteen-hour days because they were not working—they were having fun building innovative organizations—Apple Computer, 3Com and Microsoft—all to some extent on PARC intellectual property. These people also had no preexisting focus on plain-paper copiers to blind them to the opportunities inherent in the PARC technologies. Their golden cycles looked further out than Xerox's; they took the capabilities Xerox developed and learned what they needed to build revolutionary businesses.

The overall pace of progress toward excellence depends on how often your firm checks, how much you learn, and how well the results of the checks lead to improvements in the other cycles. As the Xerox PARC experience shows, surging forward in capability while wearing blinders about market opportunities limits innovation almost to the extent of a competitive death wish. Just imagine how differently things would have turned out if a *Check* step on Xerox planning in the early 1970s had led Xerox leaders to design a new organization with individual and organizational values relevant to exploiting PARC's technology. History shows that such an organization could have outgrown its parent.

Now you have seen three supporting cycles of learning and improvement that work together to enable an organization to pursue golden cycles of wealth creation—and how dialog synthesizes the four cycles into a whole whose purpose is to generate excellent performance for customers, employees, owners and other stakeholders. At this point, you should be convinced that it is time for your organization to build a management system designed for high performance, basing its design on principles of world-class management:

- Powerful individual and organizational values strongly held and acted on every day
- Knowledge of why processes work as they do with ongoing improvement
- Deep care and insight into why customers and other people behave as they do
- Appreciation for how parts of a system work as a whole to pursue a common purpose—innovating to deliver ever more customer value at a profit, to create and share wealth

Such a system will allow your organization to grow and share benefits with all who have a stake in it. Furthermore, developing a management system ensures that the organization remains stable as it grows and that it does not outgrow the capacity of one or a few executives to manage. Management embodied in a system exceeds the capability of any individual or small group of individuals.

If you are ready to begin the transformation in your own organization, chapters 10 and 11 should put you in a frame of mind for action. They describe how you can use the *Baldrige Criteria for Performance Excellence* to improve your management systems. They give you a sense of what you need to commit to do and provide a road map to follow. If you believe your firm is ready to begin its transformation to high performance, read on to find out about readiness for a Baldrige assessment. What assessment level fits your needs? What kind of—and how much—work must your firm do to participate? Part IV tells you what's in store and what you will get back.

PART IV

Achieving High Performance

CHAPTER 10

Assessment: Roadmap to Excellence

And this above all—to thine own self be true:
And it must follow as the night the day,
Thou canst not be false to any man.
> —William Shakespeare, *Hamlet, Prince of Denmark*

To achieve greatness: "Start where you are. Use what you have. Do what you can."
> —Arthur Ashe

If you have read this far, by now you understand the power of a system to transcend the performance of any of its parts. You may have tried to sketch a flow diagram of your own organization as a system. You know how the parts of an organization can function as a social system of purposeful stakeholders that develop their capabilities to innovate and achieve new heights. You also know that it takes a foundation of strong individual and organizational values and systematic cooperation within the organization to build a high performance management system on cycles of learning and improvement. By now, you are convinced that your firm can benefit from building a management system designed for high performance, but where do you start?

Firms as diverse as Solectron, AT&T Universal Card, The Ritz-Carlton Hotel Co., and Delta Dental Plan of Massachusetts regularly assess and improve their management systems. They all begin by comparing themselves against a high standard, the *Baldrige Criteria for Performance Excellence*. These firms and many others tried one thing after another in their search for excellence—TQM programs, re-engineering, Six Sigma—however, they have gone beyond wandering from management fad to fad, or tinkering with one business part after another. Now they assess their whole management system every year or two and consider such an appraisal as an all-important input to aligning their business for high performance. With assessment as a guide, they know which tools and approaches will benefit performance the most, and why. So why not start where all these leading firms started, by taking stock of where your management system is now?

Most publicly traded U.S. firms operate management systems that would score between 200 to 300 on the Baldrige 1,000-point scale. They take justifiable pride in several outstanding strengths, but many gaps in their systems prevent them from sustaining high performance through market and economic ups and downs. Their results fail to emit powerful signals of high performance management such as extraordinary customer retention and loyalty, high employee satisfaction and industry-leading returns for shareholders. To make rational decisions about investing, smarter investors realize they must seek out firms with management systems designed to produce excellent results. Such firms regularly assess their management system and then act on what they learn from the assessment to follow the path to excellence.

ASSESSMENT DEFINED

What is an assessment? It is the organizational equivalent of checking yourself in the mirror before a night out. High performance firms step back, take a comprehensive look at their management systems ("warts and all"), and compare them to a model of excellence. Assessment replaces ad hoc, reactive change with purposeful, systematic and continuous learning and improvement. Repeated assessments—especially against a rigorous set of requirements such as the Baldrige criteria—usually transforms managers' thinking. Thought patterns shift from the old philosophy of making every department, every process and every product a little bit better, while hoping that overall performance will improve as a result. Managers come to understand that all your firm's parts should fit into a whole system pursuing a common purpose. This understanding helps them see how isolated system gaps and disconnects harm performance of the whole business. The assessment identifies and provides feedback about the strengths in your management system and the gaps that block better performance.

Most organizations use assessment and follow-up in a cycle of four basic stages that you can repeat annually or every other year, as your business deems appropriate:

1. Select and understand a model (the standard against which your firm's assessed)
2. Gather the data needed to apply the model
3. Draw and document conclusions about where your firm compares favorably with the model and where it falls short in a feedback report
4. Decide what to do about shortfalls and take needed steps to correct deficiencies

With assessment feedback in hand, teams of managers decide which follow-up actions will exert the highest leverage on better overall performance. They implement actions to close the gaps, strengthen weaknesses, and improve performance. Rerunning the cycle annually—assess, investigate, follow-up, re-assess—puts a PDCA cycle to work on the firm's management system itself. The best case is to build assessment cycles right into your overall leadership and planning cycles.

MOTIVATIONAL BARRIERS TO
ACHIEVING EXCELLENCE

Although the four-step assessment cycle to achieve excellence is highly rational, those receiving assessment results often react as if the findings were personal criticisms. Organizations often react to assessment feedback the way that parents of a newborn would react when told, "Your baby is ugly." This defensive reaction demotivates follow-up on needed improvements and discourages ongoing assessment. Please recognize that assessment feedback has important implications for how people feel. If your organization tolerates audit reports and survey results without fear and blaming, then its culture will very likely accept and benefit from assessments. If your organization's culture finds fault and assigns blame, however, assessment feedback may prove threatening to some.

Managers who have been in a job for more than a few years own the way things are, and are understandably reluctant to embrace change, no matter what they say. You may encounter resistance to assessment as such, or specific objections to the Baldrige model as a basis for assessment. Assessment by nature requires some standard of comparison and the Baldrige model is the best validated standard now available. Objections to assessment usually arise for one of two reasons. Resistance may be a defense against a culture of criticism, blaming and fault finding. Resistance may be due to fear that organizational learning and change may undermine stakeholders' self-esteem and diminish pride in past accomplishments. Making assessment part of your organization's way of life means focusing on what managers can learn and gain, maximizing the wins and minimizing or overcoming apparent or felt losses.

How do you remove the fear factor? Make sure that people know that an assessment of their management system is not a performance appraisal of them personally. People who are working hard within a lousy system often generate poor results because the system is bad, not the people. You will need to focus on management methods, data, analyses or lack of analysis, processes and interrelationships among these parts, but without criticizing or seeming to criticize individuals. It can be done, and it must be done to succeed.

A "blaming" culture constantly puts people on the defensive because they fear for their job security or prestige. Concern with "political correctness" blocks action on improvement opportunities. As a blaming culture takes hold, those who blame become more and more out of touch with what is really going on. Everyone knows how fear drives good but timid people to falsify or hide the truth. For assessments to work, it is necessary to face reality in a way that people can hear and deal with it, and not become so defensive or fearful that they turn away from it. It is sad that the real role of consultants in many assessments is to "speak truth to power" because those in the organization who know the facts too often are afraid to present the truth themselves. Obviously this type of a culture cannot generate sustained high performance. If it could, Hitler or Stalin surely would have conquered the world.

Another common motivational barrier to assessment is that gathering data for the assessment takes time and effort. Since everyone is already too busy, gathering data for an assessment carries a low priority. The expedient way to avoid data gathering is to rely on managers' opinions about your firm and its management system. Basing your assessment on opinion is much faster and simpler than gathering facts. However, a pooling of opinions is not a fact-based evaluation of a well-defined management system. Self-interested opinions are likely to be biased or even invalid; assessment finding can be no better than their input data. Remember that at one time most learned men agreed with the opinion that the world was flat and at the center of the universe—so much for a pooling of opinion. Opinions unsupported by observation and facts are usually inadequate as a basis for important actions.

CHECK READINESS FOR ASSESSMENT

Many a firm gets into assessment for the same reason the wicked witch in *Snow White* asked "Mirror, mirror, on the wall, who is the fairest one of all?" Its leaders want and expect to hear that their firm is the best. Unfortunately many firms—even hugely successful firms—find that they do not like the answer when they assess against a rigorous framework like the *Baldrige Criteria*. So they conclude the mirror must be flawed and give up running assessments after two or three tries. When considering whether or not to run an assessment, look before you leap: Check whether or not your firm is ready to see the whole picture, warts and all, and prepared to take a step at a time for as long as it takes to make the picture better.

A preassessment check on your organization's readiness for real assessment and follow-up is a good starting point. An organization that decides to start something new has to pay a price in terms of effort. That organization and its management must perceive enough benefit from the assessment to make it worth the cost and time. The payoff from a high performance management system usually takes the form of business growth, profitability and sound management by relying on a management system to spread the task of maintaining progress. A readiness check can reveal if your organization has the foundation in place to make constructive use of assessment feedback; it may also give a sense of how much benefit the firm might obtain from assessment and follow-up. Such a check lets you determine that an honest assessment will not threaten those in the organization who will have to make changes based on assessment results.

One way to check readiness is to have an outside consultant spend two or three days interviewing your firm's top managers and a cross-section of employees and other stakeholders. A few days before the interviews, the consultant usually alerts interviewees to the topics to be covered. This advance warning is not just courteous; it also gives people time to organize their thoughts. Each interview lasts about an hour and follows an outline that searches for information on your firm's future direction, management system, cultural values and management approaches relevant to the assessment model. The interviews also seek profiling information about long-term trends in competition, customer requirements, supplier and partner relationships, expenses and management. By exploring peoples' recent experience with changes at the firm—both positive and otherwise—the consultant can also assess your firm's capability to learn, innovate, manage change projects and adapt. The idea is to anticipate roadblocks so you can avoid them.

Uncovering an organization's real values is an important aspect of the readiness check, because organizational behaviors shaped by those values determine whether a high performance management system is feasible. The readiness check has to consider both current organizational values (what is really important in your company now), as well as gaps your organization may have in the list of eleven high performance values. Closing some of these values gaps may become really important for successful change and improvement. In addition to assessing organizational values, the interviews also need to assess resistance to change and the following three factors:

1. The degree of dissatisfaction with the as-is situation
2. A shared vision of a better way of operating that offers enough benefits to all parties to motivate them to undertake painful changes
3. A roadmap showing how the organization can progress from *as-is* to the *should-be* with its existing capability

More often than not, your firm's readiness check will find that the organization lives by two or three organizational values that together are inadequate for building a high performance management system. Usually one of two situations exists. The first is to find few organizational values other than financial results. The second is to encounter different, conflicting sets of departmental values in each part of your organization with no organizationwide shared values except usually some focus on financial results such as profit, cost or revenue. For example, sales and customer service departments value customers while finance and operations place high importance on immediate revenue and cost avoidance. So when customers have a problem, sales and customer service propose an accommodation, but accounting sets up stringent justification criteria for issuing a customer credit or incurring cost. The result is organizational strife that delays resolution of customer service issues, which makes customers unhappy. The lack of organizationwide values provides little common ground within the organization for strengthening the business.

Exclusive focus on near-term results—making it the only organizationwide value that matters—will interfere with following up on assessment findings with longer-term implications. Without high performance values such as innovation, focus on the future, employee involvement in improving work processes, management by fact, partnering with suppliers, and agility, your organization will fixate on quick remedies and immediate incremental opportunities. Assessment findings that offer high long-term leverage will be ignored because only immediate results are important. (This is what happened in the case of the utility company described in chapter 3 except that a takeover changed their values for them.)

When a preassessment check reveals a lack of readiness for full assessment, the question becomes How can your firm prepare? Preparing must make change safe for all participants. The ideal preparation for assessment involves leaders and managers in:

1. Figuring out why the same old methods, management system and strategy need to be upgraded to higher performance and why now as opposed to waiting until a more auspicious time. Answering the question: "Where is the pain?"

2. Reviewing and critiquing the results of your firm's readiness check and obtaining introductory training on the Baldrige Criteria

3. Gaining general agreement that the high performance model is a standard against which they want to assess their management system

4. Having your senior executives talk to counterparts and peers at customers' or suppliers' firms that have used assessments to upgrade company performance, reporting back on what they learned from visiting other firms

5. Organizing a senior-managers' leadership task force and assigning shared accountability to this group for improving your company's performance for customers, employees, owners, suppliers, and the community

6. Preparing a written charter that spells out commitments and ground rules on top-management accountability for the assessment and follow-up

Preparing an organization for assessment may take a year or longer. Your organization's planning process may provide the best opportunity for dealing with two key issues that help pave the way to making assessment and improvement of the management system safe. The first issue is the desirability of change at your firm. Why now (why not put off change until some later date)? What should you change to? Those who object to the Baldrige performance excellence model as a basis for improvement should be asked to explain their alternative business model. The only unacceptable performance model is to manage without any model at all. The second issue is how to make the change? The current system of management at your firm probably took years to evolve, so assessment and follow-up will take time to overcome resistance to change. During that time, individuals with the character, values and leadership skills to make improvement will show up. Encouraging these "plate breakers" will speed progress.

Once your organization is ready to begin, the next step is to run the assessment. Assessments vary from informal, one-day brainstorming sessions of managers and executives—like an oral quiz with no grade—to a formal corporate process sponsored by the CEO and integrated with the firm's planning and performance cycles. At this point, you want some nuts and bolts about how to match an assessment level to your firm's needs.

THREE LEVELS OF ASSESSMENT

Assessments come in several formats, depending on how much time and effort can be spent gathering data on the management system, and who applies the Baldrige model. After twelve years of experimentation by management consultants and for state quality awards, three types of assessment have emerged.

A *level-1 assessment* surveys a sampling of employees, using a written questionnaire derived from the *Baldrige Criteria*. It is quick, easy, and generally able to detect glaring gaps in an organization's management system. It is also possible to elicit suggestions from survey participants on their priorities for improvement.

A *level-2 assessment* moves beyond surveying people with a written instrument. For a level-2 assessment, a team of trained assessors conducts a site visit and interviews a similar sampling of people as those chosen for the less formal level-1 assessment. These interviews give the assessors more information about what the firm is doing than does a paper survey. They also yield direct insight into how well the parts of the management system work alone and in cooperation, what is not working, and what requirements in the *Baldrige Criteria* are not currently addressed. From these data, the assessors prepare a report on strengths, system gaps and areas for improvement.

In a variation on the site visit approach some level-2 assessments combine training with the actual assessment. In this type of assessment, a cross-section of managers, executives and other leaders, usually numbering between twenty and forty people, spend two or three days with a team of two or three assessor/facilitators. Attendees may be asked to fill in data-gathering forms before coming to the assessment session. During the session the assessors train attendees on the *Baldrige Criteria* and then facilitate small groups in working out strengths and opportunities for improvement. This variation is usually referred to as a facilitated assessment workshop.

A *level-3 assessment* (the usual, full Baldrige assessment) involves writing a narrative "application" which describes how the management system meets requirements of the *Baldrige Criteria*. The organization being assessed may be a department, a plant, a division or even a whole company. This description simply speaks of "the organization" to be assessed. A team of independent examiners then assesses the application against the detailed performance excellence model. From their point-by-point assessment the examiner team prepares written feedback.

What do you need to know about the three assessment levels? Besides an estimate of your firm's assessment readiness, you need enough information to choose the level of effort you and your firm are willing to expend and the return on expenditure you can expect for your efforts. Here are brief overviews of level-1 and level-3 Baldrige assessments and a rather complete explication of a level-2 assessment—a reasonable initial compromise between the extremes.

For Beginners: Questionnaire-based Assessment (Level-1)

The questionnaire-based, level-1 assessment is at the opposite end of the spectrum of data gathering and formality from the level-3 assessment. Many firms begin their very first assessment here, often at the initiative of just one or two senior managers. (In some even less formal self-assessment formats, managers and executives may spend one day of their strategic planning process, agreeing on their organizational profile and brainstorming their firm's strengths and opportunities for improvement in each of the seven categories of the *Baldrige Criteria*. Then, they bring their findings on weaknesses into the session in which they develop business strategies and action plans for the coming year.)

A level-1 survey usually takes a modest step beyond this top-management huddle by administering a questionnaire (known as a level-1 self-assessment) based on the *Baldrige Criteria*. Level-1 self-assessment surveys ask a cross-section of managers and employees to fill in the questionnaire. Respondents to a level-1 survey may come to a conference room for an hour or so, have the purpose of the survey explained, and be given a chance to fill in the questionnaire with a knowledgeable proctor in the room to answer questions. The questionnaires usually ask respondents to rate their level of agreement with statements about the management system, such as "Our top managers create a climate which encourages everyone to learn, take initiatives, try out new ideas, and make improvements." Analysis of questionnaire responses provides a feedback report and often suggestions for follow-up actions.

A list of seventy or more agree/disagree questions has limited ability (at best) to highlight major gaps in the firm's management systems. What's more, the level-1 survey usually cannot detect breakdowns or disconnects between parts of the management system—usually, the most significant areas for improvement found in an assessment. Because of these limitations, such a survey has to be considered a first step in a progression.

The Baldrige office at the U.S. Department of Commerce, NIST, is developing an entry-level assessment survey which is available over the Internet. This instrument is likely to become the single best baby step toward assessment for several reasons. First the NIST survey is backed up by the knowledge and expertise of hundreds of Baldrige examiners and subject to continuous improvement as the *Baldrige Criteria* evolve. What is more, NIST plans to let its web-based survey provide you with a comparison of how your input compares with similar inputs from other firms within your industry.

This feedback falls far short of what more rigorous assessments can provide, but it gives you a rough impression of where you may be ahead or behind a sample of practices in your industry.

The Gold Standard: Typical Baldrige Assessment (Level-3)

A level-3 assessment is modeled on the process used to determine recipients of Baldrige awards. It usually involves outside examiners as a guarantee of objectivity. As a result, it represents the "gold standard" against which you may judge other assessment approaches. A conventional, level-3 Baldrige assessment is only worth the effort if the organization really has a management system in place and it is well enough understood so that someone can write a description of that system. (Most organizations doing their first assessment do not have enough of a management system in place to justify beginning with level-3.)

A firm conducting a level-3 assessment must first describe its organization and environment in an organizational profile. The organizational profile sets the stage for the assessment by providing examiners with insights into the needs of the business. This profile requires the applicant company to describe its organizational environment, staffing, culture, etc. as well as its relationships with customers and suppliers. Then the profile moves on to ask the business to outline its organizational challenges in three areas: competitive environment, strategic and systematic performance improvement. The overall themes and requirements outlined in the profile provide the examiners with insights they need to assess how well the management approaches meet the needs of the business. Assessing the management system in the light of the challenges facing each business adds great value to the resulting feedback.

The fifty-page body of a Baldrige narrative contains diagrams, flow charts and tables as well as narrative that detail how the organization's management approaches meet the requirements outlined by the Baldrige criteria. An application usually is detailed, technical and occasionally daunting reading. However, the discipline of preparing the application yields tremendous benefit to organizations that do it. The attempt to document how the company meets various requirements often turns up important requirements (such as strategic planning, new product development or customer relationship management) for which the organization has no systematic approach. Those preparing a level-3 narrative should be taught to prepare a list of gaps (requirements of the *Baldrige Criteria* that the management system does not meet). This list of gaps and areas where the organization falls short of high performance requirements is traditionally referred to as a gap analysis. Most firms say that their gap analysis prepared them for much of their formal assessment feedback received later from the examiners.

Once an organization has prepared its Baldrige application (or narrative if the firm has no interest in really applying for an award), an independent team of examiners or assessors, either insiders from the company or outside consultants (or both) "grades the paper." (Some companies find that applying for the award, even though they have no real interest in winning it, is a source of tremendously valuable consulting feedback for the price of just an award application fee, less than it would cost from paid consultants.

Whether they are award volunteers, or your own team, the examiners assess the narrative, evaluate the facts, and identify the strengths and areas for improvement. In an in-house Baldrige assessment, they usually make a site visit to spot-check gaps and to confirm important strengths and areas to improve as well as resolve questions that arose during the assessment (called site-visit issues). Finally, from the narrative plus the site-visit spot checks, the examiners prepare a feedback report on their findings. The quality of feedback from a formal assessment depends to a great extent on how well the data gatherers and narrative writers document their organization's management approaches, deployment and results.

The writer of a Baldrige narrative absolutely must be trained on the criteria and preferably should have some experience with examining. Often, however, novice writers consider the criteria outline as suggestions; they exercise their creative-writing skills to explain vividly how their business manages itself. Unfortunately, for examiners to assess a Baldrige narrative effectively, they must be able to find the approach and deployment facts they need, and where they need them. A good assessment application may not be creative, but it is comprehensive, fact-filled, to the point and clear. If a firm has enough of a real management system to make a level-3 assessment worthwhile and wishes to do so, it must train its writers and assessors rigorously.

The Compromise: Interview-based Assessment (Level-2)

You may have decided that a Level-1 Baldrige assessment will not yield the kind of information your firm needs, but that the level-3 assessment appears overly challenging for a start. Is your firm ready for an assessment that lies in between the detailed examination of level-3 and the "quick and dirty" level-1 survey by questionnaire? This middle strategy, known as a level-2 assessment, is more rigorous than a level-1 survey; it consumes much less time and effort than a level-3. It has the advantage that it is rigorous enough to evaluate main approaches and linkages within your management system. As a result, the feedback can be much more thorough than is possible from a questionnaire-based approach.

The increased rigor of a level-2 also comes from having a team of trained examiners (usually outsiders) interview members of your organization. The team derives its assessment from the interview data. In the course of interviewing anywhere from several dozen to several hundred persons in your firm, the examiners find out if the organization's left hand knows what its right hand is doing (alignment and integration). The examiners are able to see if the pieces fit together into a system with cycles of improvement. In fact the ability of an interview-based assessment to evaluate how well your management approaches are integrated into a system is the greatest advantage of a level-2 assessment. A second great advantage is that the interviewers can close their interviews by asking people what they see as the greatest challenges and recommendations for raising performance.

The assessors' findings of strengths and gaps in your management system arise from what the assessors learn from their interviews. If your firm does not choose to begin assessments at level-1, you will probably use a level-2 assessment as your starting point, because this approach features speed, relative simplicity, and ability to provide relatively high-leverage feedback. If you choose level-2, what will you be doing?

SCENARIO FOR YOUR LEVEL-2 ASSESSMENT

Now that your organization is ready for an assessment, the first step is to charter the assessment.

Charter Your Assessment

The assessment process begins when you or some other senior executive or manager decides to look into ways to get your organization growing faster and running better. Most organizations treat their first assessment as a "special project." Once they gain experience from a few cycles of assessment and follow-up, however, they either give up or build assessment into their management system. While assessment is in the special project status, someone has to sponsor it. Since you can hardly be expected to sponsor something you do not understand fully, you or your sponsor's first step is to review, understand, and select the Baldrige model as the standard against which your management system is to be assessed.

About one organization out of twenty or so modify the published criteria to fit their unique business circumstances. For example, a multidivision firm created a whole category for technology transfer and cross-divisional innovation and cooperation. Another firm added an entire category on learning and innovation, while yet another added its own category on environmental, health, and safety management. This practice is acceptable, so long as it does not compromise the Baldrige system's integrity. It is also increasingly common to find firms integrating their approaches with ISO9000 and with certain requirements of the Baldrige business model. Although your firm could choose another model, the following scenario assumes that you adopt the Baldrige model as your assessment standard.

Some time prior to the actual assessment, your assessment sponsor picks members of the organization to serve on a steering committee or steering team. Ideally, this team includes the executive sponsor and other executives who the sponsor designates as "category owners" or "category champions." The sponsor should clarify that owners or champions are responsible for following up on assessment findings in their respective Baldrige categories. The champions' assigned categories usually relate to their regular organizational responsibilities—for example, finance for the results category, marketing for the customer- and market-focus category and operations for the process-management category and so on. The champions take responsibility for progress on their assigned categories; they then coach and facilitate improvements. These executives will need some training in Baldrige and will often benefit from personal coaching themselves as they coach follow-up.

Organize Your Assessment Team

Once your assessment is chartered, the next step is to set up and train an assessment team. Typically, your organization designates a program manager—usually a middle manager from a quality or service responsibility—to manage the logistics of your firm's assessment. If the program manager has no prior experience with Baldrige assessment, his or her first step usually is to hurry off to a Baldrige assessment training program and to buy several popular books on Baldrige. The assessment-program manager usually is accountable to the assessment sponsor for the assessment program's success.

The program manager usually prepares an executive briefing on the Baldrige framework and gets agreement with the sponsor on expectations for the assessment. Most program managers also run daylong training sessions for their firm's category champions. This training is a first step designed to help sponsoring executives understand their Baldrige category-ownership roles within the assessment and follow-up framework. The program manager also begins preparing for the assessment by selecting a team of assessors. An ideal assessment team would include:

- *A general manager* from a site comparable to the organization being assessed—to cover leadership, planning and organizational issues, as well as to ensure that the assessment team has strong internal credibility;

- One or two *quality managers*—to cover the deployment of quality improvement methods and process management throughout your organization and to participate in the *supplier focus group* (discussed below)

- A *human resources professional* or someone with a strong HR and training background

- A *sales, marketing or customer-service person* with experience to cover the customer- and market-focus category and to partici- pate in the *customer focus group*

- An *information systems or financial person* to cover the informa- tion and analysis category

Occasionally, an outside examiner from Baldrige or from a state award program is included on a firm's team to ensure objectivity.

This team will interview your organization's subject-matter ex- perts to gather information on your management system. Usually, the team talks to or interviews all executives, a majority of manag- ers and supervisors, and a representative cross-sectional sampling of all other employee categories. When your assessment team visits a site, interviewing is intense. Indeed, during this interview-based assessment, your organization may feel that the three- or four-day visit from a team of assessors is the whole assessment process. However, these interviews and the accompanying discussions among the assessment team members is just the tip of the iceberg— only the visible part of a larger whole. Your organization will need to make a lot of preparations before a typical site-visit-based level-2 assessment. Here is a typical scenario drawn from field experience.

Once the assessment team forms, the next step is to train them. Typically, your program manager puts together an examiner train- ing program based on what he or she learned by attending a pub- lic seminar. The usual training for internal assessors consists of a brief review of the criteria, together with practice examining a Baldrige case study application. Assessment team members usually take a week or more to score individually an entire Baldrige train- ing case study. Then, they meet to hold a consensus session, during which they discuss their individual assessments and—as a team— arrive at consensus about the case study assessment findings.

Since NIST Baldrige training cases always have a pre-prepared "book solution," your assessment team-in-training may compare its consensus findings against the official Baldrige book solution. Much of their learning about assessment comes from the team consensus discussion; comparing their agreed-to assessment with the book solution helps acquaint your assessors-in-training with the expectations and standards that apply in Baldrige. Training cases, together with book solutions in the form of sample feedback reports and assessment scorebooks, are available for little cost from American Society for Quality (ASQ) in Milwaukee, Wisconsin. Usually costing about $50, they may be ordered by calling ASQ at 800-248-1946.

Your assessment-program manager may also coach your team in interviewing skills and create opportunities for your assessor trainees to role-play interviewing, thereby building up their questioning and listening skills. Finally, your assessment team begins planning the logistics of its site visit. Often, team members use laptop computers to document their findings and prepare their feedback. It is helpful if one member of your team serves as the technology coordinator, ensuring that each member can read all others' files and arranging on-site equipment to print output documents.

Some preparation is needed to ensure that the assessors have a common understanding of what your organization is all about. (Even if the assessment team is from the same organization, surprisingly, there may not be much agreement on fundamentals.) To that end, your assessment-program manager usually facilitates a session in which the steering team writes a profile of your firm—four pages of facts about your organization and its business. To be most useful, the organizational profile must follow the outline appearing in the *Baldrige Criteria*. The profile's content covers the environmental, strategic, competitive and performance challenges that your steering team wants the assessors to consider in examining your organization's key business requirements.

Gather Assessment Data

In practice, firms vary widely in how they gather data to assess their management systems. An interview-based level-2 assessment can touch dozens or even more than a hundred people within your organization, so the jumping-off point is to alert your organization that the assessment will happen. In the level-2 approach, assessors gather the data they need for the assessment in direct, face-to-face interviews with subject-matter experts throughout your organization.

Notify Your Organization of the Coming Assessment

Part of the preparations for assessment consists of getting people in your organization into the right frame of mind to host the assessment and open up to your assessors. Your assessment-program manager's communications and internal public relations task is to condition peoples' expectations. The manager usually drafts a communication from the assessment sponsor, announcing to all hands the assessment and its purpose. Copies of relevant portions of the *Baldrige Criteria* may accompany this communication to managers and supervisors, who may post charts explaining the assessment process and *Baldrige Criteria* for interested employees. Your team may even run a brief training program on what the criteria are and how the assessment will work. Everyone in your organization needs to hear this message: *The assessors are not auditors or faultfinders. They will not blame or criticize anyone.* Instead, they are examining the strengths and opportunities to improve your firm's management system to help your firm compete more effectively and improve job security.

Perform the Site Visit

When site preparations are complete and your assessment team is trained, that team travels to the site on what is known as a *site visit*. Assessment team members usually come from outside the organizational unit being assessed; often, they will not have worked with each other previously, except for their experience in Baldrige assessment training.

The night before the site visit starts, members of your assessment team usually assemble at a hotel near your organization's site and introduce themselves to one another over dinner. After dinner, the team members agree on lead- and backup-category assignments and pair up into interview teams. Typically, individuals will take responsibility for gathering data, assessing and writing feedback on one or more of the Baldrige categories—leadership, human resource focus, information and analysis, for example. Individually, team members read the criteria for their assigned categories and prepare questions for their interviews. Then, over breakfast on the first day of the site visit, they review these questions with one another. The site visit begins when they arrive on your organization's site and introduce themselves to the site host, each category owner, and others involved.

Organizations hosting a site-visit assessment usually designate an on-site host who is responsible for getting the assessors to the people with whom they need to meet. At this point, your organization's assessment sponsor usually explains your firm's business by briefing the assessment team with the previously prepared organizational profile. The assessment team members let your on-site host know whom they need to interview (usually by job title since they will not know the individuals personally), and the assessment begins.

The assessors usually cannot predict ahead of time precisely who they need to interview, so the process of arranging interviews and appointments goes on continuously over the several days of the site visit. The host schedules interviews to begin as soon as the introductions and organizational profile briefing end. Usually, non-executive interviewees come to central interviewing points—small conference rooms—where pairs of assessors interview persons for about twenty minutes or longer. (Working in pairs ensures that assessors hear and understand all of the information they are gaining.) Assessors usually visit executives in their offices where they have access to reports, documents and other data. The interviewing process continues throughout the day, interrupted only by the previously scheduled *customer* and *supplier focus groups*. Typically, the whole assessment team meets with your site's senior management team for a somewhat longer interview—an hour or ninety minutes.

Understanding Customers, Markets and Opportunities

Assessors gathering information on customer and market focus and strategic planning usually interview senior marketing, planning and general managers to seek information about how your organization spots expansion opportunities (new products, customers, distribution channels) for long-term development. As they interview, the examiners look for evidence that your organization looks beyond its current customers to identify future markets full of prospective customers. (The term *market* describes buyers that are not yet your customers.) They invite the people they interview to show how your organization systematically learns about and understands what customers and markets care about and how customers value what they get from you, your products and services. They may review survey methods, customer relationship database designs, purchased market data, or other approaches used to segment and understand customers and markets and how they are evolving.

During two or three days of interviewing and analysis, the customer- and market-oriented assessors usually discuss whether or not your firm has a systematic method or methods for identifying customer or market segments by growth, attractiveness, and size. They may examine sample market research studies, trace how their findings were put to use, and examine whether listening and learning from customers is systematic or sporadic. As they gather information they discuss among themselves such questions as whether or not your firm has effective market research methods to uncover top customer "care-abouts" by customer group and market segment.

In parallel with finding out what customers care about, the assessors will be on the lookout to see that functions across your whole organization know where they stand with customers on each "care-about." In other words, they will seek evidence that you know which customer requirements your offerings excel at, and on which they are in need of improvement. This usually is in the form of data on customer satisfaction and dissatisfaction with your products and services. The assessors also seek information on how your organization handles complaints. Is your process systematic, improvement-oriented and the like. Customer dissatisfaction is usually a leading indicator of a revenue downtrend just as rising satisfaction is a leading indicator of increased customer loyalty and revenue.

Checking for the Golden Thread

Properly trained assessors usually try to follow the golden thread throughout the whole management system and across the organization. In so doing, they focus first on how your company creates a customer and market focus. They seek evidence that you start the focus by defining your big-dollar opportunities in planning for the immediate and long-term future. They usually interview along a crosscutting chain of personnel from marketing through strategic planning to operations, to trace the flow of customer knowledge through organizational activities. Frequently such cross-cutting interviews turn up disconnects. For example, the marketing department knows that electronic equipment customers no longer view reliability as an issue but prefer equipment that is easy to train people to use. However, engineers in the same firm are spending more development effort improving reliability than improving usability. Such disconnects or misalignments are surprisingly common; feedback on them helps the firm to make a "quick fix" that boosts results sooner rather than later.

As the customer and market assessment team members gain clarity on your current and future customers and their requirements, their counterparts interviewing in the area of strategic planning trace how well your management system (1) defines competitive and market strategies and (2) links action plans in all work units and processes with the few vital customer requirements or "careabouts." They may seek to interview managers responsible for action plans, or leaders of new product development efforts to obtain information on how effectively market and customer knowledge links to the organization's direction- and priority-setting. They may also review the agendas of planning sessions, review the notes produced and seek evidence that strategy is based on valid customer and market information, rather than assumptions and guesses. This lets them check that information on customer and market focus is really used in planning.

Assessors interviewing senior leaders also explore how your organization answers the competitive question, "In each segment, how does your company make customers 'your' customers rather than 'their' customers?" The answers allow the assessment team to identify and evaluate how your firm's strategy builds and maintains a competitive edge—a position of being the best in your chosen customers' minds. They also consider how you systematically ensure that customers know and benefit from being "your" customers. They look at how you maintain relationships with customers, how you find out what makes customers loyal, and what drives them away. Interviews of customer contact and sales personnel usually provide solid insights into how your organization cares for customers and maintains relationships. As interviewers move through the customer relationship areas, they also look for evidence that you measure your capability to maintain a close and mutually profitable relationship with your customers and that you check to see that the measures are improving over time. They need to answer the question of how you know your customer relationships are healthy.

Assessment team members who gather data on process management and quality improvement will interview those responsible for production and delivery processes. They may interview operators on the line or in production and service jobs. They consider whether your process improvement efforts align with your competitive strategy. They check that the in-process and end-of-process measures used on the line link and align with the higher level strategic metrics that top management is using to guide and evaluate the firm's strategic performance. They may do this by interviewing process improvement teams, or by examining several past process improvement efforts.

Checking Leadership, Planning and Alignment

The assessment checks that your organization's leadership and strategic planning approaches point toward future market opportunities. For example, they may start with the agenda from strategic planning and identify a major strategic initiative. Then by interviewing participants responsible for that initiative, and interviewing each individual who subsequently became involved they follow the chain of actions from strategy to specific tasks, completing a "vertical slice" through the organization. The information from such interviews establishes whether the firm has an effective method for deploying its overall strategies to each relevant work unit and process.

The assessors concerned with leadership and planning also interview throughout the organization to assess how effectively your organization's leaders give people a common purpose. In interviews and during an open-ended activity known as a "walk-around" they ask people questions that reveal what expectations the leaders create. For example they may ask everyone they meet: "What is really important around here and how do you know?" By asking the same questions of personnel throughout the organization, all the assessors check on whether or not people across your whole organization share the same mission and organizational values. When twenty interviewees give nearly as many different answers to the "what's important" question, there may be an opportunity to better align the organization around an overall mission and high performance values. Another objective during a walk-around is to find out if your organization's leaders inspire people to aim high—do they set standards that lead to excellence?

The assessors concerned with leadership issues also investigate what makes the leaders tick—are they striving for business excellence because of a need for personal glory, to get the next promotion, or are they trying to build an excellent organization so that every participant can share in being the best that they can be? Such questions shed light on whether the organization's management system will survive changes in individuals, whether it is more permanent than just the personal practices of the managers who happen to be in charge.

Knowing that a high performance organization's mission needs to consider all stakeholders' prosperity, the human resource focus and process management assessors seek evidence that organizational commitments to customers are backed up with commitments to employees, shareholders, suppliers and other stakeholders. Employee considerations are crucial, because the employees of an organization have more at stake in its success than any other group of stakeholders (often more than even the owners). The assessment team members also interview for evidence that the company understands and attends to the interests of suppliers, shareholders and surrounding communities. If the organization's activities raise environmental, health or safety issues, interviews would explore this aspect of company citizenship.

In the service side of every business, the leadership and human resource assessors seek insight into how the company ensures ethical behavior in all of its dealings. Assessors usually obtain first-hand data from interviewing organization members about executives' behaviors relevant to achieving the organization's mission. Simply asking people "what is important in your organization," and then listening as interviewees give examples, provides clear insights into what the organization really values and whether those organizational values are consistent with high performance values.

Somewhere during the interviews, the leadership and planning assessors question how your leaders have systematically involved your organization's managers, supervisors and work units in planning for the coming one to three years. Does your organization's planning process also include a one-year plan and profit budget consistent with the plan? These assessors interview those involved in planning and budgeting to spot-check whether or not they've set measurable goals and targets to show improvement; without forecasts of what to expect, it's impossible to check results.

Assessing Capabilities

The process management assessors usually narrow their focus to the processes key to the success of your competitive and market strategy. They may interview product and marketing managers, however their focus will be on working level people to check how your organization manages processes. Does your firm's approach to managing processes ensure that everyone knows the right way to do his or her job, to check the quality of that job and what to do when there is a problem? They look for evidence that your process management includes measurements and a corrective-action system. Do you employ improvement teams to tap the knowledge of your work force? Are teams properly trained in methods of identifying repetitive (process) problems and initiating corrective action—does your firm mandate such training? For the most customer-significant issues, does your firm's process-management approach investigate the sources and root causes of waste, error, and delay in key processes? Do root-cause investigations use systematic statistical and experimental methods that result in conclusions that really work—or do they rely on opinions and guesses that relate to risk taking?

The assessment team members concerned with process management also investigate how your firm's process managers select appropriate control tactics for each process. They may look at daily in-process measures and controls. In their interviews, they seek evidence that things have been changing for the better in key processes. They question whether process improvement is systematically driven by strategy, or just in reaction to complaints and cost pressures.

Interviewing personnel who are in contact with customers often highlights whether customer relationship management methods are systematic and effective. When the assessors hear of opportunities for improvement from front-line staff, it also raises the broader issue of how the organization systematically obtains such staff input as a basis for improvement. The human resource assessors interview those concerned with teams, suggestion systems, recognition and other ways of involving employees in managing. These assessors also seek information on how the organization deploys lessons learned and retrains personnel as processes and work practices improve, to see if the golden thread reaches into human resource development.

If suppliers are critical to your organization's mission, some of the process management interviews will extend to purchasing and contracting personnel who manage supplier relationships. The assessors will look for systematic methods of communicating requirements to suppliers. They will also seek measurements to demonstrate that your organization knows which suppliers are meeting or exceeding requirements. Finally, interviewers will seek evidence of genuine partnering with suppliers, especially in areas where close relationships with suppliers will confer a strategic or competitive advantage, say in new product development or through reducing costs or working capital requirements.

Diane Schmalensee, a noted authority on customer loyalty and Baldrige assessment, adds another element to the best-run level-2 assessments. She holds a series of focus group interviews to obtain data directly from customers and suppliers. These focus groups usually take place as part of the site visit; the assessors in charge of the customer- and market-focus category and the process-management category lead them. The site-visit host usually arranges for three to five key customers to send representatives to the assessment site to meet with assessment team members. Similarly, three to five key suppliers send representatives. They provide the assessment team with limited but powerful independent data on customer relations and supplier management methods. Arranging these focus groups takes some advance work with customers and suppliers. Each of the two focus-group interviews usually lasts for ninety minutes to two hours.

The human resource members of the assessment team will look at workforce issues in the light of the golden thread—what customers care most about. If something is important to customers, it is included in your firm's strategy, and it affects your firm's processes. What does the golden thread demand of your firm's people? After interviewing human resource managers to gain perspective, the assessors will usually take their human resource questions to wherever work is done. At the most basic level, the assessors interview those in management, supervisory and support functions responsible for your work systems. They are seeking to understand how your management system taps motivation and fosters high performance. How do you design jobs? How does your organization select people to hire? Does your organization have a systematic way to identify the critical skills and educational requirements of all jobs? How does each activity and job relate to what customers care about and benefit from? Do you have ways to identify and develop the employee skills your firm needs and the work demands? Do you assess employees' job-related training and development needs as part of performance appraisal, or do you simply give feedback to employees and leave it to them to figure out how to improve?

Another aspect of human resource management relates to how well your firm expands the empowerment and initiative of its work force—how it achieves better-managed work processes with fewer managers, doing more with less. Assessors may take selected customer problems or complaints and examine whether or not people in contact with the customers are trained and encouraged to make the customer happy. Your assessors may explore how the firm identifies its leading subject-matter experts (SMEs) in key skill areas.

How do you share knowledge within the firm and expand work-force learning? Does your firm systematically encourage its experts to take "train-the-trainer" training and upgrade key employee and workforce skills? Does your business systematically ask individual employees to help generate personal development plans and then train supervisors to coach employees in carrying out those plans? Just how does your organization maximize the return on its human assets?

Finally, your Baldrige assessment team wants to see how your firm seeks employee input and involves them in decisions affect-ing their satisfaction and motivation. Human resource-oriented interviews will look at whether managers treat members of the workforce as internal customers; how do they work systematically toward higher levels of employee satisfaction and motivation? They will join team members concerned with information and analysis to interview whoever is in charge of measuring employee satisfac-tion, motivation and morale, to see whether your organization uses employee data to drive improvements. Reviewing trends tabulated from answers to employee survey questions lets the assessors check the effectiveness of management actions and behaviors. Do employ-ees consider their leaders trustworthy? Are leaders compensated on performance measures that reinforce high performance values throughout the organization? Do employees clearly understand the organization's mission and values? Do employees get cooperation and coaching when they need it? How effectively does the firm follow up on gaps in employee satisfaction? These questions give you an idea of the human resource issues that arise in a high per-formance organization.

At the end of each day of your site visit, assessment team mem-bers caucus briefly before dinner to review what they are learning. After dinner each evening, the team continues to share data and summarize findings and issues from that day's interviews. Often, the assessors present summaries of what they are learning to the other team members as preparation for documenting their most significant findings. During most site visits, individual assessors work far into the night, summarizing their findings on strengths and on areas to improve. As they develop clear pictures of the man-agement system's most important elements, they begin exploring its subtleties and refinements, its strengths and opportunities for improvement.

Usually, by the third or fourth day of a site visit, the team is well on its way to digesting data from dozens of interviews as it clarifies and substantiates its main findings. At this point the team begins to focus on important findings that either need to be double-checked or further validated. They schedule follow-up or "double-checking" interviews they need to wrap up data gathering on all key issues, usually by the middle of the last day of inerviews.

Prepare the Assessment Feedback Report

Once your assessment team finishes its wrap-up interviews, team members work individually to summarize findings in their assigned categories. In the evening, they come together as a team to share strengths and areas for improvement by category and to discuss the content and wording of their feedback with each other. Their usual approach is to identify the system-level or crosscutting issues where improvements will give the greatest boost to organizational performance. Experienced examiner teams try to identify the essential gaps and disconnects between the approaches of the management system as a basis for effective innovation and learning, rather than dive into tremendous detail.

As a group, the examiners identify the "high leverage" conclusions from the assessment—the management system gaps that will produce major gains when fixed. The attitude is one of trying to help the organization upgrade its own management system. If the assessment team included outside examiners—for example, from a state quality award program or from a consulting firm, they work with the internal assessors to eliminate bias and ensure validity of the feedback from the assessment.

As they prepare their consensus feedback report, the assessors identify the top areas for improvement that can help your organization achieve leadership in your top-priority customer and market segments. Does your organization have the capabilities it needs—people, skills, information, processes and resources—to lead in your chosen market? Are all organizational units aligned with the strategy with consistent metrics? Does the organization's strategic plan address the key issues raised in the organizational profile? Are facts and analyses used as the basis for planning, tracking progress and decisions, or does the organization rely on opinion and guesswork? All of these data are summarized and presented either orally, or in writing, and often both ways.

Feedback usually contains both good and bad news. The good news lists the strengths of your management system; it gives you and your people reasons to crow, since it highlights areas where you are already on the road to high performance. The bad news arrives as feedback about gaps in your firm's management, processes and policies; bad news also describes opportunities for improvement, presented more as challenges to improve than as news to feel bad about. Once you read or listen to and digest the assessment findings, you will have a good idea both of your firm's strengths and of your corporate opportunities for improvement.

The written feedback from a Baldrige assessment is "the envelope that nobody really wants to open" because no one really wants to be told, "Your baby is ugly." Baldrige feedback (and most state award feedback) is nonprescriptive; it states the strengths, the areas to improve and the evaluation. Nonprescriptive feedback does not recommend or advise your firm on what to do for improvement. When your organization runs its own assessment, or hires a consultant to do it for a fee, however, you are free to request prescriptions of the assessment team in response to their feedback.

Unless your firm's assessors have broad skills and experience that qualify them to make prescriptions, they may wish to stick to nonprescriptive feedback of the form that says, in effect: "The criteria require X; you address this through method Y; which does (or does not) respond to scoring requirements A, B and C." The feedback comment would also include a "So what?" comment that states the implication of the strength or opportunity for improvement in terms of business consequences.

Once the team reaches consensus on your firm's strengths and areas for improvement, the team members prepare a presentation of findings by Baldrige category. The usual presentation explains what each category seeks and then reviews the top three to five strengths the assessors find and a like number of opportunities for improvement. If the assessors asked those they interviewed during the assessment to recommend improvement in the organization's management system, quotes from this "voice of the organization" help to bring assessment findings to life.

It is becoming more common for firms to train teams of senior managers to perform assessments. Solectron and other organizations have spoken about how their senior executives participate in assessments. With upper management involved in the assessment of each unit, less need arises for outside assessment expertise. Also, in Solectron's case, the assessment team makes prescriptive recommendations to the managers of the unit being assessed. The long experience of the assessment team members gives them the necessary understanding of the firm's business model to mandate adoption of those elements where the assessment finds gaps.

Preparation for the Feedback Briefing

It is never too early to begin thinking about how you will get results from the assessment. Planning for results usually begins with a short face-to-face meeting between the assessment team leader and the assessment sponsor before the detailed feedback briefing. During this meeting the assessment leader

- Previews the most important findings with the sponsor
- Works with the sponsor to strategize how to integrate the assessment findings with ongoing business or strategic planning
- Helps the sponsor focus on the vital actions that will maximize short- and long-term performance improvement
- Invites the sponsor to think about who should be involved in follow-up, including key middle managers in areas presenting major opportunities
- Forewarns the sponsor about the desirability of having an answer to the question: "What's in it for someone to take responsibility for, to champion or to work on follow-up tasks?"

Timing of feedback is also critical to results. When one assessment finished about a month after the company's annual off-site planning retreat, no follow-up on the assessment occurred for nearly a year; the feedback came too late for inclusion in the annual plan. Usually, the best time for a feedback presentation is a few weeks before the start of annual planning activities. The time between the feedback briefing and the annual planning cycle helps senior leaders overcome defensive objections.

Implementing a few vital actions to create one or two early successes generates positive word-of-mouth witness about the assessment and boosts follow-up momentum. Having some breathing space between feedback and planning lets your top management reflect on actions that will most strengthen the management system. This thought process often is very intuitive and creative, and is best done in a relaxed background mode over a few weeks, rather than under pressure in front of peers and subordinates.

Quality of follow-up counts more than quantity in achieving excellence. Organizations that pick the most vital 20 percent of their opportunities and actually complete them, progress much faster than those that try to act on all their opportunities but finish few. Focusing on the most vital chunks of follow-up action avoids squandering time and energy on local improvements that have little systemwide performance impact.

Now that you see how the typical organization coordinates assessment feedback with planning, we will observe a typical feedback session that sets the stage for the organization's leadership to decide who should do what.

The Feedback Briefing

Most assessment teams present their findings at the end of a site visit. Usually this happens in a two- or three-hour briefing to your site's managers and category owners, and ends the assessment. Often, assessment sponsors are interested in the team's opinions about what should be done ("prescriptions," in Baldrige terminology). If the team has prepared prescriptions, presenting them as requested adds greatly to the assessment. After the briefing your team members head for home or back to their offices. Typically, within two weeks of the site visit, your team provides a written report that expands upon the findings presented orally at the site visit's conclusion.

During the feedback briefing the assessment team spends about half an hour on each Baldrige category, presenting major strengths and areas to improve. The assessment team will undoubtedly list several dozen areas for improvement. This pace allows time to answer questions from the steering team about what each feedback comment really means. All organizational leaders need to be made aware that it is NOT necessary to act on all reported opportunities in order to dramatically improve performance. Only those gaps or areas for improvement that meet real and pressing needs in the business or that bottleneck organizational performance need immediate action.

At the end of the briefing, the sponsor usually thanks all who contributed to the assessment and outlines the next steps. Typically the sponsor assigns follow-up responsibilities by area and selects champions for each Baldrige category (leadership, strategic planning, customer and market focus, etc.). These champions and the sponsor will take ownership of the assessment findings of strengths and opportunities for improvement and bring them into the organization's strategic planning process. The sponsor usually asks designated champions to take responsibility for studying the written feedback report prior to the start of planning, and for presenting the major findings for consideration during planning.

Misinterpreting constructive criticism of a management system as personal criticism produces anger, defensiveness, even aggression—but does not promote change. This transition point between assessment feedback and follow-up action takes an intellectual and emotional breakthrough, as managers learn to separate how they feel about themselves from their feeling about their management system. Unfortunately this emotion is often misdirected because of confusion between an opportunity for improving a system and criticism or condemnation of the system's owners: Criticism of a management system is not criticism of a manager in that system. For follow-up to succeed, it must move beyond blaming and must stress understanding causes. The fact that a management system offers opportunities for improvement is something to celebrate; it does not automatically reflect badly on individuals. Although individual managers may change little over time, your management system is capable of great change and improvement.

Congratulations on Completing Your Assessment

In many organizations participation on an internal assessment team often is a significant professional accomplishment and opportunity for career advancement. Assessment team members meet and work with each other on an intense program whose sole purpose is to improve the performance of their whole organization. They have access to the top executives of the organization and they have the training and framework to look at the whole system and to ask insightful questions. What is more, the experience of synthesizing assessment data into an understanding of the whole management system is stimulating and instructive. Ultimately, assessment experience produces managerial insights that eventually benefit the assessment team's organization in many significant ways.

The final step in all assessments? Both assessors and the assessed organization summarize lessons learned and recommend improvements for future assessments. What then remains is for your organization to turn the assessment findings into actions that strengthen your management system.

Now that you have been introduced to several assessment formats and have read through a detailed scenario for an interview-based, level-2 assessment, please read on to find out how organizations follow up on assessment feedback. Chapter 11 outlines how the single assessment team leads to the formation of multiple, coordinated follow-up teams that enhance the management system and raise performance.

CHAPTER 11

From Assessment to Improvement

Since Solectron adopted the Baldrige Criteria, progress has come in a very accelerated fashion. Improvements are deployed much more efficiently as measured by recognition from our customers and bottom-line financial results.

—Ko Nishimura, President and CEO, Solectron Corporation

Understanding your opportunities for improvement and gaining insights into systems are worthless if you are unable to turn them into improved results. So it is appropriate to end this book by describing the most commonly used approach to getting results—organizing teams to take follow-up actions based on the results of the assessment. Not all organizations that perform assessments benefit, however. Many firms can find out what needs to change, but lack the resolve or the resources to make the needed improvements. Other firms work on improvement for a while, but slack off on their improvement efforts once their crisis ends.

Payoffs from assessment cover a wide range from no improvement at all to a steady progression of better results. The reasons for failure to generate results vary by organization—everything from tackling too much change too quickly, to fading commitment when results improve enough to solve the short-term performance problem. The successful organizations all combine improvements into projects they can handle with the time and resources allowed and *they get them done.* They make improving the management system into a core responsibility of managers. The successes follow a cycle of assess and follow-up. Repeating the cycle again and again builds discipline and accumulates improvements and lessons learned from the last cycle. Integrating follow-up with all other priorities is critical to long-run success. As mentioned in the previous chapter, fitting assessment into your organization's planning process is a key step toward integration.

Most organizations hold their strategic planning sessions off site, away from interruptions. Whatever the format and agenda, such planning sessions are usually facilitated by an in-house professional or outside consultant. At some point the participants will have defined their view of the future as a context, and worked out their major objectives and strategies to achieve them. This is the point in the planning process where improvements in the management system usually fit in.

STRATEGIC PLANNING SESSION

The planning session deals with assessment feedback as you would any other issue in planning. Participants seek to select the highest leverage areas of improvement for inclusion in the next year's list of priorities. If your current planning approach has a sound basis for setting priorities you may simply add assessment follow-up items to your other planning issues. If you want examples of how other firms integrate assessment follow-up items with strategic planning, the following examples work well.

The easiest improvements to implement in a management system are changes in things—for example, policies, procedures and systems that the assessment has found wanting. Learning how to succeed with these changes can usually be accomplished through investment and training. The slowest and most difficult changes in a management system usually involve changing individual behavior or organizational culture. These changes take a lot of feedback, coaching and hard work. Most assessment feedback will involve a mix of both easy and difficult opportunities for improvement. The ease or difficulty of implementation is important to the costs and benefits of acting on assessment findings.

When your assessment follow-up items relate directly to your strategies a facilitator may lead participants through a formal analysis (known as an interrelationship diagram). This tool shows clearly how assessment findings support or reinforce each of the organization's plans and strategies. The second tool that facilitators often use to help those involved in planning select initiatives is known as a prioritization matrix. Prioritization involves participants in ranking all opportunities for improvement from top to bottom, based on a combination of strategic impact and ease of implementation. Either exercise usually reveals that the most immediate items for follow-up are actions that will increase the flow of business, revenue, and profits.

Assessment follow-up initiatives often close gaps in your organization's golden cycle to expand revenue opportunities. (Increased revenue makes up for a multitude of sins.) If the golden cycle is sound, then high-leverage opportunities usually address needed improvements in one of the three supporting cycles. In fact, OMI, Inc., winner of the Baldrige award for 2000, requires that *every* improvement initiative it launches relates to at least one of four *strategic objectives*, one or more of the 150 *processes* that it has formally identified in its process model, one or more of the *measures* in its balanced score card, and to *a key customer requirement*. In this way OMI specifies the entire Plan, Do, Check, Act content of the golden cycle for each improvement initiative, a good model to follow.

By setting organization-wide priorities on the few vital assessment actions, you ensure maximum strategic impact for minimum expenditure of resources. Other actions—many of them beneficial—can safely wait until they restrict strategic success. Once they restrict your future success, you will naturally act on them. Now that you know that the assessment feedback must be integrated with organizational plans, we next look at the work of making changes to improve actual performance.

COACHING THE FOLLOW-UP EFFORT

To maintain momentum after the strategic planning session, executive follow-up champions must coach progress in one of the Baldrige categories. Collectively we will refer to all the follow-up champions as the business excellence team. Often this team is just the organization's executive committee, which becomes a de facto business excellence team by adding excellence follow-up items to every executive committee agenda and working those items consistently. Usually, a senior executive, for example the general manager, chairs the business excellence team personally and also champions follow-up action on leadership or strategic planning opportunities.

Each member of the business excellence team now becomes a coach of an action team responsible for one of the high-level action plans that came out of strategic planning. For example, an information systems executive on the business excellence team might be responsible for developing and deploying a balanced score card of leading indicators that aligns a balanced set of nonfinancial measures on people, processes and strategies with measures of financial results. Such a scorecard will give division management three months advance warning before upsets cause unfavorable financial results. Or a marketing executive may own a follow-up action to improve the response time in the customer-service function by enough to reduce attrition of customers due to service problems by 50 percent. The top operations executive may be champion for re-engineering strategic operational processes. Each member of the excellence team is personally responsible for some area of management system improvement that defines his or her coaching challenge.

Like you, most people in your organization are already so busy with their "day jobs" that they have very little time to take on major new initiatives. Members of the business excellence team must sell people on the need to get involved in pursuing "excellence." Of course sponsors such as the general manager have the authority to direct people to work on their top priorities. However, most sponsors choose to lead rather than direct, so they first try to sell their vision of a more excellent organization that generates high performance.

The best way to engage the organization in follow-up is to find people who like to do the necessary tasks, and who can do them well, and let them take responsibility for those tasks. You can do this by inviting the key people to plan implementation of follow-up objectives. The business excellence team may champion follow-up, however planning for implementation reaches out to assemble all the resource people needed to make planned improvements happen. For your key resource people to take follow-up responsibility, they must work out detailed tasks and project management ground rules they will follow to get the job done themselves.

If you are the sponsor, you need to consider the up- and downsides of involving people in follow-up implementation. The upside is the education, networking, skill building, visibility and recognition that participants in building a high performance organization gain personally from their involvement. The downside consists of lost enthusiasm, commitment, and hope if champions and follow-up teams falter on high priority action plans. Can there be any acceptable excuse for failing to invest just two days per month in making the organization a better place to do business, to work, to invest in, to sell to and to be a neighbor to? Firms that transform to high performance consider implementation commitments a serious job performance matter.

Coaching an excellence effort takes ideas from the best minds and diverse sources. Members of the business excellence team would do well to keep the following advice in mind:

- Search your soul to find the real reasons why people should trust your leadership. Teams follow coaches they respect and trust. When sponsors make a solid factual and emotional business case for change, they tend to connect emotionally to those they lead. Trustworthy leaders (who need not be people in positions of power) work for the good of the whole organization as a system, rather than solely for personal, selfish interest. Such leaders are not complete altruists; they realize that their personal success comes through the success of their organization. How many winning coaches have you heard of that coach chronically losing teams?

- Listen to audiotapes of business books and motivational speakers to gain greater understanding of improvement from other leaders. When you paraphrase books, magazine articles or comments from other leaders to kindle desire for improvement throughout the organization, you are leading. With good taste and judgment you can pick up ideas from other leaders that will help you nurture creative genius and steady purpose in those you lead.

- Use encouragement liberally to get team members to stretch what they believe to be their capabilities and help them to win. Coaching is a high-leverage activity for leaders. Because leadership behavior is on all the time, coaching does not displace other activities, and it gives corrective feedback and encouragement to novices as they use new skills.

- Use progress checks and reviews of progress to keep follow-up efforts on track. These meetings are opportunities to spotlight the vision, communicate successes, gauge progress and coach teams lagging behind plan. Spot checks also provide first hand insights into barriers slowing progress. Translate failures and mistakes into learning (just as a great teacher or coach does), so that the organization learns to anticipate, avoid and prevent future mistakes. Coaching also makes your leaders visible and provides them with direct observations on how well people understand and participate in making lasting improvement. This will help you solve another major problem— knowing who you can count on in the future to get things done.

- Keep assessment follow-up activities focused on overall direction and priorities. Hardworking follow-up teams often focus on their own goals and objectives and become isolated from other teams working in parallel. Link the several team efforts into harmony within the management system. Use progress reviews to seek opportunities to improve integration of follow-up action; constantly check if the left hand knows what the right hand is doing and where the left and right hands should work together. If you are a sponsor, one of your titles will be "chief problem solver" when your follow-up teams run into conflicts and barriers.

- Appreciate that changes are painful, so help people to understand where they are and where they need to be. People who care do not want to disappoint those they lead, which makes them worthier of trust.

Leaders that prove untrustworthy usually are those whose need for change arose from personal political ambitions, goals or objectives. As the politics change, or these people move to different positions, their commitments change, leaving those they lead feeling abandoned—if not cheated. It takes a year of hard work and patience to overcome the residue of organizational cynicism that a few months of poor leadership breeds. Focus your sponsorship around the organization's mission and its business issues, and your sponsorship will provide a trustworthy, enduring foundation, even if the personalities change.

The action plans resulting from strategic planning should identify what is to be done, which business excellence team member is the champion for follow-up and spell out major actions. The how-to level of tasks would be left up to a working level team to specify in detail. Now that you know what to work on and why (in terms of strategy) the next step is to select the right team for the job at hand.

Select Follow-up Team Members

Your improvement objective and its challenge should guide team member selection, not the other way around. If individual participants pick the team they want to work on, many will join teams that are best connected politically. So you find all the ambitious talent asking to join the leadership action team because the CEO is champion; or they join the customer and market focus team, because the CEO is on that team, implying that it is a good team to be on.

Selecting team members to work on an action plan must consider who has the expertise and skill and who wants to be on the team. Actually, if you are willing to coach intensively, it usually is best to pick high potential team members who do not have all of the ideal qualifications for higher responsibility. Select team members whose skills need polishing and development for further promotion. Cover gaps in team member skills through training and coaching. Each executive sponsor needs to negotiate team makeup with potential team members.

Working on a team is a tremendous educational opportunity and it usually provides opportunities for members to qualify for promotions to greater responsibility as a result of skills honed through team participation. Also, working on follow-up teams is a good way for candidates for promotion to attract the attention of senior executives. The best teams tend to be people who develop a dedication to the team objective. Select team members that are ambitious to learn, desire to become involved and who seek greater responsibilities. They also must be willing to become ambassadors for their team or its accomplishments, so they need good people and communications skills.

Individual team members bring differing functional skills, working styles and people skills relevant to the team's goal and areas of action. The issues of time commitment must be clear with participants' superiors so that each member can devote time willingly to the team effort. Some experts base team member selection on behavioral characteristics such as the Meyers-Briggs system. However, sponsor and team judgments about who has good people skills, work task completion habits, discipline and desire to learn and develop appear to be as effective a way to select team members as present psychological methods.

Team size is important in determining team success. Whatever its size, the team's mission will be to work together to design and implement a key opportunity to improve how your organization manages. Team sizes of four to six usually are best because they allow enough airtime for everyone to participate in discussions. (A two-hour meeting of twelve only allows ten minutes airtime for each participant.) However, larger teams are often necessary. In such cases members subdivide themselves into smaller subteams, each of which handles assigned tasks on behalf of the whole team. Meetings of the whole team then serve as a communication vehicle for communicating and integrating the subteam efforts into a whole. These whole team meetings also tend to exert peer pressure on subteams to complete their task assignments.

Successful team leaders use peer pressure to motivate members to keep their time, effort and quality commitments to the other team members. Dale Crownover of Texas Nameplate tells of a tradition that arose in his firm when a team member tries to give an alibi or make an excuse for letting the team down on some task. The first person on the team who hears the alibi coming starts a chant, "Alligator, alligator, alligator . . ." which the other team members pick up and chant loudly in unison until the excuse making stops. Needless to say, people keep their team commitments at Texas Nameplate rather than be embarrassed by alligators.

Overlapping membership on teams also helps to coordinate separate teams as they make progress. So, a minority of participants may serve on two or more teams. The overlap in membership helps ensure that each team understands what others are doing beyond linkages that the business excellence team itself can make.

The final step in selecting the team is to arrange for training any members who may need upgraded skills to succeed. If you are the team sponsor you need to ensure that your team leader has proper training in project management, and that all members have been trained in interviewing, listening and problem solving. The team usually begins by analyzing the opportunity for improvement from the assessment and the plan of action. After identifying the gap and agreeing on its implications for performance, the team performs a formal root-cause analysis to determine why this management system gap exists. This analysis usually involves brainstorming the gap's causes and using a tool known as an affinity diagram to organize the causes identified. At this point, the team may survey members of your firm and gather data to verify its root-cause analysis. Much of the routine work of the team consists of brainstorming and organizing information, performing analyses of data, and mapping out processes as they should be. It is also very helpful for both leader and team members to be trained in team methods and tools such as process mapping, brainstorming, root-cause analysis, prioritization, nominal group technique, action planning and project management. Some Baldrige winning firms have sent large numbers of team members to Dale Carnegie training. The point is that you cannot just pull together a group of people and expect something to happen by magic; sponsors frequently need training in the communication skills they need to guide and coach teams.

Sponsors who go through training with their teams show enthusiasm and commitment to the teams' success and get a chance to see their colleagues in action during the training. At a minimum, team leaders and most team members must train on the high performance business model. A solid training program in process improvement is the next step beyond the minimum. They need to understand what the whole management systems looks like and how it works. They also need to understand your organization's strategy—"how we plan to win this business race we have entered."

In addition to members of the business excellence team, having follow-up team leaders who participated during strategic planning helps provide focus on how opportunities for improvement relate to overall strategy. Such team leaders may be asked to provide background briefings on what has gone on before the follow-up team formed.

Kickoff Session

After you (as champion or sponsor) pick an initial team, you bring four to ten people from all levels into a room. The first time everyone—sponsor and team members—gets together in the same room (perhaps with a few attending by speaker phone) is referred to as the kickoff meeting. The team's kickoff meeting includes background briefings for members unfamiliar with the assessment and its feedback. The team and sponsor also discuss how this team's assignment or project fits into longer-term priorities. The sponsor ideally will have provided training for all team members in the business excellence model, or it should be scheduled during this kickoff session. The sponsor may also arrange for a presentation of the full assessment feedback findings to the team members as well as background on what priorities for follow-up emerged from the strategic planning sessions. It helps if everyone on the team understands the full scope of improvements needed by the management system. The more they know, the more effective they will be as work progresses.

Also during the kickoff session, the executive sponsor may designate one member of the team as a leader if no one was designated previously. Usually the team leader is a person the sponsor can rely on, as well as having good project management and team leadership experience. An assessment follow-up team is not an opportunity to ask someone to lead his or her first team project. The leader usually will be a forward-thinker who can stay several steps ahead of the team he or she leads. The leader also needs the emotional sensitivity to keep in touch with individual members' feelings and attitudes.

The team leader's most important function is to return the team to a focus on its goals when it wanders; the second most important function is to make the team effort fun, productive and to maintain involvement. People will soon drop off a team if they feel that the team wastes their time or disrespects their contribution or point of view. At the first session, the team leaders usually will ask their teams to draft a written charter. A charter is a memorandum or e-mail that states what the team will work on, when it will meet, and what rules of conduct it will follow, general milestones and goals, timeframe, membership and responsibilities.

In addition to the sponsor, a facilitator may also support the team leader in carrying out the follow-up project. A facilitator helps the team do its work, without injecting him or herself into the task. Facilitators tend to be experienced team leaders, and they usually stay in the background, intervening only when teams are going off the track or making preventable errors. A good facilitator will have expertise on the team process, tools used, and analysis of data necessary to develop high performance business approaches, but will never usurp the role of the team leader. One way to check on a facilitator's effectiveness is to have team members periodically evaluate one another's (and the facilitator's) performance. A facilitator helps strengthen your team by keeping it focused. Eventually as a team and its leader gain skill their need for facilitation dwindles.

Now that the team is selected, trained, oriented and chartered for the particular action plan they will work on, the real work begins.

How a Typical Team Works

To begin, team members work out the opportunity for improvement, the business case for working on it, and then develop their plan. Each team outlines its own project plan—a roadmap and timetable that maps the steps, how long each will take and members' task assignments. To anticipate—and, if possible, avoid—problems, teams may rate each planned step's difficulty on a 0 to 9 scale. Breaking the difficult tasks down into simpler tasks eliminates all really difficult tasks and increases the likelihood of success. The most common form of team plan is a simple Gantt chart or time line, which graphs when each task starts and stops. As the team checks this time line every meeting or two, it reminds them of what they have done, and what they still have to do. This checking builds a feeling of accomplishment, but also focuses them on what they have yet to accomplish.

Once a team has its time line and plan, it reviews this roadmap with its sponsor or follow-up champion, laying the groundwork for team accountability. Usually the content of the plan follows an improvement or problem-solving approach that the team has been trained to follow. Once the sponsor agrees to the team's plan, each meeting usually follows an agenda drawn up at the end of the previous team session. Although team members propose added agenda items as they go, the team's project plan and improvement approach dictate most of the tasks. The team leader's responsibility is to ensure that no team meeting ever wastes team members' time. Once team members realize that they have more important things to do back on their desk than they are doing in the team session, morale, attendance and performance all become problems.

Teams combine different points of view; the team leader should encourage team members to ignore organizational rank and rely instead on members' expertise and willingness to work on team goals. As the team works along, it may need a small internal infrastructure for documentation. One team member may take on the role of team scribe and another the task of meeting timekeeper. Many teams rotate these roles among team members on some equitable basis. The scribe or note-taker records work done in each session, records who agreed to take responsibility for which tasks, picks up documents, charts, and diagrams the team produces, and writes a report, usually by e-mail, a few days after each meeting. Some firms prefer to have team facilitators be the official note-takers. Either way works.

The role of meeting timekeeper helps the team leader keep things on track by reminding team members and the leader of the agenda. Usually the team leader involves the team in setting its next agenda at the end of each meeting. During the meeting, the timekeeper watches the clock and warns the team when it is running over its allotted time for an agenda item. Team member accountability directly impacts efficient use of team time. Team members who are responsible for bringing data or presenting some work product to the team but who do not do their work, waste the time of all team members. Peer pressure to keep members and the leader accountable is critical. A team leader who can generate peer pressure and maintain team member accountability (usually with an iron hand in a velvet glove) is worth her weight in gold and then some.

Teams borrow, learn from and share approaches both from inside and from outside your firm. Many teams may charter a subteam to benchmark or study how leading firms address a system need. The idea is to identify the underlying factors (often referred to as drivers) that a sound management system includes. The idea of benchmarking is not so much to copy best practice from elsewhere, but to understand why the best practice gets great results in an effort to use that knowledge on the team's own problem. Benchmarks from literature searches, vendor contacts and referrals and from visits to outstanding firms can greatly accelerate a team's progress toward its goal, and increase confidence that the team will arrive at a workable solution.

Nearly every team needs outside help at one time or another. Guests, consultants, subject-matter experts, or visitors from customers and supplier partners fill these needs. When the need for an expert is identified early in a team project—for example, an information-systems specialist or a market researcher—inviting such a resource person to the team's initial few meetings is a good idea; then, as the team needs their help, the expert understands its purpose and has a higher comfort level with its meetings. Occasionally resource people invited to provide input for a meeting or two wind up becoming full team members.

Facilitators usually coach several teams, and carry lessons from one to another. Some firms keep a central archive of team-meeting minutes and reports, providing a basis for learning. More often, however, the team scribe keeps the records locally. As a firm gets more sophisticated in its use of teams it usually creates a process in which the facilitator polls team members after completed efforts, or runs a post–project review session to find ways to improve future team efforts. Often executive sponsors will poll teams on lessons learned at the end of their project. Some such executives actually develop personal process steps for ensuring team success.

Once in full operation, teams tend to work in relative isolation. Using data and cause-and-effect analyses is time-consuming, but vitally important. To offset the tendency for team members to overfocus and become isolated from members of other teams, they periodically present their work-in-progress to each other. Such cross presentations ensure that their separate efforts link into an effective system in which the whole exceeds the sum of its parts. For example, a team designing a balanced scorecard measurement system, upon hearing another team present a proposed performance appraisal system, suddenly realizes that the metrics used in performance appraisals must coordinate with its balanced scorecard. Unless the two teams work out how to coordinate their efforts, neither team will obtain its desired improvement. This cross-fertilization of team efforts is very important, it provides feedback to each team presenting and ensures that various follow-up actions will fit together and enhance the management system, rather than simply graft isolated patches on to a tired old system.

Reviewing Progress and Problems

If you are team sponsor, be aware that your behavior affects its morale and work effort. Employee teams usually involve members most willing to work to make your business better. To show that the team is important, send memos announcing its formation; state your support; host the first meeting and highlight the team's objectives and your expectations. As work progresses, give invitations to attend team meetings high priority and stay in touch with progress but avoid "managing the team." If as sponsor, you do not wish to read detailed team meeting minutes, have the team leader brief you informally on progress and problems.

Most sponsors meet monthly with their teams or their team leaders as representatives of the whole teams. In sum, as sponsor, you are on the hook to keep the team focused on its goal, to check that they are following their own roadmap, to help them with problems when they get off the road at the wrong exit, and to encourage the team to drive on to results. Do not accept alibis and excuses, but maintain the team's accountability. Periodically checking the team's progress against plan lets you as sponsor or champion spot mission drift, scope creep or other problems in time for you to act to keep the team on track.

The team's detailed project plan also helps the team leader and champion ensure that members keep their team commitments. Champions often ask the team leader or facilitator to track meeting attendance and report weekly on status or completion of assigned tasks. This information gives the champion routine feedback and helps deal with the accountability issue; it may suggest how the champion can help the team be more effective and highlight who is and who is not working on agreed responsibilities.

Meeting with teams that you champion also gives you an early indication of what changes, improvements, or remedies your team may be identifying. Give the team feedback based on your expectations and its progress. Involve employee teams in deciding what additional training is needed for future teams. Ask teams themselves to recommend specific ways to engage other employees in improvement. Make team progress visible through bulletin boards, displays of work products, or broadcast e-mails to lists of interested people throughout the organization. Provide a mechanism for teams to share their experiences, so struggling teams learn from more effective teams. Provide facilitators to help teams use tools and gain skill in improvement approaches, but carefully define their roles.

Major team projects vary in duration from sixteen weeks to a year or more. Soon your team will arrive at the point where it wants to make some change in the way the organization works.

Pilot Test of Change

Common sense dictates that you insist on a pilot test of all process or management systems changes to see how they fit with normal operations and the rest of the management system. Ideally the pilot test will confirm that the planned changes benefit all stakeholders and meet their requirements and those of the organization. However, the purpose of any pilot is to learn, even if what you learn is that the planned change has undesirable side effects that call for more work. Pilot testing helps determine if everyone wins. If there are rough edges, or portions of the proposed change do not address management system or stakeholder requirements, there will still be time and resources left to improve on the pilot before deploying it further.

Once a pilot of some new approach succeeds, the team homes in on its final changes to the management system. It usually prepares action plans to deploy the new methods and approaches to all relevant areas. The team's action plans describe the change, its impact, why it is necessary, who is responsible and who must buy in or commit to making it happen. At this point many sponsors ask teams for reality checks on their plans. These reality checks can be based on benchmarks from elsewhere or on results from the pilot tests of new approaches. Sometimes, reality checks show before and after result projections to highlight the benefits of change. Reality checking helps to link improvements to results measurements. Usually, at this time, the team shifts into project-management mode; some of its members may continue to expand a successful pilot into full deployment while watching for evidence of improved results.

Participation in a successful team can be its own reward, but tangible benefits often arise. It is not unusual for most members of successful teams to be promoted to greater responsibilities within a year of serving on such a team. Working on teams also helps individual members build leadership skills, sharpen their abilities to manage change, and construct linkages throughout your organization. Relying on follow-up teams can kill two birds with one stone: you can use teams to develop people and a stronger organization, as well as to build a more effective management system.

SUSTAINING THE ORGANIZATIONAL CHANGE

The first rule in sustaining the organizational change is to be patient. Except for the rare exception, such as a startup like AT&T's former Universal Card organization, transforming an organization to sustained performance excellence happens over three or four years, not five or six months. Some business leaders want fast change because they need fast results. When it comes to people, this attitude spells trouble. Force-feeding change—rather than involving people in making changes—causes resistance; the harder you push change, the greater the resistance and push-back. Permanent, companywide change takes several years of adjustment as people come to terms with new approaches in your firm's management system and learn to operate at a higher level of performance.

Responding to assessment feedback requires learning and growth at two levels—your whole organization and your individual stakeholders. The organizational view of change considers the change strategy itself: what actions must the organization take to increase the maturity of its management system? The second level considers individual reactions to change—from why they should change to helping them get through the change to play significant roles in a better organization. Here is a vivid example of how such change alters your peoples' ways of thinking and working.

A Baldrige videotape once featured an employee of an award-winning firm talking personally about the transformation to a high performance company. He told how he used to come into work to do his job. In a tone of voice that grew increasingly enthusiastic, this factory worker reminisced that through training and coaching he gradually began to understand quality, that he learned how he had a customer—the next person who worked on what he had just completed. He explained that now an important part of his job was to improve how he related to his customer, which let him do a better job for his customer while making his own job better at the same time. He ended on the idea that now quality was a part of everything he did at work. Eventually, your whole organization learns new ways to relate, work, and make decisions. But it takes time.

How Individuals React to Change

The noted management psychiatrist Barry Greiff says that except for a minority who experience change as a stimulating experience, most people face change with a wide variety of feelings: loss, ambiguity, uncertainty and fear. Understanding this individual response to change helps you coach people through the loss that change causes. When an organizationwide change occurs, as people learn about the change their attitudes toward the change may be thought of as forming a bell-shaped curve along a hypothetical scale measuring resistance to change. At one end of the scale about 15 percent of the people fall in the tail of the bell shape that is most prochange. They welcome change and embrace it with no feeling of loss. At the other extreme on the scale, about 15 percent of the people fall in the opposite tail of the bell shape because they experience extremely painful losses from the change, so they will ask "Why, why, why" and push back against it. Most people's reaction to major change lies somewhere between the prochange and antichange tails of the bell-shaped curve. In the middle ground some fall on the pro side of change, an equal number fall on the antiside of change and the bulk fall right in the middle –neither "pro" nor "anti;" they will wait and see.

Each of the five groups has different needs and roles in making the change to high performance. The 15 percent or so at the extreme in welcoming change never saw a change they did not like. They are the change-makers, the leaders and the innovators who welcome the new when it looks better than the old. These people like change and innovation, and they will teach and coach those who are interested into accepting and mastering what is new. These "early adopters" only get into trouble if the new situation turns out to make people worse off than did the old—a circumstance that should not occur as your firm builds an excellent management system. (You, the readers of this book, are most likely in this 15 percent.)

The largest segment contains people with attitudes toward change somewhere in the middle. How they work through change depends on the examples and the influence of the innovators. Helping these middle-grounders to change, especially those who are nearer the antichange end of the distribution, will take coaching from your firm's innovators and leaders (the ones who make the change first). The last group, the extreme antichange group, may never make the transition and nonthreatening provisions will need to be made for them.

For change to succeed, your people must overcome their loss through a process like grieving—the downside of change. Individual employees experience not just different amounts of loss, but also different stages of grieving to overcome their losses. Those who feel little loss readily move through their feelings to accept new ways. Those who feel changes as immense losses may need help working through their feelings. You and other leaders acknowledge honestly that change involves some pain, and you articulate a vision that makes change worth the pain. You also listen to people's problems, working on underlying concerns and emotions as your firm transforms its management system.

The Organizational Reaction to Change

In parallel with the personal changes people undergo, the organizational level of change usually considers cultural and behavioral issues. Your organization's senior managers are in the best position to promote an organizational climate that is not toxic to improvement and innovation. In some organizations, a culture that favors and enables cross-functional action on important opportunities sometimes seems beyond mortal means, but with conspicuous and sustained leadership effort it can be a certainty.

At the cultural level, the issue is to identify how senior management behaviors must change to raise your firm's management-system maturity to high performance levels. As follow-up progresses you need to take stock of the behaviors and cultural rules that stimulate success and encourage them. Your overall concern at this level is to create a climate that reduces resistance to change—one that reinforces and recognizes even small steps in the right direction. Such a climate weakens attraction to the old ways and strengthens the appeal of the new.

Human resource practices such as measurement, reward, recognition, succession planning, employee-selection, training and planning approaches all must unfold and evolve as a system to re-inforce high performance values and behaviors. Creating a bias toward leadership in human resource practices takes time, especially in organizations that have previously favored those who resist change.

Leading change at the organizational level takes attention to changing management behavior. Of course, your firm has to balance these changes against the daily operational needs of running the business. Is the amount of change affecting your people adversely? Check it out, regularly, so you know factually the benefits of changes being made. Feedback can include data-gathering from performance reviews, all-hands meetings, informal surveys, employees' town hall meetings, employees' focus groups and the like. Human resource practices are among the most important areas for learning and improvement within the capability-development cycle.

Feedback can be very helpful in changing top management behavior. AT&T Universal Card had an observer sit in on all major management meetings and give feedback at the end of the meeting on how well the decisions and actions during the meeting upheld the company's high performance values. After a few months, management behavior and decisions were consistent with the high performance values they talked about. One Baldrige award-winning leader observed that for every top-down communication channel promoting change, he needed three bottom-up feedback channels telling him how change was coming along.

Two rules will help you get honest feedback to sustain the transformation to high performance: "Don't criticize the messenger when you don't like the message." Another, slightly more general rule is closely related to it: "Find cause, not fault." Firms with fault-finding cultures that have turned in ten years of marginal performance can be turned into stellar performers in just a year or two when a new management team switches the emphasis to finding and eliminating causes of problems. Once people know they are not going to be blamed for things that go wrong, they become more willing to discuss what is going wrong, and why. Once you understand in concrete terms what the root causes are, you can do something to remove the problems permanently.

Respecting and managing time commitments is another important aspect of the successful transformation to high performance. Senior people in some organizational cultures get so impatient for quick results that they show little respect for people's time. Carried too far, this breeds a climate in which no one has any time to take on new tasks. Higher-ups dump follow-up tasks onto overloaded middle managers; these "dumpees" cannot possibly finish everything dumped on them, so they second guess their superiors, do what they want to, and ignore tasks that do not have painful consequences if left undone. Politics determine what gets done in such a culture. Unless the politics of sticking with the status quo look forbidding, the safest course is to ignore follow-up responsibilities with explanations like, "We are too busy." Highly motivated, task-oriented people tend to leave such impossible environments—and this attrition weakens firms that do not respect people's time.

CHANGE BEFORE YOU HAVE TO—AND PERSIST

The advice to begin transforming your organization to high performance before some competitor or new development forces it on you is easy to give but very hard for most organizations to follow. When business is good, there is little time and even less motivation to begin learning and changing. However, waiting until business is bad and your organization is forced to change is a riskier strategy. It makes you try to force-feed change, rather than letting your people be participants; it invites resistance. Setting up an assessment and follow-up routine also takes time, which gives people time to adjust to changes if you start before you are forced to.

In the author's experience, most firms run one or two assessments and then slip back into business-as-usual mode when results improve. These organizations survive, prosper to an extent, but never excel. As your organization executes its action plans and actually gets results, it may build the process of assessment and follow up into its planning and management cycles. Some firms like Solectron run their assessments every two years; others run them when they complete all of the follow-up actions from the last cycle.

Experience suggests that small to medium-sized firms benefit from assessing their management systems every year; larger or more complex organizations are safe in assessing every other year. The rule on how often to assess is to do it as often as you must to keep your pursuit of excellence going. The cycle's purpose? To expand the wealth-creating capability of your whole business by balancing opportunity, strategy, motivation, capability and risk with return.

It takes several cycles of assessment and follow-up to get your golden cycle in high gear and to mesh with the three supporting cycles. Each success helps your firm recognize barriers. Then, your next cycle removes or overcomes some of these roadblocks, inconsistencies and clashes in rewards, priorities and cultural values. The result? High performance. Here are some words of practical wisdom on trading in worn out ideas about change for new ideas that work.

Good Advice About Making Change

Professor Jeffrey Goldstein of Adelphi University says that businesses are using nineteenth-century theories to make twenty-first-century changes. Goldstein has identified four old ideas that need to be exchanged for new ones to manage change making.

First old idea: Change has to be driven from the top down in your organization. Pressure a system to change, and it changes. Goldstein says that pressure from top managers raises lower-level resistance to the change. Instead, he advises setting up spontaneous, self-directed processes that evolve change from within. Provide change agents who guide, teach and support the process, but don't pressure people to change. The management team that sponsors your assessment can split up into multiple follow-up teams; each follow-up team takes responsibility for implementing improvements in one management system category or across categories to strengthen one of the four cycles. The team members listen to those in the areas where change is needed. Then, they search for approaches that address the gap or opportunity for improvement. By involving those most directly affected by change, your firm can enlist their help in keeping the change on track. Tailor each follow-up action resulting from an assessment to also meet real needs of the people on the scene.

Second old idea: You need an accurate assessment of where you are now, a big emphasis on anticipating what will go wrong, and detailed plans to prevent it. Instead, Goldstein insists that detailed planning is only a start. He advises letting go of plans early in the change process as long as you stay clear on the objective; seize opportunities that turn up as your business implements plans. Instead of rigid adherence to plans, he advises managers to gather lots of data on how things are going. When unexpected events and random accidents point in the desired direction, build these serendipitous events into your program. Happenings during a change program can produce unplanned experiments. Ignore those that work out poorly and fit the good ones into your firm's change effort.

Third old idea: Anticipate resistance to change (since no one likes change) and become adept at overcoming such resistance. Instead, Goldstein advises managers to view resistance to change as an attraction to something that people consider important. In a coercive environment, resistance to change may simply be an attraction to old ways that let people keep their personal dignity intact. He advises using this attraction to generate change. Understand what the people in your organization really feel is important, and then redesign the needed change to raise and reinforce their dignity. When the process of transforming company performance leads to greater job satisfaction and joy in work, resistance to change dissolves.

Fourth old idea: Organizations need to define their purpose and spell out formal roles and responsibilities to fulfill that purpose. In its place, Goldstein advises that organized work groups should have feedback loops to reshape roles and responsibilities from the inside. He advises giving people training in creativity and information gathering, so they can find better ways to reorganize their work. When people standing around the water cooler organize spontaneously for some purpose, others don't want to be left out so they naturally join in. Enthusiasm and desire to accomplish things attracts people, puts them in a cooperative frame of mind, and brings them into the change process. Goldstein tells businesses to tap this natural, spontaneous urge to get things done, instead of overreacting to spontaneous events or accidents as though you are losing control. He says to set boundaries and objectives to guide the change process and then let your groups reorganize spontaneously around what they learn.

THE BOTTOM LINE

This book's main purpose is to help you look at your own business as a system so that you can improve it for the benefit of all who have a stake in it. Anyone knows that to improve a system you must understand how each part works in the context of the whole; this takes a thinking process known as synthesis. Improving parts in isolation, no matter how much they need improvement, wastes resources if system bottlenecks remain.

At this point, the task of building a high performance management system may seem overwhelming to you; the next step of assessing your organization's management system and then following up may also seem daunting. Where do you begin? Begin with your organization's mission, and aspirations for where it wants to be in the future. Then, gather support for assessing your firm's relative strengths and areas for improvement against a world class standard—the widely accepted Baldrige model.

Begin to familiarize those around you with the Baldrige model. Show how it links seven areas of management—called categories— into a whole-business model or system. You may find it easier to explain the roles of the categories within the management system in terms of Stankard's Baldrige bicycle (see the appendix):

- The *strategic triad* of the Baldrige system model, categories 1. leadership, 2. strategic planning, and 3. customer focus, steers the organization to innovate and capture market opportunities that create profits and wealth
- The result triad of the system model serves as the power source. Categories 5. human resource management, 6. process management and 7. business results represent the people and operating aspects of the business, its costs and its capabilities
- The alignment subsystem, categories 2. strategic planning and 4. information and analysis, provides *direction and power alignment* to ensure proper performance of the whole organization.

Begin thinking in terms of ever improving versions of your management system beginning with whatever you have now. Your as-is management system can be called Version Zero. In a year or two after your first assessment, you can have a Version 1.0 management system with a full golden cycle. In short form, a minimal golden cycle would probably consist of:

- Strategic planning—focused on revenue-producing market opportunities—defines a set of strategies, a balanced set of objectives, goals and measurements, and action plans.

- Action teams that take scorecard goals from planning and carry out action plans for strategically important improvement in products, processes and your organization's management system. These in turn lead to reviews.

- Systematic listening to market and customer reactions, which provides learning on how well your improvements worked out, as well as revealing further opportunities to increase customer value and cut cost. In addition, reviews of scorecard measures align units around critical steps on the way to overall objectives.

- Finally, the golden cycle closes on itself with careful review of lessons learned in the past year to kick off next year's PDCA golden cycle.

To build this Version 1.0 management system, link new approaches with existing methods and practices that already work for your organization. Sticking with what works (even though it could be improved) minimizes disruption and speeds up achieving a full cycle and management system as quickly as possible. After one or two years you will feel the time is right for another assessment. Call the management system at the time of your second assessment Version 1.0. Your second assessment will set the stage for system improvements that will result in your Version 2.0 management system. Eventually, you will find that you must progress in some or all of the other three cycles to sustain overall improvement. Guide changes in your management methods by assessing them periodically against the Baldrige model and acting on the high leverage opportunities for improvement.

Gradually, through follow-up, learning and innovation you will evolve a more effective management system; with effort this management system will improve business results dramatically. Another advantage of thinking about your management system in terms of versions is that you get out of static thinking and create an expectation of steady progress toward newer, better, more integrated, higher performing management systems as time goes by. Remember, even Microsoft seems to need three versions to succeed with something new.

Like the song lyric about how a night in Bangkok makes a hard man humble, assessment takes self-confidence and humility. Many firms begin out of stark terror at the prospect of failing—but many of these quit when the peril disappears. Jim Collins refers to leaders able to transform a company as "level-5 leaders" (Collins 2001). Their careers represent "a triumph of humility and fierce resolve." That is what it takes in most cases where there is no terror, no burning platform.

Only steady leadership (fierce resolve) can create high performance in your business by focusing people on improving the system for satisfying customers and developing markets profitably. Your system of organizational values organizes all of the methods, approaches and actions within your firm into a management system. You and your organization's other leaders move your firm by your vision and observable behaviors that consistently show— rather than tell—what you truly consider important. Over the years of the Baldrige program, experience has shown that the highest performing firms in the world share eleven high performance organizational values that lead to extraordinary performance. Leaders who adopt and embody those values are the leaders of organizations in which they can take pride.

Your firm can use the Baldrige model as a system template to embark on "virtuous" cycles of learning and improvement that cause *durable* high performance, gauged by growth in market share, shareholder return and employment. The golden cycle of wealth creation focuses activities throughout your whole firm to innovate customer-satisfying products and processes that create wealth. The golden cycle also provides a framework that seamlessly integrates three supporting virtuous cycles: leadership and planning, capability-development, and risk and return. These powerful cycles define your firm's fundamental path to enduring high performance.

As your firm sets out to build a management system to excel, you can use the *Baldrige Criteria* to base that design on principles of world-class management:

- Powerful individual and organizational values
- Expanded opportunities to create wealth by delivering more customer value for less resources
- Deep insight into what makes the organization's people behave as they do
- Significant understanding of how the parts of a system work as a whole pursuing a common purpose—innovating ways to raise customer satisfaction

Make assessment a regular part of your overall business management system, and include feedback from each assessment on your firm's planning and action agenda. Remember, you want next year's version of your management system to be improved in ways that give you the most leverage in meeting near-term objectives and goals. But, you also want the changes to be a lasting part of a system that ensures a golden future.

When your organization understands itself as a system and improves that system, it will outperform the averages, shifting to a new, higher level of wealth-producing capability based on profound new knowledge it learns for itself. It competes on excellence and innovation, rather than on penny pinching, small-time tricks, and also-ran tactics. Having a management system that strives to go beyond merely satisfying customers generates wealth: Your business can be one of the firms that excel through stellar high performance and you can be a leader of this transformation. Get out in front and spread the word.

Appendix:
Stankard's Baldrige
Bicycle Analogy

We can draw only very weak inferences (if any) by analogy.
. . . In analogy we know only that two situations have certain
properties in common; we know nothing abut the correspon-
dence of the structure of the two situations.

—Russell L. Ackoff, *Scientific Method*

This appendix reduces many of the implications of high performance management systems and businesses to common sense that
you can understand in a few minutes. If you rode a bicycle as a
child, you already have an intuitive understanding of the most basic operating principles of complex, multi-loop, dynamic feedback
control systems. That may sound complicated, but the realities are
not complex. In the next fifteen minutes you will see how to translate your understanding of bicycles into powerful insights into business improvement—as long as you look at your business as a whole
and understand it as a system.

A management system that satisfies the *Baldrige Criteria for Performance Excellence* puts a company ahead in the race for markets

and customers. The trick to understanding this clearly is to think of the Baldrige system flow chart in Figure A.1 as though it were a two-wheel bicycle. Figure A.1 overlays a bicycle moving from *right to left* on the system diagram. Just as a bicycle multiplies how far you can travel by 500 percent or more relative to walking, management systems of Baldrige-winning firms generate wealth at three to four to five times the rate of the Standard & Poor's 500 large capitalization firms.

A BICYCLE AS A HIGH PERFORMANCE SYSTEM

Chapter 2 explained the strategic and result triads and alignment subsystems of the Baldrige high performance model. This appendix creates a parallel between these subsystems by analogy to the three subsystems of a bicycle. Each main subsystem of a bicycle maps neatly to the Baldrige framework and makes its operation easier to understand as a system.

Front Wheel: Strategic Management Triad. In the Baldrige bicycle shown in Figure A.1, the front wheel on the left points in the direction of future profit opportunity (shown by the large, left-pointing arrow). It represents your choices about how your organization will create wealth, and whom you want to have as your customers. The bicycle front wheel overlaps the strategic triad, a triangle formed by the three categories on the left side of the diagram: 1. leadership, 2. strategic planning, and 3. customer and market focus. Next comes the Result Triad at the right-hand side of Figure A.1.

Successful organizations must choose long-term directions and gain long-term competitive advantage. Choosing this direction is like picking a bicycle race to enter, based on the size of the prize, how good you are, how tough the course is and how strong the likely competition will be. Once in the race, the front wheel and handlebars of the bicycle let the rider choose a destination and steer toward the objective; steering represents strategic choices. As the race progresses, the front wheel, handlebars and rider form a continuous feedback cycle for guiding the system in the planned direction and avoiding obstacles along the way. When the destination is out of sight, the rider must have a road map or route along which to ride; the business's roadmap is its strategic plan.

Figure A.1
Stankard's Baldrige Bicycle (Traveling Left)

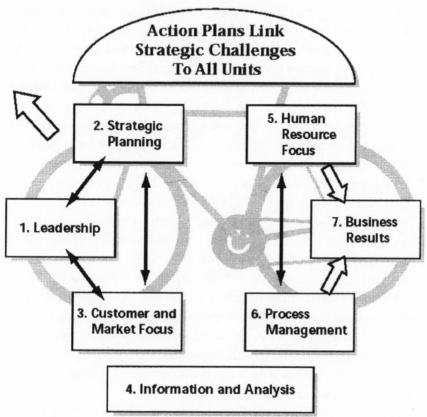

Rear Wheel: The Power Source. A bicycle's back wheel and the rider's legs set up a feedback loop that propels the bicycle forward. If the bicycle goes too slowly, the rider pumps harder; if it goes too fast, the rider pumps more slowly or less forcefully and applies the brakes. In business, cash flow and profits from producing and selling products and services push the business forward and fund investments. Similarly, in the Baldrige bicycle framework shown in Figure A.1, the rear wheel overlaps the three Baldrige categories that drive your business forward: 5. human resource focus, 6. process management, and 7. business results. These categories form the motive power, delivering goods and services every day to incur expenses and generate income and profits that fund investments to propel your business toward its strategic objectives.

The Frame: Aligning Direction and Power. The bicycle frame aligns future strategic direction and opportunities with ongoing results and cash flow. Two companywide elements in a business management system perform corresponding alignment functions: (1) deploying strategies and action plans to meet the firm's challenges and (2) relying on information and analysis for checking plans, setting priorities and guiding decisions. These functions link and align the strategic (front) and operational (back) parts of your business into a management system that turns in excellent performance. Strong organizational values and a shared mission are important elements in creating structural integrity in an organization.

Stakeholders who depend on your organization ride the Baldrige bicycle; like the rider in a race, they all gain something from winning and are worse off when a competitor wins. Your customers are important stakeholders as are those who supply the raw materials, capital, managerial know-how, labor, innovation and creativity that drive your enterprise. Of these, the workforce has the largest stake in overall success of the business (they usually suffer most if the business fails). Still other stakeholders provide the environment and the community within which the business operates, and also have a stake in its performance.

The essential difference between the mechanical bicycle and your organization as a system is that parts of a bicycle have no purpose of their own—they merely function. Parts of an organization —individuals, work units, teams, and even whole companies—all have their own purpose. Each part of the social system can learn many functions; it can develop its own capability. Any part of a social system can even alter its purpose. Your organization consists of people with diverse skills, experiences, attitudes, personal missions and idiosyncrasies—a management system builds on these uniquely human characteristics of social systems. High performance emerges from the uniquely human elements of learning, invention, competition, cooperation, communication and motivation that a management system harnesses in pursuit of its mission.

IMPLICATIONS

The following implications of the bicycle analogy will help you think about your business and its management system and clarify what actions will improve its effectiveness. The points below follow the five conditions outlined in Chapter 1 that Russell Ackoff identified as defining a system (Ackoff 1994).

1. *The whole system serves a purpose or mission.* An eighteenth century challenge by a French mathematician to develop a human-powered device that would increase personal mobility led to the earliest bicycles. A modern bicycle increases mobility over walking by more than 500 percent. The high performance model of Baldrige yields a business designed to outperform competitors.

1a. *A change in a social system's purpose or mission changes its elements and how they work together.* The choice of what to include in a system depends on its mission or purpose. Consider three different bicycle situations:

   • *Improve mobility*: Each part of the bicycle is designed to optimize human-powered mobility.

   • *Race*: When the purpose of a bicycle is to win a race, every part of the bicycle, as well as the rider's athletic conditioning and training, is designed to gain the greatest competitive advantage.

   • *Biking vacation in Vermont*: For a biking vacation, bicycle, conditioning, traveling companions, route, choices of inns and sights to see all form a system designed to provide a relaxing, enjoyable vacation.

   The boundaries of your business also depend on its mission or purpose. For example, if the only purpose of a firm is to generate profits for shareholders, customers are not part of the system (business). However, if the business purpose is to build lasting and satisfying customer relationships, customers are an integral part of the system (business). The choice of purpose impacts your business's long-term performance; including customers in how a business works helps both business and its customers do well.

1b. *Making missions attractive gets more people to work toward them.* Ackoff says that leadership is about aesthetics—one of the ideals that attract (Stankard 1995a). People in your business are not bound together mechanically like bicycle parts; they choose how they work. Even on a bicycle ride, picking destinations attractive to riders taps their motivation to get there. As your organization's workforce includes more professional and knowledge workers reluctant to be pushed and managed, missions must attract their loyalty and energy.

1c. *A system's mission or purpose (and its environment) needs to change slowly enough that your management system can adjust or evolve to pursue it effectively.* A bicycle that confers high performance on a smooth road will not help a nonswimmer cross a smooth lake. Environmental changes that are not matched by changes in system mission or purpose affect performance. Every management system, no matter how competitive, presents vulnerabilities in some environments that are not amenable to strategic correction from within the management system. Such intrinsic vulnerabilities result from the very definition of system capabilities or its intended range of environments.

2. *Every element in a system can impact its performance under some conditions; there is no most-important element.* When you ask people to name the most important part of a bicycle, someone usually answers "the rider," someone else says "the wheels," another person guesses "the handlebars," or "the rear wheel," and so on. Without a rider, a bicycle will not run. Put the rider on, but remove the wheels and it will not run; replace the wheels but eliminate the handlebars, and the bicycle cannot run straight or in control. Each part of the bicycle impacts the performance of the whole. Lose any part, and the whole system no longer performs as intended. In business, extra (often heroic) human skill and effort often compensates for system deficiencies. (After all, some people ride unicycles!) NO part is most important. Each part either plays its role, or the system is better off without it.

3. *Many elements must work together to carry out the mission of the system. No part or group of parts can do alone what the system as*

a whole does in all circumstances. You cannot ride a front tire, a handlebar, a frame, a set of pedals or any other group of parts that works together. No part of the whole or group of parts can increase human mobility as well as the whole bicycle. However, a complete system is not essential for high performance all the time in all situations. Sometimes (and under certain conditions), a system can fulfill its purpose without all its parts. For example, you could probably ride a bicycle that had no brakes if your entire route were uphill; as soon as the road goes downhill, however, your bicycle without brakes performs badly.

3a. *High performance arises from how well parts of the system work together, not from how good each part is in isolation.* Assembling the parts of the bicycle leaves them all with the same individual properties they had when they were scattered on the floor. Because assembly does not change the parts in any way, the bicycle's high performance arises from how those parts now work together. Improving how isolated management methods work together within your management system adds more to organizational performance than investing in better methods until all methods are part of the system. Then some set of methods becomes the business bottleneck.

4. *No part of the system has an independent effect on how well the whole carries out its function.* The way that the handlebar works to steer a bicycle depends on the air pressure in the front tire. Turning a flat tire generates friction that makes steering more difficult. The implication is that improving isolated elements of your business cannot directly improve the performance of the whole, unless the improvement considers how the element in question works with other elements of the management system.

4a. *Every system has a set of elements that bottlenecks accomplishment of its purpose or mission.* If any system could exist without a performance bottleneck, that system could achieve infinite results. Since no system produces infinite results, all systems must have limiting factors or bottlenecks. Since your business cannot generate infinite profitability, there must be limits to its performance.

4b. *Deleting the group of elements that bottlenecks overall performance will not improve the performance of the whole, without redesigning the rest of the system.* If deleting its bottleneck elements improved the operation of a system under all conditions, then those elements were not actually part of the system. They were accessories at best, or extraneous.

4c. *The quality of change in a system's components and working relationships has greater impact on improving performance than the quantity of change.* Suppose that your bicycle is ready to ride except that its handlebars do not connect properly with the front wheel, which means you cannot steer it. Someone who has improved bicycle performance by changing the gearshift suggests that a new gearshift will also improve your results. Another person suggests improving the tires. Yet another suggests a better frame will help. Will these changes improve *your* bicycle with its nonfunctioning handlebars? No. None of the changes relieve the bottleneck to performance, which is the handlebar problem. So the amount of improvement in a business is much less significant than how well focused all improvements are on impacting the business's mission.

4d. *Small performance differences can lead to big wins.* To win a bicycle race, you must cross the finish line ahead of your competitors. But the winning margin need not be large, just enough so that the judges can see you are ahead. Astoundingly higher performance in the marketplace can rest on surprisingly small differences in system outputs. In business competition customers and shareholders judge performance. How much better do your business's products and services have to be? They must be just enough better for your customers to see a difference that they care about. How much better does your financial performance have to be to attract investment? Again, just enough for investors to see a difference worth investing in.

4e. *Improving isolated elements produces little payoff when the system-level performance bottleneck lies within the system design.* During hard riding, the treads on your tires wear from fast braking and skids. To reduce tread wear you buy harder tires.

Now in panic stops, your new tires no longer screech across the pavement, burning rubber off; instead they slide smoothly. But because harder tires slide over pavement, the bicycle crashes. Moral of the story: what is good for one part in isolation may harm the whole system. Change in elements or functions of a management system must be judged by their impact on overall system-level performance.

4f. *All the best parts do not equal the best system.* Imagine obtaining the best parts of a bicycle, regardless of price or source—perhaps a French derailleur, an American frame, British tires—simply every part the best in class. All these parts, however individually excellent, will not produce the best bicycle, because they were not designed to work together as a system. Technical excellence of the parts is secondary to the objective toward which the whole system (firm or bicycle) is striving.

5. *The effect of each subset or subsystem of elements on achieving the mission of the whole system depends on the behavior of at least one other subset of parts.* For example, the steering effectiveness of the handlebars and front wheel depend on how fast the pedals and back wheel are turning. Turning the handlebars when the bicycle is moving too slowly makes steering unreliable.

5a. *Two apparently identical systems can yield vastly different performances, based on how their parts work together.* Suppose two seemingly identical bicycles stand side by side. Although they look identical, part for part, bicycle A was properly assembled using the right tools. Bicycle B was assembled by hand, without tools, so that its parts are only loosely fitted to each other. In a side-by-side comparison, they look identical, but how they work differs in many important ways.

5b. *Putting together the parts of a system without proper tools may get them to resemble a working system, but does not necessarily generate high performance.* For example, all the parts of a bicycle scattered on the floor are not a bicycle; they are just bicycle parts. If you lack the proper tools to assemble them but you put them together by hand, every part may fit so the final assembly looks like a bicycle, but it will not work properly and will soon fall apart. Using the right tools helps the parts of a system work together as a whole. Tools that help your organization's people, units and other parts work together for the good of your whole business reinforce the effectiveness of all parts of the management system. Such tools include:

- Tying everyone's performance-based compensation to measures, such as customer loyalty, customer satisfaction, or overall cycle time
- Forming teams to flow chart all processes in the business from start to finish
- Maintaining feedback loops on each process to stimulate learning and improvement
- Defining quality and responsibility in each job relative to each other in customer-supplier pairs
- Partnering with suppliers and customers to include them in the management system
- Involving each unit or individual in planning how best to achieve the organization's purpose
- Designing jobs that put responsibility, flexibility, and innovation into the work place
- Training everyone in his or her job, how to do it right, and how that job relates to the organization's mission
- Combining diverse sets of skills, personalities and knowledge on cross-functional teams
- Letting future leaders of the organization develop by taking part in cross-functional teams
- Recognizing and rewarding cooperation, sharing and win-win working relationships
- Avoiding the practice of labeling individuals or units as to winners or losers
- Sharing lessons learned throughout the organization
- Linking financial and nonfinancial measures of daily actions in all units to overall strategy

5c. *Continuous feedback and corrective action are essential for a management system to maintain progress.* A bicycle and its rider are stable as long as they recover from the bumps and obstacles encountered during a race without falling over. Stability is a system's ability to tolerate internal or external shocks or perturbations and return to equilibrium. Feedback in the bicycle-and-rider system controls steering, pedaling, and balancing to take the rider where she wants to go in spite of potholes, bumps, obstacles and curves. High performance demands constant vigilance and corrective action, however. Think about riding a bicycle blindfolded, even for a minute—the result will be a crash. A loss of feedback and corrective action on a moving bicycle—even for a moment—can bring disaster. Organizations that are busy with Plan, Do, Plan, Do, lack the feedback and, like the blindfolded bicycle rider, are heading for a crash. High performance organizations are much the same, their managers must act on constant feedback to maintain control over the dynamics of opportunity-seeking, leading and planning, building capability and risk-taking.

Because this appendix uses the bicycle analogy to make statements about systems, please re-read Ackoff's caution (quoted at the beginning of this appendix) that even close analogy is not proof. Despite Ackoff's caveat, the Baldrige quality improvement bicycle offers a number of useful lessons. Of course, the proof of these lessons will be in terms of results you get; try your new understanding out, use what works for you, discard what does not.

References

BOOKS

Ackoff, Russell L. 1962. *Scientific Method: Optimizing Applied Research Decisions*. New York: John Wiley & Sons, Inc.

———. 1994. *The Democratic Corporation—A Radical Prescription for Recreating Corporate America and Rediscovering Success*. New York: Oxford University Press.

———. 1981. *Creating the Corporate Future: Plan or Be Planned For*. New York: John Wiley and Sons, Inc.

Argyris, Chris. 2000. *Flawed Advice and the Management Trap*. New York: Oxford University Press.

Christopher, William F., and Thor, Carl G., eds. 1993. *Handbook for Productivity Measurement and Improvement*. Cambridge, Mass.: Productivity Press.

deBono, Edward. 1992. *SUR/PETITION: Creating Value Monopolies When Everyone Else Is Merely Competing*. New York: HarperCollins Publishers.

Deming, W. Edward. 1989. *Out of the Crisis*. Cambridge, Mass.: Massachusetts Institute of Technology, Center for Advanced Engineering Studies.

———. 1993. *The New Economics: For Industry, Government, Education*. Cambridge, Mass.: Massachusetts Institute of Technology, Center for Advanced Engineering Studies.

Feigenbaum, Armand V. 1991. *Total Quality Control.* 3rd ed., rev. New York: McGraw-Hill Book Co.

Goldratt, Eliyahu M., and Cox, Jeff. 1986. *THE GOAL: A Process Of Ongoing Improvement.* Croton-on-Hudson, N.Y.: North River Press.

Goleman, Daniel. 1995. *Emotional Intelligence: Why It Can Matter More Than IQ.* New York: Bantam Books.

Hamel, Gary, and Prahalad, C. K. 1994. *Competing for the Future: Breakthrough Strategies for Seizing Control of Your Industry and Creating the Markets of Tomorrow.* Boston, Mass.: Harvard Business School Press.

Kaplan, Robert S., and Norton, David P. 1996. *The Balanced Scorecard: Translating Strategy into Action.* Boston, Mass.: Harvard Business School Press.

National Institute for Standards and Technology (NIST). 1991–2001. *Criteria for Performance Excellence.* Revised and published annually by the Baldrige National Quality Program, National Institute of Standards and Technology, Technology Administration, U.S. Department of Commerce, Gaithersburg, MD 20899–1020. Available for download by accessing <http://www.quality.nist.gov>.

Stankard, Martin F. 1981. *Successful Management of Large Clerical Operations.* New York: McGraw-Hill Book Co., Inc.

ARTICLES AND OTHER SOURCES

American Society for Quality. ANSI/ISO/ASQ Q9000: 2000 Series Quality Standards. 2001. Reprinted by American Society for Quality, Milwaukee, WI.

Balastracci, Davis. 1998. "Data 'Sanity': Statistical Thinking Applied to Everyday Data." 1998, summer. Special publication of the ASQ Statistics Division. Available from ASQ Quality Information Center, at (800) 248–1946.

Butler, Timothy, and Waldroop, James. 1999, September–October. "Job Sculpting, the Art of Retaining Your Best People." *Harvard Business Review* 77, no. 5, pp. 144–152.

Cappelli, Peter. 1995. Personal conversation between the author and Dr. Peter Cappelli, Director, Center for Human Resources at Penn's Wharton School of Business concerning Cappelli's investigation of the link between training and productivity in his study "The Other Shoe: Education's Contribution to the Productivity of Establishments."

Collins, Jim. 2001, January. "Level 5 Leadership: The Triumph of Humility and Fierce Resolve." *Harvard Business Review* 79, no. 1, pp. 66–76.

Colvin, Geoffrey. 1998, August 17. "What Money Makes You Do." *Fortune*, p. 213.

Drucker, Peter F. 1990, May–June."The Emerging Theory of Manufacturing." *Harvard Business Review* 90, no. 3, p. 94.

———. 1994, September-October. "The Theory of the Business." *Harvard Business Review* 72, no. 5. pp. 95–104

Editors, *Fortune*. 1997, December 8. "How Toyota Defies Gravity." *Fortune*.

Hammond, John S., Keeney, Ralph L., and Raiffa, Howard. 1998, September-October. "The Hidden Traps in Decision Making." *Harvard Business Review* 76, no. 5, pp 47–58.

Helyar, John. 2001, June 11. "Sittin' Pretty." *Fortune*, p. 133 (see particularly the article's sidebar "An Obscure Book Makes Rainwater a Fortune." p. 138).

Hendricks, Kevin B., and Singhal, Vinod R.1997, September. "Does Implementing an Effective TQM Program Actually Improve Operating Performance? Empirical Evidence from Firms That Have Won Quality Awards." *Management Science* 43, no. 9, pp. 1258–1274.

———. 2001, March. "The Long Run Stock Price Performance of Firms with Effective TQM Programs." *Management Science* 47, no. 3, pp. 359–368.

Kotter, John P. 1990, May-June. "What Leaders Really Do." *Harvard Business Review*, 68, no. 3, pp.103–111.

Madrick, Jeffrey. 1998, July-August. "Computers Waiting for the Revolution." *Challenge* 41, no. 4, pp. 42–65.

Mintzberg, Henry, and Van der Heyden. 1999, September–October. "Organigraphs: Drawing How Companies Really Work." *Harvard Business Review* 77, no. 5, pp. 87–96.

National Institute of Standards and Technology (NIST). 2001. *Criteria for Performance Excellence*, American Society for Quality, Milwaukee, WI. Updated annually. The complete *Baldrige Criteria* are available for download directly from the National Institute of Standards and Technology <http://www.quality.nist.gov>, a unit of the U.S. Department of Commerce.

Porter, Michael. 1996, November-December. "What is Strategy?" *Harvard Business Review* 74, no. 6.

Quest for Excellence—The Annual Baldrige Award Conference. 1990–2001. The Quest for Excellence, The Official Conference of The Malcolm Baldrige National Quality Award, 1991 through 2001, held in Washington, D.C. Notes available at the conference. Audiotapes of conference speeches published by Audio Archives, International,

La Crescenta, CA 91214. Usually twelve to sixteen tapes per volume.

Quinn, James Brian, Anderson, Philip, and Finkelstein, Sydney. 1996, March-April. "Managing Professional Intellect: Making the Most of the Best." *Harvard Business Review* 74, no. 2.

Reuters, Limited. 2001, May 28. "Worldwide IBM Staff Swarms Online Meeting." Published online in AOL Personal Financial News—IBM.

Rucci, Anthony J., Kirn, Steven P., and Quinn, Richard T. 1998, January-February. "The Employee-Customer-Profit Chain at Sears." *Harvard Business Review* 76, no. 1, pp. 82–97.

Schulze, Horst. 1993. Acceptance speech by Mr. Horst Schulze to the ASTD National Conference, Atlanta, on "How the Ritz-Carlton Won the Baldrige Award." See videotape of speech, 92ASTD/V-T0, American Society for Training and Development, Alexandria, VA.

Sichel, Daniel, cited by Jeffrey Madrick. 1998, July-August. "Computers Waiting for the Revolution." *Challenge, The Magazine of Economic Affairs* 41, no. 4, pp. 42–65.

Spears, Steven, and Bowen, H. Kent. 1999, September-October. "Decoding the DNA of the Toyota Production System." *Harvard Business Review,* 77, no. 5, pp. 96–106.

Stankard, Martin. 1990, July–August. "Giving a Team Control over a Workflow without Regretting It." *Productivity Views* 7, no. 4, p. 11.

———. 1994a, November-December. "Redefining Productivity." *Productivity Views* 11, no. 6, pp. 1–2.

———.1994b, September-October. "Employee Selection." *Productivity Views* 11, no. 5, pp. 1–2.

———.1994c, January-February. "Delta's Design for Service." *Productivity Views* 11, no. 1, pp. 1–2.

———.1994d, July-August. "Eliminate Inspections." *Productivity Views* 11, no. 4, p. 3.

———. 1995a, September-October. "Training That Pays." *Productivity Views* 12, no. 5, p. 3.

———. 1995b, March-April. "Ackoff on Leadership." *Productivity Views* 12, no. 2, p. 7.

———. 1996a, September-October. "High Performance in Financial Services." *Productivity Views* 13, no. 5, pp. 4–5.

———. 1996b, July-August. "The Improvement Paradox." *Productivity Views* 13, no. 4. pp. 1–2.

———.1996c, March-April. "All or Nothing in HR Management Practices." *Productivity Views* 13, no. 2, pp. 4–5.

———. 1996d, July-August. "Does Planning Pay? The Survey Says. . . ." *Productivity Views* 13, no. 4, pp. 6–7.

———. 1996e, July-August. "USAA Employee PRIDE." *Productivity Views* 13, no. 4, p. 3.

Struebing, Laura. 1997, September. "Suppliers Team with Chrysler for $1.2 Billion in Cost Savings." *Quality Progress*, p. 14.

Zangwill, Willard I., and Kantor, Paul B. 1998, July. "Toward a Theory of Continuous Improvement and the Learning Curve." *Management Science* 44, no. 7, pp. 910–919.

Index

About the Author

MARTIN F. STANKARD is a consultant and author based in Westford, Massachusetts. He holds an M.B.A. and a Ph.D. in Operations Research from the Wharton School and an undergraduate degree in mechanical engineering from the University of Pennsylvania. He has been a senior staff member at Arthur D. Little Inc., has taught at Wharton, and conducts seminars and consults on the Baldrige business excellence model.